# BARKING MAD

R SOLE

The incredible true story…

# BARKING MAD

…of the former Serious Organised Crime Agency detective who went Mad in spectacular fashion after 17 years undercover with 5 identities infiltrating organised crime, but survived and came out the other side dancing

## R SOLE

(aka, I Can't Reveal My True Identity, or
I will Have to Kill You)

Copyright © 2023 Robert Sole

All rights reserved. No part of this book may be reproduced, stored in any retrieval system, or transmitted in any form or by any means, electronic, mechanical, photocopying, recording, or otherwise, without express written permission of the author or publisher.

The moral right of the author has been asserted.

First published in 2023

ISBN: 9798863037295

Cover art: beingjohnstockley.com

*For Jane, the love of my life*

'… the only people for me are the mad ones, the ones who are mad to live, mad to talk, mad to be saved, desirous of everything at the same time, the ones who never yawn or say a commonplace thing, but burn, burn, burn like fabulous yellow roman candles exploding like spiders across the stars and in the middle you see the blue centerlight pop and everybody goes "Awww!"'

- Jack Kerouac, *On the Road*

## TALK ABOUT SHITE

'If you are having a shit life, blame yourself. You are restricted by the boundaries of your own mind and ambition. You are not responsible for what happens in your life but you are responsible for how you dealt with what happened. This book details white privilege at its finest. If you think life has been crap, would you swap your life with the author R SOLE?'

- R Sole, circa somewhere in 2023, British wisecrack, detective, actor, author, NOT a TV host, artist, all round 'roustabout'


'Life is a shit sandwich. The more bread you have, the less shit you will have to eat.'

- Jonathon Winters, circa in the '80s, American comedian, actor, author, TV host, artist, all around 'roustabout'

# CONTENTS

| | |
|---|---|
| *Prologue* | 15 |
| *Introduction* | 16 |
| Mania, Baby | 19 |
| My Story | 49 |
| Secret Agent Man, aka Danger Man | 165 |
| A Long Way Home | 349 |
| *Acknowledgements* | 357 |
| *About the Authors* | 359 |

# PROLOGUE

You'd be kind for caring why I went literally barking mad. But then I'd have to kill you. Just kidding. Maybe. So now, knowing this, do you dare to board this runaway train to get the answers? Am I pulling your leg? Then dare ye and enter well.

# INTRODUCTION

The Author has written a book which provides a warts and all account of his amazing and provocative life from 1959 to 2023, taking you into the highly secretive world of a successful, skilled operative for the United Kingdom. He deployed on operations around the globe, targeting anyone who by their criminal activity was having a detrimental impact on British society.

In recounting his story, he has changed some locations and details to protect innocent parties. If he has annoyed anybody in his writing of this book, including police and criminals alike, he makes no apologies for that. He has absolutely no regrets in his life, and if he lived it again, he would do everything with the same passion.

If you recognise yourself as having been subjected to an undercover operation involving the Author, and you now feel aggrieved, his advice to you is to let it go. It was never personal for him; it was only business. Indeed, the Author liked a number of the people he infiltrated, some of them even more than his personal friends; but if you choose to be criminally active at a high level, you must accept infiltration as an occupational hazard.

In the past, there have been contracts put on the Author's head by criminal organisations. He would like to think that they have by now expired, but if they haven't and someone decides to come looking for him to exact some form of revenge, make sure you kill him. If you fail to do that, rest assured Mrs Glock 19 handgun and her babies will come out of retirement with him to visit you and your family ... and it won't be pretty.

Mad Jack McMad is not dead; he's just in hibernation.

The author using a handgun at 10 metres from target

# MANIA, BABY!

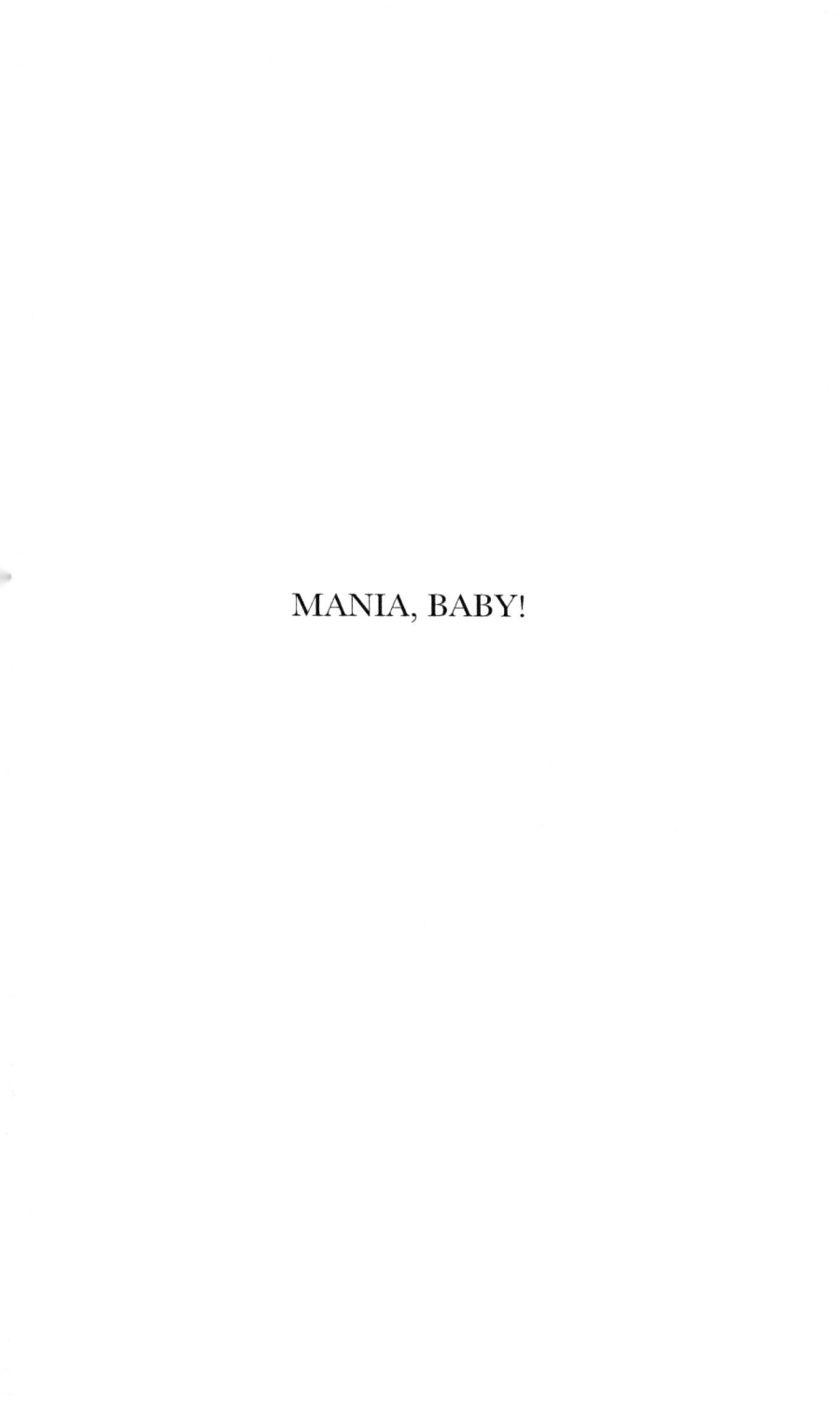

# ONE

Hands braced firmly between the door frames, I'm standing at the doorway of my house in Hampshire, itching for trouble and eyeing like a hawk the gathering police squad. Already, word has spread throughout the neighbourhood like wildfire that I, R Sole, am in a standoff with a whole SWAT team of specially trained police officers.

They haven't received orders to shoot me, so I'm not worried yet. But as I observe these cowards, they are crouching behind their patrol cars no doubt with adrenaline pumping wildly and readying the battering ram – not unlike the new Netflix series, 'WACO: American Apocalypse', except this here is Hampshire, England, mate, across the jolly ol' pond.

Growling and clenching my teeth, manically determined to stand my ground, I suddenly slam the door shut – KAPOW! - and retreat to dwelling. 'I need to— Ah, yes!' I need to engage my ritual in preparation for what may come.

Moving back inside, I rummage in the kitchen cabinet and find a bunch of stubby candles that I place on the credenza. Then I jerk out a kitchen drawer and scoop up a half-dozen carving knives. At every entrance to the house, I stick a carving knife in the stubby candles to signal my willingness to allow these marauders to skedaddle peaceably.

I have a Bic lighter in my pocket that I remove and flick. 'Flick your bloody Bic,' I say, laughing. One by one, I light the candles and peer through the windows, gauging their level of activity.

Now, facing the door from five metres in, I brace myself for the inevitable onslaught. Only to hear a familiar sound. 'What?' My friends have come knocking at the door. Someone says, 'Rob! Don't do anything daft. Please come out holding your hands up for bloody sake. Please, mate!'

Bless their hearts. These chaps are making a last ditch effort to talk me out of doing anything silly or dangerous which, given the powder keg outside, portends to be more than explosive.

'Go away!' I yell, and then a police negotiator intervenes and tries to talk me out as a last resort; but my determination is unflinching and, as far as I'm concerned, it is worse than hopeless. In fact, the whole stinking mess only serves to agitate me more. 'Fuuuuuuck, you!!!!' I scream bloody murder from my bowlegged stance inside the house, practically shaking the rafters.

Suddenly, there's a loud crashing noise punctuated by boards splintering, and down comes the front door with a 'KA-BOOM!' The riot squad storms the house, smashing through the patio doors and quickly overpowering me despite my peace candles blowing in the wind.

Once I'm rough cuffed and slammed hard to my knees, a fat bald guy punches me square in the face. It hurts like hell, but I smile, thinking like Mike Tyson, the great heavyweight fighter, when asked if he was worried about fighting Evander Holyfield: 'Everyone has a plan, until they get punched in the mouth'.

'Well done, fatty', I say, blood spurting in all directions from my face. 'It takes a lot of bravery to punch someone when they're handcuffed'.

All of his mates burst into laughter at my wry humour.

Despite my violent kicking and screaming, the EMTs manhandle me onto a gurney, tightening the straps across my chest, arms, and legs. Then I'm rolled out the door, thudding and bouncing on the foray and steps and into the triage ambulance outside.

Believe you me when I tell you this: there are people fuckin' everywhere. Swat police, regular Hampshire blokes, ER medical staff, my neighbours, and the odd assortment of general gawkers that rubberneck all of life's miscellaneous disasters.

And this is one, meant for prime time.

For the benefit of all, I let out a thunderous 'WHOOP! WHOOP!' and make a shit-eating grin as the doors are slammed at my feet. From here, the EMTs drive me straight to the intensive care unit at Basingstoke Psychiatric Hospital where, at this moment in time, I damn well belong.

# TWO

When I arrive at the hospital strapped in the gurney ala Hannibal Lector, I squirm and wriggle and spit and scream as if the staff will just up and set me free with profuse and profound apologies. But exhaustion soon overtakes me, and instead I'm reduced to drooling and mumbling and buzzing. Yes, buzzing. I'm buzzing from repeated blasts of adrenaline, even though I'm soon fully sedated, transitioning into numbness and darkness.

I wake up in a small, single bed to an eight-foot square cell surrounding me on all sides. It feels to me like the forces of evil are shrinking me into oblivion, squeeze-wrapping my effervescence, blood-sucking their tentacles around me. There is no sink, no toilet, no dishwasher, no cupboards like in my house -- no anything, just a lightbulb dangling from the ceiling, slick whitewashed walls, a small table, and a square window located centrally to the door that serves as a window to my demented soul.

The first thought that runs through my broken mind is, what am I fuckin' doing here in this hell hole?

I sit up a bit terrified, a tad disoriented, and walk over to the door, still not knowing exactly where I am – and truly trying to get my bearings within my larvae-like cocoon. I jiggle and push and pull the door, heaving it hither and thither, but it is tightly locked like a drum. The sounds of traffic, birds chirping, and people talking, which float about my ears, are punctuated with the occasional errant scream – all seeming to permeate the heavy air with a low, ambient 'hummm'.

I knock on window – 'RAP, RAP, RAP, RAP' – until someone comes. A thirtyish white male gawks at me through the window and turns and walks away. He comes back with reinforcements in the guise of a diminutive Asian lady older in age, and the two of them flick the lock and cautiously open the door.

Taking my arms, they lead me to a conference room consisting of a table and three chairs. The Asian lady starts talking and says a few words before I hook onto them. '... you have been detained in a mental health facility pursuant to section 3 for a further assessment', she states.

'I've been sectioned?' I ask, and she nods. 'I shouldn't be here. There's nothing wrong with me. You got this all wrong? How long will I be here for?'

'Just a couple of days', she says, though I immediately sense that she's lying. That she probably says this to everyone.

My head spins at the thought of being here even for the day. Drawing from some my deep space in my mind, from another lifetime, I start quoting line and verse regarding the ins and out of the psychological commitment regulations.

'You can only detain me to a hospital if I have a mental disorder that is of a nature or to a degree that requires treatment in a hospital...' I pronounce as if I'm channelling the authority of King Henry the VIII I am I am, or a barrister pontificating some spiel before a magistrate.

The Asian lady just nods her head and stares into my eyes, obviously assessing me in that way. Really, I want to reach out and choke her.

'It must be necessary for my health or safety or protection of others… You can only detain me against my will for 36 hours without a warrant. I want to speak to someone now!' Rattle and hum, rattle and hum, rattle and hum.

The un-dynamic duo return me to my cell promptly for getting too aggressive – perhaps they could sense it from my veins popping. Though they lock my door behind me, the next morning I find the door unlocked. They have come in the night and unlocked it.

Walking out tepidly at first, peering down one hallway and then the other, I yell to someone down the way whose back is turned to me.

'Hey! HEY!'

A nurse turns around and faces me. Honestly, she could be Nurse Ratched in the fleshy flesh flesh – a pure battle-axe but with smooth skin like an expensive British doll and baby blue eyes, a button nose and full, womanly breasts. I undress her with my eyes, right then and there.

'Do you know who I am? *Do you?!*' I stomp.

Nurse Ratched purses her lips in obvious contempt, then smiles back in a flat, mechanical smile, as if she is a robot repeating a task to which she had been doomed for all eternity.

'I'm with the Flying Squad, nurse…' I protest, as if the gates of heaven will suddenly and dramatically swing open for all to behold. Actually, I have to strain my eyes to see her badge and am finally able to confirm that she was indeed a nurse not just my fantasy of one.

'Nurse, ah, ah, Nurse whatever... I am a member of the London Metropolitan Police Service, eh?'

She nods robotically, as if to imply, sure you are, you crazy mutha fucker. *Sure you are.*

'You know, the Robbery Squad, the Specialist Crime Directorate 8, the SO8, the--' I rapid-fire the words, imagining her head spinning from my verbal onslaught.

When I feel I'm not getting through this spinning, thick skull of a person, I yell: 'Lady, the fuckin' Sweeney, you know? Rhymes with Sweeney Todd for mutha fuckin' Christ's sake'.

At some point, I become more fully aware of my surroundings and realise I am truly in a real psychiatric hospital. It's like I've switched dimensions.

Suddenly, I imagine long, endless hallways going round and round and round and round. You know, the feel and effect of 'The Shining', if there's a word for that particular feel and effect.

Maybe it's the feel and effect of being utterly forlorn. I feel an overwhelming pang of loneliness...

Before long, I find myself alongside some young white males who apparently are suffering major mental issues stemming (no pun intended) from cannabis abuse (aka, weed). My first clue comes when someone says this other guy fancies himself as a Rasta man.

Even though this other guy is died-in-the-wool British, not an islander, in other words, he speak with a very heavy Jamaican accent and wears his baseball cap back to front. For some reason, don't tell me why, I take an instant disliking to Rasta man, and when I take an instant disliking to a guy, things typically do not go well for him from that point forward.

So, on a whim, that night I decide to buy all the lads a truck load of Kentucky Fried Chicken – except, of course, for Rasta man, who has earned a premier spot on my shit list. Pointing to him, I say with relish, 'but *YOU* mate are not getting anything. Zippo! Zed! Nada!'

The food arrives at the same time as my sister Gail, so I take my KFC in the visitation room. Since psych detainees are generally allowed to keep their mobile phones and wallets (at least until they abuse their privileges), I had called Gail first as she was the only family member located anywhere near Basingstoke Psychiatric Hospital.

'What the fuck is going on?' she had said.

'I'm in an asylum', I had said. 'It's a long story but you need to come and get me out of here pronto. There's been a mistake'.

When I enter the visitor's room, I know she has already been required to run the rigmarole of being a guest to a looney bin. Having been already patted down and bags searched, she cannot hold back her emotions any longer and breaks down into a flood of tears when she sees me in my bizarre and dishevelled state.

'It's been a mistake', I assure her. 'They're going to let me go when they realise that'.

'Rob', she says sternly. 'No, they are not. They told me they are not letting you go'.

'Listen', I tell her quite assuredly and seriously. 'Go home, come back with an angle grinder, and break me out of here, okay?'

She raises her small fist to her mouth and coughs, stifling a small laugh at my ability to keep a sense of humour anywhere; but what she does not know at first is that I am not kidding around. And then she sees it.

'Are you really serious?' she says. 'I can't bloody do that'.

'If you love me, you will', I say serious as a stone to the head. 'If not, don't bother to come back'.

It's impossible to describe the look on her face, other than mortified.

When I return to the ward from scaring Gail, I notice at once that all the bags of KFC are gone. I figure that the bags must have been dispensed to the other patient inmates, but when I learn that Rasta man has nicked one of them, my blood starts to bubble and boil.

So I conceive a plan, if I cannot get out of this place.

The next day, the staff takes me for an assessment. Already, more than three days has passed. Clamouring to be set free at once, I say, 'you don't mind if I record this meeting, do you?'

All of them were taken aback, as they obviously haven't had this happen before. I continue unabashed. 'This is obviously a stitch up and you all are bent', I say matter-of-factly.

Hands to the hips convey a clear message: no fuckin' way are you recording this.

In reaction, I say, 'if we're not recording this, we're not meeting and you can all fuck off'.

The three-man riot squad promptly returns me to my cell for being patently aggro. Then they lock my door with a big 'schlunk' and keep it locked until the next day. They also take my mobile on the grounds that I am causing trouble by ringing the police to tell them an ex-cop is being held against his will. Which, between you and me, and I am.

Meanwhile, since I'm not getting out, I return to calculating my revenge for Rasta man, deciding to bide my time until night falls.

There is typically a female staff member on night duty (call her 'the night lady'), supported by a little admin team of psych-ward enforcers if trouble were to break out, God forbid.

Conveniently, when Rasta man belches to the night lady, 'hey, bitch, get me a cup of tea', I see the perfect opportunity. Standing up, I say, 'Who the fuck do you think you are talking to, *you piece of shit*'.

Then, leaning across the table that separates us, I give him a heavy backhanded slap and proceed to rudely swipe his hat. 'Hats in here are banned from now on', I say with a Joker's crazy grin.

Because I have knocked Rasta man off his chair from the force of my swipe, the night lady pushes the blasted alarm, erupting a shrill, mind-piercing 'BUZZ, BUZZZ, BUZZZZ'.

Whereupon, the three-man security team promptly arrives and tries to get hold of me, but because I am quite agile and squirmy and very very strong, all hell breaks loose like one of those barroom fights in the old American westerns.

After dropping into a Karata stance and warning everyone, 'I know Karate, watch out', I back into the kitchen arm to the hilt with a knife in one hand and a $CO_2$ fire extinguisher in the other. Imagine that!

It's not long before the full tactical team arrives, complete with a gaggle of snarling dogs.

Facing a Mexican stand-off of sorts, the tactical team

forthwith tasers me and wrestles me down into handcuffs. Someone injects me with a sedative strong enough to drop a mule dead in its tracks, and I sleep the whole night, waking with a massive headache and groggier than Sony Liston after he threw in the towel to Cassius Clay.

Maybe they've had their fill of me, maybe not, but before long it's time for my reassignment. From Basingstoke, I'm transferred to The Priory Hospital called back then Thornford Park in Newbury. I use the term 'hospital' loosely, as this is essentially a prison for the criminally insane that functions as an overspill for Broadmoor, the oldest and most notorious psychiatric hospital in the Kingdom.

## THREE

Thornford Park has a 20-foot high perimeter wire fence with deadly razor wire swirled across the top that would cut a fleeing madman to ribbons before he hit the ground. Alcatraz, San Quentin, Strangeways, Wormwood Scrubs, Broadmoor... and Thornford Park – all send shivers up the spine of all but the most criminally insane.

Which I'm surely not.

On arrival, I am gingerly greeted with a stay in solitary confinement with my very own padded cell. There are pads on the walls. Pads on the roof. Pads on the doors. Pads everywhere. A place where a madman can bang his head and spill out his brains any time of day or night, just for shits and giggles.

I get the five-star treatment, of course, because, well, I guess my reputation has preceded me. My food is served through a hatch in the wall, and I am forcibly injected in the arse every day with who knows what concoction of drugs to make me calm and sedate. There is no silverware or wooden spoons. There is only smooth plastic that can barely cut or gouge a mound of sand.

For making me stay in this God-forsaken place, I am determined to make it as hard on them it can be. So, at first, I'm so out of control that they usually need a team of eight staff with shields to wrest control of me to administer my injections.

Left alone in my padded cell after the injection, I scream, 'I'm crazy! I'm fuckin' crazy! Don't you believe me now? I'm ker-ray-zed!'

But the hollers and echoes just fall on deaf ears because these sounds are commonplace. Not getting a rise in anyone, I stop and reconsider my strategy to fool the fools and somehow escape by my wits.

I have a small exercise area just outside my padded cell where I'm allowed to take short breaks and breath in some clean, fresh air. Whilst outside one day, I speak to one of the inmates in an adjoining ward (out of his window only), and he clews me in to the ward that I occupy.

Wards, you see – bottom line - are the sections of prison or a psych hospital that tell you whether you are likely to live or die. Some wards are mostly safe, some are most certainly not.

'You're in the Bucklebury Ward', my neighbour says.

'Oh?'

'Yeah, you're in with the Bucklebury gang and I'm a member of that gang', he says.

He's black and the Bucklebury gang consists of two black guys and ten white guys. He tells me that his gang was originally from Birmingham and that he was, more specially, from the notorious 'Burger Bar Boys' gang. The Burger Bar Boys were a nasty lot from the Handsworth and Winson Green areas, who got their name from a Burger Bar on Soho Road.

Anyway, in about 2003, this gang had infamously used an Uzi submachine gun to shoot two 18-year-old girls, name of Letisha Shakespeare and Charlene Ellis. These girls were just unlucky, having simply been caught in the crossfire outside a New Year's Eve party. Point being, they are ruthless.

Meanwhile, my behaviour improves over time and I'm allowed to interact with three young black males (not psych inmates) outside the padded cell area in what's called the 'seclusion unit'. Untrained and only pulling down minimum wages, these blokes help me re-connect with my sanity, at the various stages of my recovery process.

As contradistinguished with the seclusion unit guys, there is one Dr Williams. He's bad applies.

When I first met him in the reception area upon my arrival from Basingstoke, I had greeted him with a pleasant, 'Who you fuckin' looking at?' because, when I was a kid in the council dregs, this was the classic preamble to a fight. And I was itching for one that day.

Doc Williams is five-foot ten inches tall with a slim build and was dressed in a fine grey suit and prominent badge. Women must have swooned at this good-looking guy with his air of superiority and authority, and proof in the pudding, he had a woman kowtowing beside him on this day.

Knowing no other way, I started flirting with a particular woman colleague of his. 'You're a good-looking girl', I said with a bold wink. 'When I get out of here, what do you say we can link up?'

Instantly the debonair doc reacted. 'Your behaviour sir is inappropriate. Cut it out'.

This was the wrong thing to say to a maniac. I replied with a glib, 'take a fuck to yourself!'

But I've got to give it up to Doc Williams. Even

though he disliked me intensely from the get-go, as the doctor responsible for my wellbeing, he does not allow that to get in the way of diagnosing me as sufficiently stable to be transferred onto the main Bucklebury ward.

I question the merits of that decision, however, as I know from my chats with my neighbouring window-mate that the main ward is full of maniacs and certifiably insane criminals of which I am no real match.

When Doc Williams approves my release to Bucklebury ward, I say to him, 'wait a minute. Don't you see a problem with me being an ex-cop let loose amongst a criminally insane gang of murderers?'

'Ex-cop?' he says, busting a gut. '*You – an ex-copper*?'

I reply, 'yes, and are you completely stupid? My life expectancy in there will be about 24 hours'.

Not believing I am who I say I am, he tosses me a cheeky grin and says, 'don't worry none, there are staff in there'.

'Are you really that naïve?' I plead, hunching my shoulders and going into some kind of 'Columbo' character.

'If I go on the ward as an ex-cop with a group of people who are criminals and insane, there will only be one outcome: either they will kill me, or I will kill them. Pick your flavour, mate!'

'Are you now threatening to kill other inmates,' he says rudely, lifting his brows for exaggeration. 'You know what? I think you need more time in seclusion'.

The whole thing reminds me of what Carr (the prison floorwalker) said in the movie, 'Cool Hand Luke'. 'No one will sit in the bunks with dirty pants on. Any man with dirty pants on sittin' on the bunk spends a night in the box. Any man don't bring back his empty pop bottle spends a night in the box. Any man loud-talking' spends a night in the box'.

When the fine doc returns me to my padded cell, I'm thinking, what a total dipshit. So I am forced to remain in that padded cell until the top honcho in charge of all the Psycho hospitals comes by to see me (and presumably, the other recent detainees as well).

Also Asian, he has the grand title of Chief Consultant and gets right down to the nitty gritty, which I like. Nitty gritty or fuck off.

'During the last two weeks, have you ever wanted to commit suicide?' he says.

'No'.

'During the last two weeks, have you done anything to harm yourself?'

'No.'

'During the last two weeks, have you wanted to harm anyone else?'

'Yes, but just keep Dr Williams away from me and we're fine', I say with a cheeky grin.

'Did you ever want to strangle the Rasta man?' he says.

'Every single got damn day! Just kidding', I say.

We chat for about half an hour, when finally he states, 'you shouldn't be in confinement. I will get you moved onto the ward as soon as possible'.

'Hold on, hold on,' I say. 'I don't want to get *killed*, emphasis on killed, when I am allowed on the main ward. I'm an ex-cop'.

He lifts his eyebrows and says, 'Look, fine. You can

think you are an ex-cop all you like, okay? I'll make sure the staff doesn't' talk about your situation or divulge it to the other inmates, okay?' Wink, wink.

With much trepidation, I consent to be moved to the Bucklebury ward. Once there, the word spreads that I am suffering from major delusions. The PO's are saying, 'can you believe this guy? He thinks he's a secret agent! Haaaaaaaa. What total bollocks!'

# FOUR

In the general ward, there are characters of all ages, ranging from teens 18 years of age to old-time pensioners. Some are inside for burglary, some are inside for armed robbery, some are inside for murder and mayhem. There are those that have been incarcerated less than a year, and those that don't know any other life, such as the chap that has been here for 52 years.

Even in this threatening, survivalist environment, I have the knack and can make friends easily. Reaching into my bag of character types, I have made a calculated decision to create a further diversion from being a delusional ex-cop.

Instead, I have decided to use a Navy persona as my real background story, should anybody poke around and ask me nosey questions. Despite my serious mental limitations, I feel sane enough to consistently keep myself in this character and not blow it.

There is always an air of tension and apprehension in the main recreation room, a feeling that creeps into your shoulders and biceps and lingers there like a muscle ache. This feeling is exacerbated by a 25-year-old black male nick-named Linford Christie, who, the rumour was, is doing his time for street robberies with a knife.

Note that the official reason for any particular person's

detention is not made public to the ward. Though rumours fly far and wide, you never know whether any of them is true. It helps you hide in plain sight , if you're of a notion to do it. An inmate's backstory could be true, partially true, totally made up, or any combination thereof.

With wild staring eyes, good ol' Linford keeps pulling an imaginary gun out of his pocket and crouching down, pretending to shoot whichever patient, guard or staff has inadvertently rubbed him the wrong way or pissed him off on that particular day. You are waiting on edge for the one day it might be the real thing.

Bizarrely, he would also get down in the starting blocks position at one end of the ward hallway and then without warning sprint the whole length of the ward, before adopting the same position and sprinting right back again. Back and forth, back and forth. And he would do these sprints ten to 20 times a night, often spontaneously.

Because we each have our own unlocked, unsecure rooms, I feel I have to sleep with one eye open until I get the full measure of the place. And thank God I do. It turns out that when Linford gets bored with running, he often wanders behind someone simply watching telly and minding his own business, and then suddenly springs on him, smacking him brutally upside the head.

I know it wouldn't be long before he has a go at my head, so when none of the staff are looking, I kick Linford hard and fast in the balls, sure to make a painful point that he should not mess with me.

When he buckles to his knees, I kindly help him up and whisper, 'come near me when I'm watching TV, and I'll fucking kill you'. He never came within striking distance of me ever again. Yes, he was mad, and a mad man knows when a man is madder than him, and I was (pretending) to be that man.

Somewhere in all the gossip, I'm told that the Hospital get paid £250 per man per day by the NHS, and therefore empty beds mean lost revenue. That answers my nagging question as to why some inmates, on the face of it, are well enough to be cared for in the community but instead have suffered lengthy periods of commitment.

Take the example of Julian, age 65, the man confined for 52 years. He wears a pin stripe suit shirt and tie every day and could easily have passed for anyone's grandad. I speak quite a lot to him, so one day I ask him what his story is.

I can't corroborate anything he said - he could just have been making up a backstory - but if anything he said was true, it's an awful indictment of mental health care in the UK (reminiscent of what you would expect in Victorian or medieval times).

Julian tells me that, when he was 13 years old, his mum couldn't cope with the children, so he and his siblings were placed into a children's care home. As a protest, he set fire to the curtains of the care home and was taken to court and charged with 'Arson with Intent to Endanger Life'.

Consequently, he was sent to Borstal Prison, now known as HMP Rochester. Being a young pretty boy, he was regularly brutally raped by the older inmates. The only way he could stop the rapes was to fight back with a home-made weapon. He ended up being charged with serious assault and his sentence was increased but the rapes nonetheless continued unabated into his adult life in the adult prison.

Eventually, Julian ended up at Parkhurst Prison on the Isle of Wight where he was given a command by inmate Ronnie Kray. Ronnie Kray was one of the identical twins from the East End of London and a notorious gangster, murderer, and madman who's been the subject of a few documentaries and films.

According to Julian, for the duration of his stay, he was ordered by Ronnie Kray to be his prison wife, meaning he was brutally attacked and brutally raped by Ronnie Kray on a regular basis, Ronnie's insatiable appetite for violent sex being notorious.

One day Ronnie Kray told Julian that another inmate was a paedophile and that Julian had to kill him. Julian related to me, 'if Ronnie Kray tells you to kill someone, you only have two options: do what you are told, or you will be killed yourself'.

Julian cut the alleged paedophiles throat, but he didn't die, so Julian only got charged with attempted murder. He was convicted and sentenced to life imprisonment without parole as criminally insane, whereupon he was sent to Broadmoor. This man was five foot nine and ten stone dripping wet.

His story brings tears to my eyes, and I give him a big hug. In my heart of hearts, I hope what he says is not true.

As a further illustration, I am told about a patient who has killed a man whilst in confinement for stealing his £5 Binatone radio. Fifteen years added for a £5 radio; what a waste of life. When asked why he did it, he said, matter-of-factly, 'it's not the value of the radio, it's the principle. If you let someone take your possessions, they will be back with others to take your arse'.

In the centre of our ward is a pool table, and it is the

focal point for killing time, something we all have plenty of. Keep in mind that there are only certain things that you can do to pass time when in the psyche joint. Once you wake up, you have breakfast and either read a book, watch TV, stare out the window, or play pool.

I don't fancy watching TV, reading, playing pool or staring out the window, so the old guy Julian often chats with me wearing his three-piece suit. We become chat mates, and one day a guy who regularly plays pool yells, 'hey, mates, who took the chalk?'

Nobody owns up to it but the next day Julian comes out in chalk blue lipstick, having obviously nicked the chalk to look good for his man. After 53 years in the brig, Julian is what they consider 'prison gay', which refers to take a trip to the wild side because there's nary another choice.

The staff at all levels equates mental unwellness with lack of intelligence. They think we're all daft, but that's a fatal error of judgement and, moreover, the opposite could well be said to be true.

For example, one day I ring The Priory Boss at the Hammersmith in the head office from my call box made available in the ward. In the report that results from this incident, it was said that my having the phone number for the Head Office is disturbing.

But can you believe it? These geniuses hadn't even noticed that the number for the Head Office is printed on the back page of the very forms they had given all of us when we entered the place.

There also are lying incompetents, of which the social worker Gabija Knight is one – spell her name correctly, G-A-B-I-J-A K-N-I-G-H-T, because she deserves every wallop I'm about to give her.

In the flesh, she's a five-foot-seven-inch Swedish blond with a nice figure and very attractive. I imagine most of the docs and consultants undress her in their mind's eye ever moment they get, as there would be little else better to do.

Myself, I only have disgust for her. I have since seen her report about me, and it is littered with factual inaccuracies, regurgitations, and spelling mistakes. Did she not attend primary and secondary school, much less college? Because I had one and only one meeting with her, and she shamelessly lied about our encounter.

When I confront her with her untruths, she promptly terminates our meeting with great umbrage and pomposity. When I lodge a complaint against her, she denies any wrongdoing and is exonerated.

Between you and me, I would love to tear her apart verbally in a courtroom, and if she ever reads this book and wants to sue me for trashing her name, my answer is: 'go ahead -- make my day!'

# FIVE

The head consultant has promised to keep my ex-cop backstory a secret, but the promise is wafer thin, like all other promises from the psych joint. Every time anything comes on TV with a police theme, one of the staff always chirps, 'what do you think of that, Rob?'

In the end, I pull one the staff over to one side and say, 'if you mention me once more when there is a police situation on the news or television, I will knock your fucking lights out. Spread the word amongst the staff. I mean business, got it?'

Shortly after that, I am reprimanded by Dr Williams, who accuses me of threatening the staff. 'Me?' I say. 'Are they really that dumb? Just stop them inferring I'm a cop then, you fucking idiot. A threat can only be real if it has no conditions attached and I'm attaching conditions on this one'.

When medication time is called, just like the film 'One Flew Over the Cuckoo's Nest', the inmates think of clever ways to mislead the staff. I observe that many of the inmates don't take their pills when ordered, secretly spitting them into their hands.

The tablets can then be traded for cash or clothing or cigarettes. Bear in mind, most of the drugs administered are mind-altering or mind-shattering, and I dread to think what effect the wrong medication would have on the wrong type of patient.

Linford's behaviour deteriorates rapidly over time, and on one occasion, he punches the wits out of another lad without any warning. A terrible fight ensues that is quickly stopped, but I am prompted to write letter to staff asking for Linford's removal, as it has become impossible to relax with him in the ward. Everyone signs it and I hand it in, but the only result is for me to be labelled as a rabblerouser that, obviously, still is mentally unwell.

Further to me being branded a troublemaker, at one end of the ward is a payphone. One day I decide that I will take advantage of my phone privileges to ring the 'serious organised crime agency'. I get through to the control centre and tell them where I was and how difficult it has been to be surrounded by 'all these insane criminals'.

While on the phone, I ask – well, demand - to be moved to a different hospital or even a military hospital. Afterall, I was in the Navy for few years before I was a cop. Of course, nothing is done and nobody comes to give me a reprieve.

After that, I'm left to suffer the consequences of having over-booked myself a stay at Thornford Park.

The summer comes and goes -- July, August and September 2013. During that time, I only have one session from someone with psychiatric training. Ironically, helpful therapy is almost non-existent, and I truly believe it relates to the need to fill the beds.

Indeed, I witness staff deliberately winding up inmates who have impending appeal hearings, to make them (in my opinion) perform badly.

In the meantime, I have filed an appeal to my

continued incarceration, but truthfully, in my opinion looking back, I am rightly denied. I'm not ready at this time, as I clearly present a danger to myself and others.

# SIX

At Thornford Park, and after three months total in the two psyche hospitals, I again appeal in September. I now feel I'm well enough to return to the community and continue with treatment from there. As part of the appeal process, the people who want to keep me detained must submit their reports in advance to the appeal panel, to me and to my solicitor.

Principally, the reports trying to keep me detained come from Social Worker Knight, i.e., the buxom Swede, and Dr Patel, a diminutive, petite Asian woman that resembles a smarmy-looking professor.

However, the reports are full of information regurgitated from when I was first detained, because you could count the number of times they had both interacted with me since my arrival on two fingers (that is, I only saw them on one session each for a collective 30 minutes, less than the first half on a rugby game (while piled face first at the bottom of a scrum).

The date of the appeal (or meeting, as they call it) has been officially set for 16 September 2013, re Bucklebury Ward (Medium Secure), Patient's Name: Rob Sole, having been admitted from PICU, Parklands Hospital, Basingstoke with a Diagnosis purporting to be 'Mania without psychotic symptoms (F30.1).

The appeal panel consists of a District Judge, a Senior Consultant Psychiatrist, and a lay person. Both Knight and Patel fight tooth and nail to keep me here for another year. I know for a fact that if made to do another year it may kill me.

When it comes my turn, I stand up, clear my throat, adjust my imaginary tie, and prepare to tell them the truth, the whole truth, and nothing but the truth, so help me God (well, maybe with a tad bit of embellishment and literary license for good measure).

# MY STORY

# ONE

My father believes in the inalienable right to have children he cannot afford. I'll endeavour to tell you what I mean, your Worships (I'm speaking to the aforesaid District Judge, Senior Consultant Psychiatrist, and lay person, hereafter 'Ye Worships'):

First things first. I'm born on the 21$^{st}$ of May 1959, the second oldest child of Dave and Audrey Sole. There's a bit of irony in this, or fortuity, in that U.S. narcotics agents arrested a bunch of gangsters who had previously participated in the so-called Apalachin Meeting, an historic mob summit help at the home of 'Joe the Barber'. It's also the birthday of famed but little known cricketer, Isa Guha.

From the outset, my parents are mis-matched. Dad hails from a staunchly conservative Catholic background, having suffered a brutally disciplined childhood that he apparently runs from all of his life. Mum comes from a family not particularly religious, with her and her siblings raised in a relaxed liberal atmosphere.

The two opposites elope and get married. For some reason unbeknownst to me to this day, only Mum's parents feature regularly in our lives. I have never met or corresponded or talked to any of Dad's family. For reasons also unknown to me, his family has shot him with the quiver of ex-communication.

In my youth, Dad works as a Fitter and Turner, predominantly in Northeast England. During a short spell, we move to Leiston in Suffolk because Dad gets a job at Sizewell power station.

Together, my parents have a not unique talent: they are very adept at producing children, and by the time I'm five years old, there are four of us. Two boys and two girls. Elizabeth, the eldest, and Charles, Ann, and me. Age five is about my earliest recollection childhood or of having siblings.

We live in Leiston at the time. Dad works hard, Mum is a housewife, and weekends are spent at the local beach. They produce a lot of babies, but I've said that.

Looking back, I cannot understand why dad had all these children, because he has no concept of dealing with children. Whenever mum leaves the house, he line up four dining chairs, sits us on the chairs, and, if anyone dare say anything before mum gets back, whips us within an inch of our lives with his belt.

Leiston is where I undergo my first big change. Before, I'm a wimpy, skinny child, but this will change. One day the local bully, Porky Jones, who has heretofore made my life a living hell at my new school, chases me home to give me a kicking.

Upon entering the house balling, I tell Dad what has happened. He asks where Porky is now, and I point him out in the street.

'Come on, son,' he says going to the door. 'Let's go sort him out'.

We both march out of the house towards Porky like Napoleon on Waterloo, and I'm thinking Dad is going to give this big fat porky pig what's to. Instead, he says to me when we get close, 'sort him out, son,' and proceeds to retreat back to the house and shut the door.

Squaring off, Porky and I start brawling right in front of the house, thrashing and round-housing and walloping the tar out of each other, but I stand my ground. Sure, he beats the living hell out of me, but I hurt him as well, and from that day forward, his bullying ceases. Therefore, I learn from this exchange a big lesson: Don't rely on your father, and when you fight back, you draw a line without which you are toast.

Mum has her own harsh side, if you can call Dad's side harsh. When I steal a half dozen Caramac bars from the local shop, my sister Elizabeth grasses me up to Mum. Mum promptly gets hold of my ear and slaps me every other step as march back to the shop. She then makes me get on my hands and knees and apologise to the owner for thieving. I vow then and there never to steal again.

Mum falls pregnant with her fifth child, Tina, but Tina dies at home in her second month (probably from Cot death or what we now refer to as 'Sudden Infant Death Syndrome'.) It's a horrible thing, and the death of Tina has an awful effect on Mum, resulting in severe depression. From that point forward, she and dad argue nonstop.

Eventually they decide to move back north to be close to mum's family in Billingham near Middlesbrough. Funny thing, they immediately go for another child, and nine months later Lynn appears. Out of economic circumstance, we are forced to move into what can only be described as the shite hole slums, as Grangetown is by no stretch the jewel of the north.

For the first time, an awakening comes to me as to just how poor we really are. We live on a staple diet of jam and bread with an occasional treat that's pork or beef-dripping sandwiches. I find myself and my siblings wearing second-hand clothes that were often handed down from boy to girl and back to boy, regardless of how ridiculous we looked with our clueless cross-dressing.

Dad works for minimal labour wages at Smiths Dock in Middlesbrough. We have a 3-bed terraced house that's actually owned by the local church. It's sparsely furnished with a tiny record player but no tele. Three of us sleep in a single bed in one room, two of us in a single bed in another room, and Mum and Dad in the master bedroom (though it might give a new meaning to the word master).

Because we have no bedding, we use coats as blankets. When Dad goes to work in the morning, he must take a coat off the bed. We have an outside loo, and in the winter you have to boil a kettle to melt the ice to have a pooh. Toilet paper is discarded newspaper or Izal. Izal is called the John Wayne of toilet papers, because it doesn't take any shit from anyone.

Just to show how times have changed, when I'm only nine years of age, Mum and Dad allow me to rise at 5:30am, walk three miles to the local swimming pool on my own, train with the club and then go onto school -- without ever checking to see if I'd been kidnapped by some paedophile ring or made it to school on time. In those days, it wasn't done.

Because I don't remember Lynn, Mum tells me that Lynn was a victim of a tragic accident when one of us siblings (she refuses to identify which one) swung on her pram handle so as to catapult her out and smash her head against a brick wall. The resultant treatment gave her severe fits, and she has been severely mentally and physically handicapped ever since.

Whether or not Mum's story is true, it is an absolute fact that Lynn has remained critically ill in a wheelchair for most of her life, managing only the mental capacity of a bright three-year old. Amazingly, considering the doctors said at the time that she would not survive beyond seven years of age, she may outlive us all as she is presently 59 years old and still going strong.

Lynne's condition has a major impact on all of our lives, and to this day, I do not understand what possesses Mum and Dad to continue having children. But they do. They go on to have Gail and James, giving us a grand total of seven children under ten years of age -- one severely handicapped and dad still earning a pittance. We make church mice look posh.

Then one fine day Dad's proclivities come to roost. He answers the front door whilst buck naked and is reported to the police for doing so by the paperboy who ran off screaming.

When the magistrate finds out how many kids Dad has, he dismisses the case against him, noting that he obviously had to get a shag in sideways before mum got pregnant again. At the time, we have four in one bed and three in the other with no duvets or covers, just dad's many-talented, omni-purposed coat.

# BARKING MAD

The author and siblings growing up in poverty in the slums of the North-East, where even curtains can be made into clothing and handed down

# TWO

The north has always been a cruel place for Northerners, but for Northerners returning from the south with a perceived snooty southern accent, it is far worse.

To illustrate my point, one sparkling day two local lads, Jimmy and Peter, knock at our back door and ask Mum if me and Charles can come out to play. Mum says, 'of course', and when we are out they proceed to kick the living shit out of us on principle.

At 11 years old, I attend a local secondary school named 'Sir William Worsley'. There I receive numerous beatings because of my accent and am regularly forced to run the 'Gauntlet'. The gauntlet consists of ten cubicles with toilets on either side of a central aisle and a metal pole on the top of each door.

The big fun for the seniors is swinging from the poles as we run through and trying kick us in our faces. Nobody reaches the other end unscathed. My problem is exacerbated because my Mum can't afford to buy me long trousers. Meaning, of a school with 200 boys, I am the only one in shorts. That in itself entitles me to regular beatings, again on principle.

When I complain bitterly to Mum, she eventually agrees to let me have my dad's old suit pair. But there is a slight problem in that he's a barrel-chested 36-inch waist and a good 6 foot 2 inches tall, whilst I'm a skinny 22-inch waist and 5 foot 2 inches when stretched.

Not a problem for Mum, as she cuts the legs short and pinches the waist and backside together and sews up the centre. Now I'm donning a pair of pinstriped, baggy-legged trousers with a shark's fin of material sticking out of my arse.

No prizes for guessing how that is dealt with by the seniors, as I can still hear 200 kids screaming, *'GAUNTLETTTTT!!!'*

I mentioned earlier about Lynn impacting our lives, but that would truly win understatement of the year. Two incidents come to mind that I can now smile but at the time were far from hilarious.

As I say, because of her condition, Lynn is permanently reduced to sitting in a wheelchair, upon which she also has to wear a thick padded white sponge crash helmet. Because Mum makes me take Lynn out regularly for walks in the wheelchair, we encounter an example of cruelty.

One day when I'm walking her to the park, I see two seniors from school who have made it their mission to make my life as difficult as possible. One of them shouts, 'get that twat with the spakka!' (a slang term for Spastic), and they start chasing me when I turn and run whilst pushing the wheelchair.

Now Lynn, bless her heart thinks the whole thing is hilarious and put her hands high in the air and starts whooping like she's on a ride at Disney Land. Well, eventually they catch us and kick the living daylights out of me, leaving me crumpled on the ground and Lynn tipped over and spilt askance out of the wheelchair.

On another occasion, Mum tells me to take Lynn in the wheelchair to get bread from the local baker. 'She'll like that,' Whilst I'm in the queue, I take my eye off her and she picks up two fresh cream cakes and sticks them to her forehead.

'You will have to pay for those, son,' the baker said.

But since I don't have enough money, I have to leave Lynn there for security I guess whilst I hustle back home to get more cash. When I return, Lynn's entire face is covered in fresh cream.

'Looks like you'll have to put her to work in the kitchen', I say, though eventually they admit that it's as much their fault as mine. What do you expect when you put a kid in a puff pastry store!

In the Northeast, the unions are extremely powerful, and nothing happens at work without their sanction. Someone is sacked at Smiths Dock where my Dad works for hiding in a store room asleep and the unions called a strike in response. With so many mouths to feed, Dad cannot afford to be without work and so he is labelled a scab. Ultimately he is hounded out by the unions and forced to work for ICI, a Petro-chemical company.

Whilst working at ICI, Dad applies for a job with Aramco Oil, whose work is offered in the Mideast country of Bahrain. When he takes the job, all of a sudden, his salary rockets to an insane tax free amount. Under a special contract, he works six weeks on and six weeks off.

Happy days are here again, most people would be thinking. But what happens from here destroys more than a few lives (my Dad's included). It's a situation of unintended consequences of an intentional act.

All starts well and good with good money galore, but dad is such a bullshitter that he tells his new-found Bahrain colleagues that he had no kids. Most of have no children either. So, instead of returning home to England, he joins his mates in Malta for two weeks of celebratory drunkenness and the grand pursuit of chasing prostitutes.

Soon, he is doing two shots -- one in Malta and one in England, splitting his time eight weeks away and four weeks home. But since a lot of his money is not making it home, Mum is forced to get a part-time job at a pub just to make ends meet. That's when she starts drinking, to deal with all of his shenanigans.

I pass my eleven plus and go the grammar school in Eston. I still have my report from William Worsley School, an astonishingly favourable but hilarious review, especially given the entirety of the circumstances. The report says, 'Rob is extremely bright but needs to take more care of his personal appearance'.

What kind of teacher would believe I'm wearing shark-fin-arsed baggy pin stripe trousers by my own choice? 'Hey, can I have some britches that are ten sizes to big? I really need them. Really'.

Both to my delight and to my detriment, I am extremely adept at making people laugh, believing wrongly that the making-people-laugh bit is far more important than studying for school.

As you might have guessed, I don't gel with a couple of teachers at Eston Grammar. In particular, one Mr Jones takes an instant disliking to me because I can't help being a wise-arse even if I don't want to be.

One afternoon we are playing cricket on the pitch with Mr Jones in charge. Because I hate the game, I stand in my allocated field position daydreaming. Maybe it is a product of having a big family, where you can switch off the noise around you in a snap.

By all accounts, a ball comes near me that I should have caught, yet I don't even move a spec. Suddenly, Mr Jones starts shouting at me. Then he runs past me and picks up the ball and runs all the way back and throws it straight at me from close range, hitting me squarely in the balls.

'Pay attention, you puff!' he barks.

Well, having him accuse me back in the '70s of being the worst thing imaginable, a gay boy, I launch my arm and bust him square on the nose. Class is dismissed and I am sent to the office of the headmaster, Messer Hindle. Mr Hindle only has one leg and it is rumoured the other one is made of wood; but nobody has ever seen it. Meaning, he is someone to be reckoned with.

Corporal punishment is regularly used at the grammar school and Mr Hindle intends to give me six whacks of the cane for my misbehaviour. When I refuse him, however, I'm promptly sent home and told to return the next day with my parents in tow.

Ol' Hindle sets out the facts but lying Mr Jones denies both that he threw the ball at my nuts and polished it off by calling me a puff.

I speak truth to power, saying 'I'll have the cane if Mr Jones has the cane for calling me a puff'. Mr Hindle then produces my English book which on the inside back cover has a hand-drawn picture of him with a visible wooden leg with branches and nesting bird on it. Under the artistry are the words, 'I hope Hindle gets Dutch elm disease'.

I almost burst out laughing on the spot but manage to

control myself, feeling an anticipatory twitching in my buttocks. Mr Hindle asks my dad for his view, but fair play to dad means doubling down. 'If Mr Jones did that to me,' he says, 'I would thump him as well'.

Mr Hindle is none too impressed with either of us. He then stands up and says, quite caustically, 'in that case, you can take your barrack room lawyer and find another school. He is expelled from this point forward and will not be welcome back'.

Good riddance, we both think, father and son, symbolically high-fiving each other on the way out.

Going back in time for a moment, during my first year at Eston grammar, we move from Grangetown to a relatively new development owned by the council called Spencerbeck in Ormesby, on the outskirts of Middlesbrough. Home is now a three-storey townhouse. All my siblings move to the closest school, but I remain suspended and bereft of school for six months.

Of course, I don't just sit idle. I am required to do six months of assessments with a child psychologist, and it is decided by the powers on high that there is nothing wrong with me. My punishment is that I was allocated a space at Ormesby Comprehensive School when school return from the summer break.

Spencerbeck Estate has some colourful characters, and like any council estate, is fraught with crime and social issues, including our own family's. In the time during which I'm suspended, my sister Elizabeth has hooked up with one of the toughest kids in the school.

Bobby is a muscular lad who looks 20 years old when he's actually 14 and has already sprouted a beard. This relationship between Elizabeth and Bobby will last for many years (but it all ends badly with hijinks covered later in the book).

When Bobby and I become quick friends, that fact impacts on my standing at school. The three toughest lads are Bobby and Ian, who are mates, and a loner named Geoff. All of them share a mutual respect of one another.

Picking up where I leave off, I continue to clown around at school and never take anything seriously. People naturally assume that because I am Bobby's mate and have been expelled from grammar school for thumping a teacher, that I not to be messed with.

Meanwhile, Mum and Dad's relationship continues on the skids. Sometimes dad provides money and sometimes he just disappears for months and we don't hear a peep from him.

Presumably he's working abroad, going from Bahrain to Botswana and Libya, with interludes to Malta now a regular theme. While in Botswana, he develops a bitter hatred of blacks. As a result, when he's in town, he constantly blurts out tirades of abusive language whenever he sees a black person. It's downright offensive.

Mum started drinking in Grangetown and has gotten worse in Ormesby. She's averaging 12 Gold Label Barley wines per day. The kids regularly go to the off licence and bring home four-packs of Barley Wine backstopped by Capstan full strength cigarettes.

She's gets knocked out twice in the Centurion Pub in the centre of the estate after getting pissed and picking fights with men she doesn't like. She's become a downright lush.

I start mixing with a live wire named Steve who's into

motorbikes, adrenaline and speed (only of the high velocity kind). We ride BSA Bantams and Triumph Tiger Cubs with no licence, no insurance, no helmets, and no sense, often being chased by the police and turning the chase into a romping game.

At school, Bobby and Ian decide to test my mettle and convince Geoff to offer me out at lunchtime. News of our impending fight spreads around the school like wildfire, attracting over a hundred students who form a circle around us. Geoff is a lot broader and chunkier than me, and when fighting, he goes ballistic.

My numerous fights and beatings have taught me to remain calm under stressful situations like this. I know to take a few hits without folding, sort of a rope-a-dope style made famous by Mohammed Ali.

Whist Geoff swings furiously in my direction, wearing his arms out, I pick him off with a few well-placed punches to the head (also Ali style). Nevertheless, he pounds me and good, but we are both hurting each other, and I am so close to a draw that I may have prevailed in the minds of some.

The fight is stopped by a teacher and we both get detention that night. Bobby and Ian say they think it was a draw and tell Geoff he will have to go again if he thinks otherwise.

Thankfully he declines, ceding me the third place in the beat-the-shit-out-of-you pecking order. Bobby and Ian then admit they orchestrated the fight in the first place, and I have passed the test.

# THREE

My younger brother Charles has befriended a lad called Peter whose eldest brother Phil is a major criminal on our council estate. In time, I become friends with Phil and his younger brother Rob, who is my age. It's a formula for trouble if I'm not careful.

Meanwhile, Mum and Dad's relationship is in tatters. When dad is home, they drink themselves into oblivion and we the kids look after ourselves. It's a regular thing for someone on the estate to knock on our door and tell us that our Mum has passed out somewhere mortally drunk. We have to retrieve her from someone's garden or on a path where she has passed out.

Sadly, both of our parents have become chronic alcoholics, and when they are intoxicated they behave as the opposites that apparently drew them together in the beginning. When dad is drunk, he becomes docile and sleepy, often nodding out sprawled on his favourite chair. Mum becomes a violent, spiteful woman and is utterly unrecognisable.

Elizabeth has gotten herself a part-time job working in a shop that sells men's trousers called Loon Pants (these are the pants that hug your thigh and then balloon out from the knee down). When Bobby convinces her to allow him to steal an entire rail of trousers whilst she's alone in the shop, as always happens when you do something idiotic, they get caught and the police got involved. Mum has to bail Elizabeth out of jail, but she defends herself by explaining that Bobby is always hitting and abusing her if she doesn't give him his way.

Elizabeth is 16 now and her relationship with Bobby peters out. She starts dating a black man who is a nightclub DJ, but negligently omits to tell Dad. You can imagine what happens when Dad get up one morning and comes down to find a black man asleep on his sofa. He instantly throws the fellow out in his ear with a verbal lashing about 'no niggers in the house' and his daughter 'can't be seen with a nigger'.

True to form, when you impose irrational conditions on your kids, they're going to rebel and do exactly the opposite. Elizabeth soon disappears to London and we completely lose touch with her. She married a black man named Barry with whom she had had three kids in the slums back when it was called Surrey Docks. Prejudice struck our family hard.

Not unwisely, Mum is extremely worried about me mixing with bad company when I have so many opportunities to do so. When I leave school at 16 with no qualifications and no future on the horizon, Mum takes it upon herself to apply on my behalf to the Royal Navy, signing the application and purporting to be me.

Lo and behold, the application is successful, and out of the blue I get a letter inviting me to take medical, Maths and English exams. I am shocked, but Mum persuades me to go anyway as she says, rightly, that I have nothing to lose.

I end up being accepted into the Navy as a Junior

Seaman Operator with a start date in February 1976. Holy Torpedo!

Meanwhile, I have six months to kill, so I get a job working as a general labourer building the A19 roadway and earning £150 per week. Always tempting fate, I continue to ride motorbikes illegally with my pal Steve and regularly go to work on a BSA Bantam with no licence and no insurance. Who is it that said, 'a thing can be true and still be a desperate folly?'

Drugs are becoming more common place in my world, particularly cannabis, as all my friends smoke the heck out of it. Very fortunately, I practically gag like a maggot when I first try the evil weed, so I give up smoking before I even get started. To this day, I have never been one to imbibe.

Just before reporting to the Navy, I'm riding my motorbike around the estate without a helmet. I rev loudly one time too many and end up being chased by a blue and white police Panda.

The cops are closing in on me, so I mount the pavement and cross a playing field. After the steep incline, I head for the woods where I know the cops can't follow me.

Before reaching the woods, however, the cop's car turn sharply on the incline and shockingly rolls over and down the hill where it end up on its roof. I make the rookie mistake of going back to make sure the copper is alright, and he gets a good look at me. Seeing he's not hurt, I speed off.

About a week later, I'm in my room when I see a police officer trotting up our path. Dad answers the door and I hear the officer ask for me. "What's the problem?' Dad says. The police officer explains what happened on my motorcycle and says he's here to arrest me.

'That's a shame', Dad says. 'He's leaving to join the Royal Navy next week'.

Taken aback, the police officer replies, 'OK, here's the deal. I will go away and come back in two weeks. If your son is in the Navy, we'll forget about the incident. If he's not, he's going to jail'.

By his carefully calculated use of discretion, that cop changed the direction of my life forever.

# FOUR

In February 1976, I join HMS Raleigh of the Royal Navy and go through basic training, earning a piddling £11 a week. It is a harsh regime and for me a complete culture shock. I do a short spell onboard a Polaris nuclear submarine working as a sonar operator in a sub officially named the British Naval Ballistic Missile System, but I hate it with a capital H.

Maybe I'm claustrophobic and maybe not, but I cannot take the confinement, and luckily I am returned to normal ships duty where I become a radar operator. My first assignment in 1976 is HMS Charybdis, based in Plymouth. From that port, we venture out to countries far and wide, including a trip sailing around the Caribbean as The West Indies Guardship.

By 1979, I join the HMS Exeter that's being built on the Tyne in Newcastle. There I'm witness to the dockyard workers under union control coming to work with fishing rods and sleeping bags and spending the entire shift either fishing or asleep or both. It's total bollocks and a waste of the human condition.

Naturally, the ship is late being built and is massively over budget as a direct result of the unions holding the government for ransom. National security? Phooey, and at the time, the unions couldn't care less.

The next Navy contract goes to Hamburg in Germany. Surprise, surprise, the demise of the Tyne shipyards also follows. Talk about shooting yourself in the foot. That's what happens when you demand top dollar wages for doing absolutely nothing.

On HMS Exeter, I meet two men who have a major impact on my life and to this day are still friends, if you can believe that! Ian is the ship's Physical Training Instructor and Alan is a lead hand in the radar department.

I'll deal with Ian first. At that time, I am a beer swilling, curry-loving fat arse bloke and the life and soul of any and all parties who doesn't score that many honeys. Constructively, Ian says to me, 'Rob, you would pull more birds if you weren't such a fat bastard'.

Taking his choice words to heart, I instantly begin to moderate my drinking and eating. I also start training with him with a view to applying to take part in the Royal Navy Field Gun competition in a few years' time.

Ian is fit and muscular and has previously ran Field Gun for the Fleet Air Arm crew. He is also exceptionally good-looking and a smooth operator with the ladies to boot. A trail of stunning women from around the world always seem eager to put their sights on him.

Alan and I begin a friendship that will take us to new heights of excitement and to new depths of despair. Over time, we both have been around so much death and heartache that our middle names should have been Jonah. I love him as a brother and there isn't anything we wouldn't do for each other.

That last statement has been tested fully many times. It is a testament to our friendship that, since we met in 1979, we have remained in constant contact ever since, and despite our vastly different paths in life, there has never been more than a month gone by when we haven't spoken to each other (except for the psych ward).

Newcastle can stake claim to one of the best nights out in the whole of the United Kingdom. The weekends are a feast for sore Navy eyes with scantily clad women running amok and filling every bar and club, many wearing knickers to keep their ankles warm. Their arse cheeks remind me of two ferrets fighting to get out of a sack with their tops cut so low I'm sure I can see their vests. A Navy bloke's wet dream, in other words.

My mates Alan and Ian are like rats up a drainpipe. I'm convinced they are trying to make sure they don't let any woman in Newcastle miss out on the benefits of their sexual prowess. On the other hand, I have always been more of a relationship guy than an out and out shagger. Unless I'm mortally pissed, I am never keen on bedding women I don't really know. So the women I do wake up with seldom compliment me on last night' performance, and I often reciprocate by legging it without giving my name.

I do start a relationship with a young woman named Carol who has blonde hair and blue eyes and a body that most women would die for. As her brother-in-law is a mechanic and wily as to the ways of hot cars, he convinces me to borrow £2000 from a bank buy a Ford Cortina 2000E with huge, Carlos Fandango alloy wheels and fat General grabber tyres. But I can't get comprehensive insurance on the car due to my youth and have to settle for third party fire and theft cover.

Not long after meeting her, I am impacted by impeccably bad timing, as the ship sails from Newcastle to Portsmouth. I would spend the weekends with Carol and then set off at midnight on the drive back to Portsmouth to join my ship. That proves to be a fatal error of judgement. As I travelled down what was once the A34 (being built close to a village called Whitchurch), I close my eyes and nod out at about 6am.

The first thing I hear is a gut-wrenching bang only to open my eyes and see my car flying in mid-air with nothing visible out of my windscreen but dark sky. That view changes as my car rolls over and heads back to earth, roof first. For some reason, I scream 'MUM', and then it's lights out. When I hit the road, I have lost all consciousness.

I'm not sure how long I'm out, but I awake in pitch blackness to find the roof flattened with me lying across the handbrake and my head resting comfortably on the passenger seat. The smell of petrol is horrendous, so I quickly gather myself and start kicking the doors for what seems like an eternity until I manage to get the driver's door to open … only to entangle my jumper on the handbrake lever.

To release myself, I must rip off the arm of the jumper and drag myself out of the car. Once free of the wreckage and reek of petrol, I stumble about 100 yards up the road and sit down on the road and cry, uncontrollably.

Whilst sitting there, a car pulls up to the wreckage that had once been my car and then drives off at a speed oblivious to me sitting where I am. About 15 minutes later, I hear the whoop whoop of sirens and a police car skidding onto the scene in a long trail of dust and debris. Jetting from their police vehicle to the crash site, the officers peer into the mangled car until I shout to them from afar and they spot me sitting there all alone.

Shortly after the ambulance arrives, I'm taken to hospital where I'm detained 24 hours for observation. It clearly is not my turn on the roulette wheel of life to die that day. Despite the fact the car is totalled, I only suffer a small scratch on my face and am thereafter made to pay off a huge loan without the benefit of insurance and now nothing to show for my wear.

'Easy come, easy go', is the motto of the day. Ironically, the only thing that isn't smashed to pieces on the car is the spare wheel. That was recovered, and I now take great pride hanging it on the wall of our mess deck where the sleeping quarters are on the ship.

Meanwhile, I continue training with Ian with brilliant results: my lardy, 18 stone body miraculously starts to shift and change shape. Oddly, my face is the first place to show a difference because I previously had had more chinny chin chins than the Hong Kong phone directory. One by one, the chins started to disappear, leaving only one behind in their place.

ROBERT SOLE

The author in the Royal Navy as a young man

# FIVE

HMS Exeter is a Type 42 Destroyer, and because her base port is Portsmouth Harbour, that is where we end up. In 1980, Portsmouth is a thriving Navy city with ships anchored everywhere in the dockyard. When you go out at night, there are thousands of matelots (slang for sailors) getting mortally pissed and trying to empty the plethora of takeaway shops of all their food inventory.

Matelots never walk anywhere, so taxi -drivers who don't mind working long shifts and taking Navy flak earn good fortunes. The locals called us 'Skates' based on a rumour that in olden days sailors used to shag fish by the same name in that their orifice is not unlike a woman's. Skate-bashing has thus become a local past time, and drunk sailors regularly find themselves the victim of a serious boot-kicking by disgruntled locals who are jealous of us taking their women.

Ian, Alan and I go out regularly together and at least part of us thinks we are God's gift to woman. Ian's right, that my huge weight loss is in direct proportion to my success with women. So one night, Alan and I go to Nero's night club and there we notice a stunning blonde staring at us. Unfortunately, her wing woman is far from attractive, as is often the dilemma presented to two carousing young lads.

We both are wearing matching white cap sleeve t-shirts, white jeans which are so tight you could see the veins growing in our balls, and white POD shoes. In true cocky Alan style, he says, 'come on, Rob, we are in like Flynn here and you're having the fat one.' My heart sinks, as how could I expect any less.

We start chatting them up but to our collective surprise the blonde grabs a hold of me and the other one grabs Alan and they whisk us off to the dance floor. After several twirls later, Alan calls time out and we go to the bar for a fresh bevy of drinks. Turning to each other, we have a heated discussion in which Alan let me know in no uncertain terms that he was not shagging the fat one. 'No F_N way!'

I remind him of his obligations as a wing man and the horrors I have woken with in support of his various romps. Eventually he backs down and we return to our new-found friends, with Alan trying desperately to get pissed and me deliberately staying reasonably sober so I can do the deed that I'm destined to do.

When two o'clock closing time comes, we left the club and walk only a short distance to the girls' flat. We have just sat down in the living room, but before we even make small talk, the big girl grabs Alan and says coyly and forcefully, 'come with me, little man. I'm going to fuck your brains out'.

The last thing I see on Alan's face is her marching him out of the room like a condemned man. Within minutes, me and blondie can hear the obvious sounds of her trying her best to empty Alan's balls on a bed which badly needs oiling. Between her orgasmic screams, Alan shouts the immortal words, 'the fucking things I do for you, R Sole!'

I almost wet myself laughing and would have done so if my date hadn't reminded me of our purpose for being here by undoing my bar-tight jeans and getting down to business in the lounge, kitchen counters and bathroom sink. Eventually we're all spent, and an eerie silence prevailed in the flat.

I don't remember falling asleep on the sofa with blondie, but I am rudely awakened at the crack of dawn by a very dishevelled, very unhappy looking Alan. Apparently, he has fallen asleep with his arm around his new-found friend and is now expressing the preference of chopping off his arm in lieu of waking the monster. From that day forward, we refer to big, ugly women as 'Stumpers'.

HMS Exeter is an amazing ship with a loyal tightknit crew. As is the norm with new ships, they must carry out a certain number of hours of sea training exercises whilst being monitored by a Flag Officer Sea Training Staff -- in this instance, just off the coast at Portland in Dorset. Portland is a small community built around the naval base and Portland Prison lies about five miles to the west of Weymouth.

It's a desolate and awful place and none of us likes going there. To begin with, it means long hours at sea effectively in a war environment where the ship is simulating being attacked by a variety of enemies from submarines to jet fighters. Most of our waking moments are spent in full, anti-flash clothing wearing gas masks and sweating like Gary Glitter in a school playground.

I work in the operations room as the ship's Helicopter Controller. That position must rank as one of the most stressful jobs in the Royal Navy, as it entails using a radar screen to control an agriculture flying machine. The fact that helicopters can stay airborne by nothing more than whirring blades is one of life's mysteries, and John the pilot is a flash, cool-looking maverick who does whatever he wants once he gets airborne.

It is my job to brief the captain and the pilot about the day's flying activity as well as the weather and any other dangers that are relevant. I do that and as we walk away, John says, 'Rob, I'm going to fly to my house and wave to my wife and kids, so I'll be off radar for a while'.

Him doing that is completely against aviation rules and Naval protocol but he is so flash he doesn't give a flying fuck. And true to his word, halfway through the flight I watch him disappear into the radar clutter and land 10 miles north of our position. And true to my luck, wouldn't you know it, but into the operations room walks the Captain, who at once exclaims, 'where is the helicopter HC' (abbreviation for Helicopter Controller)?

I mumble, 'not sure, sir, I've lost it at the moment.'

The Captain turns and looks straight at me and shouts, 'lost it? It's 40 feet long and weighs three tons, for Christ's sake. You had better find it or start looking for another job'.

As if by magic, the chopper (as it is affectionately known) suddenly appears as a miniscule blip on my screen, heading back towards the ship. I wait until it is well clear of land before declaring to the Captain, 'contact has been regained, sir'. Ron thanks me for keeping stum whilst he has accomplished his mission.

A couple of days later, I'm in front of the Captain again getting a tongue lashing, which is parr for the course. Ian, Alan and I had decided to go out for a night clubbing in Weymouth. We were fortunate enough to meet three attractive and willing local ladies who had taken us back to a house and seriously abused our bodies.

Naturally, we had overslept, and unnaturally, we arrived back at the jetty five minutes after the ship had sailed. We had to be flown by a SeaKing Helicopter back to the ship and winched back onto the flightdeck, only to be greeted by the ships two military policeman, who escorted us below decks and, being a pair of characters themselves, had a good laugh at our expense.

The Master at Arms (i.e., the head honcho policeman) has suggested that if we made up a better story for the Captain at our discipline hearing – one that he had never heard before - he would probably let us go without a telling off. Happy as sand boys, we went below decks to our living accommodation and set about making up something amusing.

So, on the day of the Captain's Table (mini court hearing like a courts marshal), I foolishly volunteer to go first, with Alan set to go second and Ian last. The Captain frowns behind a lectern near his cabin and the Master at Arms stands slightly behind him. When the Master at Arms shouts my name, I march into the room wearing my Number 1 (best) uniform and hat.

Positioned in front of the Captain and at attention, I stop and the Master at Arms shout, 'Salute', which I do, followed by, 'off Cap', which I also do but in an appropriately exaggerated manner. The Master at Arms then reads out the charge of being five minutes late for the ship, which is contrary to good order and Naval discipline.

'How then do you plead?' he says.

'Not guilty', I say.

'Not guilty? the Captain exclaims. 'You better explain yourself'.

'Well sir, I was out drinking in Weymouth and met a lovely woman who took me back to her house'.

The Captain frowns. No doubt he has heard this lame excuse a million times before.

'I spent the night and set my alarm for 7am, ample time to get back to the ship. When I got up to leave, the lady said, "you're not leaving", and I replied, "I am, I must"'.

Now the Captain is pursing is lips and I can tell he's getting a tad cross.

'She said, "you're not. I'm a wicked witch and if you leave I will turn you into a frog"'.

Now the Captain is giving me an evil eye and the Master at Arms is shaking his head no just out of the Captain's view.

Suddenly the Captain shouts at me, 'this is utter nonsense. Why were you late, Leading Seaman Sole?' He is red in the face and look like he's about to blow a gasket.

But I'm past the point of no return, and I say, "of course I didn't believe her either and I left immediately, *sir!'*

'So, why were you late,' he says.

'Sir, have you ever tried hopping from Weymouth to Portland?'

The Captain can no longer control his rage, screaming 'don't be flippant with me young man. I find you guilty as charged'. Then he gathers himself and says, 'what's the normal sentence for this offence, Master at Arms?'

The Master at Arms replies, 'two days pay, sir'.

'I fine this man eight days' pay', the Captain says. 'Now about turn and get out of my sight now'.

I put my cap on, salute, spin around and march out, spluttering, 'eight days' pay for five minutes late? Holy shit'.

Alan and Ian, who have heard all of this, have since gone white. Each of them is called in separately, and each of them decides that discretion is the better part of valour, so instead of giving their made-up excuses, plead guilty and are only docked two days' pay.

That whole story is now committed to Naval folklore, and more than a few people have since laid claim to using my defence as their own.

# SIX

After finishing all our sea trials and going back to Portsmouth for some home time, we are told we will be heading soon to the Mediterranean Sea for an exercise with some other NATO (North Atlantic Treaty Organisation) warships and submarines.

Whilst in Portsmouth, I meet a very attractive young waitress named Jean and start a long-term relationship with her. Meanwhile back at home, Mum and Dad flit in an out of being together. Dad is drinking a bottle of Scotch a day and Mum is committed to eight to 12 Barley wines. My eldest siblings have all left home.

Elizabeth lives in London, Charles has gotten a girl pregnant at 16 (with a shotgun wedding following), and Ann has married a black man called Umbopo who is more than twice her age. To say that our family is fucked up, wins understatement of the year. Fortunately, Lynne, being mentally and physically handicapped, is oblivious to the carnage. But Gail and James have had an awful go of it.

The only time they have any fun or go out anywhere other than school is when I come home and take them. I become a father figure to them and make regular trips home, just to give them some semblance of normality. It always makes me smile when people blame their upbringing on the fact that they are criminals or drug addicts or benefit cheats or unable to get jobs. You would need to look long and hard to find a family with more issues than ours.

Despite our family troubles, every one of us except for Lynne have become hard-working, honest individuals. Elizabeth owned a large removal company in London until she split from her partner. Charles is a Senior Manager for a national company. And Ann tragically died at 42 from the dread gestational diabetes that she had contracted after giving birth to her first child.

It's a tragically sad story, the way she died. And ironically, her dear friend died from Type 1 diabetes at the age of 42. When Ann went out and got pissed drunk to ease the pain, she returned home and died in her sleep, at the same age, 42. Anne's death was awful for all of us, but even more so for Mum and Anne's two sons. Gail is the manager of a sought-after pub in Hampshire. James is a self-made millionaire, runs his own building company, lives in a huge house in 10 acres of land with its own lake. Not bad for a former council house kid.

# SEVEN

Jean and I get on like a house on fire. After a short while, I move in with her and her sister Lucy in a rented house in Southsea. Lucy is an attractive, lively character but after a short while she becomes more and more reclusive, stops working, stops getting dressed, and pretty much stops doing anything except lounging around in her dressing gown and pyjamas all day long.

Jean and I party hard and live an active social life. When Lucy stops having visitors, although we think it is odd as she seems mentally OK, we just leave her to her druthers -- to each his own, as the old proverb goes. She never gave an explanation for her behaviour and thankfully pulled herself together and started socialising again.

If there is one thing Jean and Lucy know, it is how to party, and we regularly trawl the pubs and clubs in Southsea, getting absolutely mullered. One of our favourite haunts is The Cambridge Pub, and that's where I introduce Lucy to my mate Alan. They hit it off immediately and my brother from another mother hitches up with my girlfriend's sister. Utopia prevails.

As with anything that is going well in the Navy, sea time bursts the bubble and we are ordered to set off to the Mediterranean to join the NATO taskforce. The girls we leave are all stunning, and we pray we have done enough to keep them faithful until we return. Life when you are married or in a relationship with a Matelot is hard. Many times a relationship buckles under the pressure, or each turn a blind eye to the other's infidelities, as we will later see.

# EIGHT

Our first stop en route to the Mediterranean is Porto, Portugal. Our assignment is an official, flying-the-flag visit designed to strengthen the United Kingdom's relationships with other countries. Porto is half the size of Lisbon, on the Atlantic and has a half dozen bridges spanning the large river that flows into the ocean, the flats on both sides of the banks looking like Amsterdam on cliffs.

As is often the case, the docks tend to be in a rough area of the city, and Porto is no exception. To have a good and safe night out, we have to walk out of our secure area across a bridge and over the river to arrive at the thriving clubs and bars in old town.

Having been at sea for a while, in true naval tradition we paint the town red and begin our return to the ship in the wee hours of the morning, absolutely shit-faced drunk with a belly full of beer and fast food.

Apparently the local hoodlums see us as easy pickings. So every night, some of our lot gets stopped at knife point and beaten and robbed of their money, returning to the ship with black eyes, minor cuts, and total humiliation. One of the lads even returns in his underpants, because the hoodlums have taken a liking to his clothing and made him remove all of his duds.

A stern warning is given by the Naval Police onboard, banning us from crossing the bridge. But banning a Matelot from anything is something akin to waving a red rag at a bull. The warning falls on deaf ears and the robberies and beatings continue because we continue to go unabated into the city. That is, until Alan, Ian and I say, 'enough is enough'.

We call together a meeting of about 40 sailors into our mess deck and decide to exact some revenge on the thieving gits who have taken too many liberties already. Someone goes out to issue a challenge, and we play fair by allowing them to go get weapons of their choice and return at 11pm dressed and ready for a fight.

They are far from shy, returning with a variety of weapons that include metal bars, hockey sticks, and socks stuffed with coins or bolts. We have already psyched ourselves up by watching the cult movie, 'The Warriors', about gangs in New York, before strategically leaving two or three at a time and re-grouping underneath the bridge over the river. Alan oversees the men under the bridge, and Ian and I walk back and forth on the bridge pretending to be pissed.

True to form, it isn't long before we are approached by five men and one woman, all armed to the gills with very bitchin' knives. As they walk towards us, Ian shouts, 'Warriors come out to play', referencing the movie. Suddenly all hell breaks loose, and Alan and the boys come streaming towards us, the knife gang hightail it into the dockside town.

A couple of them take a few punches on the way, but adrenalin is a powerful tool, and they are quicker on their feet than we are. They make it to what they hope will be a safe haven, a café bar with about ten men in it. Unfortunately for them, we have had a gut-full of the robberies and are high on the scent of the chase.

A Scouser (Liverpudlian) with a hockey stick runs up and smashes in a huge plate glass window, and we pour into the café smacking everyone in range. Even the girl is shown no mercy, with one of the lads punching her so hard her nose splits like a tomato hit with a hammer, dropping her like a sack to the floor.

Once satisfied that there is no one left standing in the café, we back out and start to walk away. As we do, we become aware of a group of thug youths approaching, and it is obvious they have heard the commotion and have no intentions of just talking. So we wade in amongst them and in short time they decide to run back from whence they have come, yelling and screaming in flight.

This late-night commotion has woken the whole town, so their numbers start growing fast and ours are diminishing even faster, until we are only about 20 strong. There is a Mexican standoff, no one daring to move first, until they number about 100 and start walking towards us like the 'Gangs of New York'. Alan shouts 'charge', and we all started running towards them.

To our surprise, even though they far outnumber us, they turn and flee. We start whooping it up and running helter-skelter until we hear the unmistakable crack of gunshots. The police have arrived on the scene and are shooting towards and at us. Despite the absolute fear factor, I shout 'run away, run away', mimicking a line from one of our other favourite films, 'Monty Python and the Holy Grail'.

We all turn and hightail it back towards the dock

entrance and the safety of the ship. It is in times like this that some people realise adrenalin is brown and a change of pants might be required. Quite a few people have arrived before us to do that, and to get back onto a ship alongside a jetty, a gangway is used (which is basically a small metal bridge with handrails).

To prevent unwanted visitors to the ship, two Navy men must guard the gangway, the most senior being the Quarter Master, so as we flood back to the ship, I tell the Quarter Master to keep stum and not identify the name and rank of anyone returning with me. I also explain that we have sorted the robbers out, but that there may be repercussions. He is a good friend of ours, so we know he can be trusted.

We leg it below docks and all come together and chat over the night's misadventures. Fifteen minutes later, over the Tannoy PA System, the Quarter Master loudly exclaims, 'Emergency stations! Emergency stations! The ship is under attack!'

We all stream upstairs onto the flight deck to find a crowd of people shaking the dock fencing so hard that it is about to give way. Out on the bridge, the Captain is shouting, 'Man the fire hoses! Man the fire hoses!' Which is what we do, in double quick time.

The angry crowd has now breached the fence and starts approaching the ship. We turn the hoses loose, pounding them with a pressure of 200 pounds per square inch, literally knocking them clean off the ground and scattering their bodies helter-skelter.

It's like playing Skittles with humans. Since more and more people are arriving fast, the Captain decides to start the engines to make an escape. We are going to free ourselves of the ropes and slip away from the jetty and anchor instead in the middle of the river. Wise move.

Thankfully, the crowd disperses without this necessity. We go to bed, but not before making sure that no-one admits to being part of the fight and subsequent riot. We – Ian, Alan and I – do not sleep too well that night, because we know the shit is going to well and truly hit the fan over the next few days.

The very next day, a Stewards' Enquiry start in earnest. Quite a few innocent members of the ship had returned oblivious to the riot and had taken quite a beating from the highly agitated and disgruntled locals. We brief as many people as we can that mum is the word of the day, but we worry we cannot control everyone.

Needless to say, this incident escalates into a huge deal. Military police are flown in from the UK, and the press gets wind of the story. The headline of the Sun newspaper reads, 'Riot in Porto Involving Crew from HMS Exeter'. Soon the riot becomes a global diplomatic event, the investigators hellbent on putting someone's head to the chopping block.

Thankfully, everyone holds firm, and despite intense pressure, nobody appears to be admitting anything. Or so we think. When the investigators return to the UK port of call, the ship's own police summon Alan, Ian and I to the office. 'Alright, you three', the head honcho says, 'we know you organised this'.

We all look blankly at them, putting on our best innocent faces.

'Look', he says. 'Junior Seaman Mackey grassed you up, but we kept it to ourselves'.

Ian says, 'he must have made a mistake. We were all

in bed asleep at the time, sir'.

We smile and honcho smiles and says, 'Fuck off now then'.

We turn and walk out and the head honcho whispers, 'good work, boys'. Then we go straight back to our messdeck and have a party, relaying tales of combat as we drink copious amounts of beer.

Not long afterwards, the Portuguese government bans British Naval visits until further notice. To be fair, that is no real loss.

# NINE

From Porto we set sail to Gibraltar, which is every Matelots dream, with roughly 130 bars and nightclubs per square mile.

Meanwhile, my new-found fitness and trim body are about to be tested in the HMS Exeter Superstar contest (mimicking a TV Programme). I have already won a couple of the heats testing various fitness disciplines, and the last event has me running to the top of the Rock of Gibraltar.

This gruelling challenge on a good day, is made worse by the blistering heat. To be fair, Ian would have romped the competition but as the organiser and Ships Physical Training Instructor, he has been banned from entering the competition. The race involves running up a series of twisting, turning roads from sea level all the way to the top of the mountain that is the real Rock of Gibraltar.

I come in second place behind a proper racing snake who weighs about eight stone when soaking wet (to my much bigger and thicker build). Each event scores 10 points for $1^{st}$ place, nine for $2^{nd}$, eight for $3^{rd}$, and so on. I have won so many individual sections that I win overall by a clear margin. At the end of the day, the Captain presents me with the trophy in front of all the ship's crew and personnel.

'Come and see me in my cabin with your divisional officer in an hour', the Captain says. And to my complete amazement, when I show up, he says, 'we have given this considerable thought, and recent events show you have great leadership skills, and the men respect you, so at the next Captain's table I will be promoting you to Petty Officer'.

Again you could have knocked me out with a feather. I smile wryly at both and humbly say, 'thank you, sir'.

His Steward gives me a beer from the Captain's bar, and once I drink that, I leave and announce to the lads below decks what has happened -- that I have been promoted for being one of the leaders in a riot. Alan is pleased as punch for me, and in true Monty Python style, exclaims, 'you lucky, lucky, bastard!'

That night in Gibraltar we get so pissed I vomit into a disgusting urinal. I am so smashed that my two false teeth and entire plate fly out of my mouth into the nasty pisser. But I am beyond caring, so I pick them up and stick them straight back into my mouth without missing a step or vomiting more. Then I return to my mates and order more drinks.

As an aside, a ship join us at Gibraltar from the Turkish Navy. It's called the T.S Tenaztepe or something similar. We are allowed to board her, but find the conditions on that ship worse than awful. When I am on the bridge, a message is sent from the Tenaztepe to Flag Officer Gibraltar (to which we are copied into), asking permission to carry out a punishment of a rating who has struck an officer.

Flag Officer Gibraltar enquires as to what the punishment is, and the reply (no kidding), is, 'we want to hang him'. Of course, permission is rightly denied, and I think that will be the end of it. I am wrong.

They leave harbour, go outside the 12-mile limit into international waters, hang him, and then return as if nothing has happened. No wonder not many people volunteer to join that Turkish Navy, relying as it does almost entirely on conscriptions to fulfil the Turk's military requirements.

Upon leaving Gibraltar, we head into the Mediterranean and engage in a war scenario. In this simulation, NATO ships have to protect the aircraft carrier from attack by a nuclear submarine for an entire seven days. All the ships are operating their sonars -- the carrier has Seaking, and the Wessex helicopters dip sonars on a cable at various depths and positions within the flotilla. A fish could not have swim by without us knowing its make and tag number.

At the end of the exercise, we signal the submarine, mock him for failing in his mission, and ask him to declare his position. The reply comes in, that 'we are underneath the aircraft carrier and have been all week'. To prove the point, he surfaces about 500 yards astern of the carrier. Hats off to the submarine Captain for having balls of steel. That week teaches me the next sea war will be won or lost by submarine superiority. Ships don't stand a bloody chance.

The exercise over, we go on some well-earned R&R, porting with fly-the-flag visits around the Mediterranean but with strict instructions to behave ourselves. Between visits, we organise a 'Sods Opera', which is a naval tradition during which members of the ship perform a variety of acts not dissimilar to 'Britain's Got Talent' (but much more hilarious).

Alan and I perform 'The Amazing Ventriloquist' with quite a lustre. Both holding mics, I sit in a chair with curtains on either side of me and then wrap my left arm around Alan's arse, on which eyes, lips, and make-up are painted. All the audience can see Alan's arse under my arm and all of me.

As soon as his arse comes through the gap, the audience erupts with laughter. We crack jokes and banter mindlessly, also messing with the audience. I then position a lit cigarette from an audience member between the cheeks of Alan's arse. When he squeezes his butt cheeks together, the cigarette glows, and then he blows smoke out of his arsehole.

Just kidding, OK, but he did have a tube running from his mouth down to between his balls, and he smokes a cigarette and blows the smoke through the tube. The effect has people crying with laughter. I then inform the audience that my pal is also the world's best sword swallower.

Thereupon, I produce a three-foot metal sword and make it disappear into his mouth (i.e., anus), with Alan demonstrably screaming out in pain. What in fact happens is that I have used a retractable car aerial and he has stopped it disappearing into his anus by blocking it and then holding the end tight whilst I pull it back out to full length.

We finish the act by getting the ship's Captain to give both of us a kiss goodnight for being a good sport, which takes place to a big round of hooting and hollering from the gallery. Then we repeat this act at my brother James's wedding many years later, and we still have the DVD capturing it all to this very day.

# TEN

Every ship has a variety of characters living together in a mess-deck with 30 Navy men so cramped that the tight quarters are bound to cause issues and personality conflicts. Alan, Ian and I are responsible for ensuring the mess runs smoothly, is kept clean, and that everyone fulfils their respective obligations.

You knew when you have pissed someone off, because when you wake up in the morning and go to put your steaming boots on, you find someone has dropped a nine-pound William the Third turd in the chamber.

Matelots are generally meticulous about personal hygiene and time keeping, but we have one Scotsman onboard who is sloppy on both counts. Although I personally warn the Scotsman many times about his failings in this regard, eventually the crew decides to punish him.

The punishment meted out is dragging him up to the showers, stripping him off, and pouring soap powder over his naked body. They then scrub him with long handled scrubbing brushes whilst he squirms in pain and agony.

That message to him has the desired effect and he starts conforming to the required standards of cleanliness and punctuality. However, he clearly blames me for his punishment, and one night whilst asleep somebody smacks me so hard in the face with a weapon that in the morning I look like the Elephant Man (with my nose four times its normal size and my eyes panda black). I have no idea why the blow didn't wake me up instantly, but it didn't. I cannot prove it was Jock, as we call him, so he has the final word on that occasion.

Every night, the ship must be thoroughly cleaned below decks. The Duty Officer or 1$^{st}$ Lieutenant carries out 'ship's rounds', by which the matelots go round and inspect all the mess-decks and communal spaces.

Matelots can be quite childish in their humour, and it has become commonplace whilst moving around the ship to pretend we are on a motorcycle, making engine-revving engine sounds and pretending to be turning up the throttle and holding onto imaginary handlebars. You can picture how childish and hilarious it must be for grown men to be doing this.

During 1$^{st}$ Lieutenant's rounds, everyone must stand still and to attention as he and his entourage walk past. One night when Alan is with him as his escort, the bosuns mate blows the whistle to warn everyone he is coming and to stand to attention. I start riding past them on my imaginary motorbike, to the amusement of everyone except the 1$^{s}$ Lieutenant.

Furious at my display of what he obviously believes is contempt, he shouts, 'Leading Hand bring that man back here immediately'.

Alan says, 'yes, sir', and then goes onto his imaginary bike, kick starts it, and then revs it up with a VROOM, running after me.

That costs Alan a visit to the Captain's table and another discipline hearing. Not amused one iota, the

Captain sentences him to seven days of no shore leave and to working in the galley under the supervision of the Petty Officer responsible for feeding everyone every day with his team of cooks.

During that week, however, two things happened that are worthy of note. Firstly, as Alan is peeling potatoes, one of the cooks moves a huge pot of stew and drops the entire contents on the floor, mixing the soup with dirt, boot scuff marks and other vile and filthy material. The Petty Officer screams at him, 'don't just stand there, pick it up with a dustpan, put it in a tray, and put a pastry crust on it'.

They all presume that, at mealtime, we will serve up the dustpan pie and no-one will be the wiser. Fortunately, Alan tips us off to give the pie a miss. Unfortunately, not everyone gets the message, and Ian ends up choking on a couple of cockroaches that he spits onto the table.

But it doesn't stop here. Ian marches up to the counter and starts hurling abuse, calling the cook a cunt (even though the cook has since disappeared into the kitchen). Ian then returns to his seat, and shortly after, the Petty Officer comes out and shouts, 'who called the chef a cunt?'

In a heartbeat, Ian replies, 'who called the cunt a chef?' The whole canteen erupts with laughter and the Petty Officer retreats into the kitchen.

I said a ship has many colourful characters, and Tim is one. We nicknamed him the 'black panther' because, if you had a black cat, he had a blacker one. One night we are all watching TV and drinking beer when competition 'Moto-Cross' comes on. Out of the blue, Tim pipes up and says, 'I used to be a world champion Motor-Cross rider'.

'Bollox', Robbie shouts, an able seaman who looks very similar to Stephen Fry.

Tim replies, 'no, its true. I was racing in the world championships, fell off and took a tumble, was seriously injured, and had to have a metal plate inserted into my head to hold my skull together.' A couple of the boys thereupon start chanting, 'Panther, Panther'. Tim protests but no-one is listening.

The next day, Ian, Alan and I decide to hold a Kangaroo court, and whilst Tim is having dinner, we dress as officers. Alan is the Judge, I am the prosecutor, and Ian is the defence lawyer. All the lads are the jury, and when Tim returns, oblivious to what is unfolding, he is grabbed by two of the bigger lads and dragged to the mess square where he is made to stand for his 'crimes'.

Alan reads out the charge. 'Tim, you are hereby charged with spinning the biggest ever bullshitting dit ever heard by any Naval rating at sea or in harbour in that you told your shipmates you had previously worked as a world class moto-cross rider... contrary to good order and Naval discipline. Do you plead guilty or not guilty?'

'Not guilty', says Tim defiantly.

'Prosecutor, present your case', Alan says.

I relay the story as told by Tim and call a couple of the lads as witnesses. I then produce a strong magnet with a handle used by the diving team as a practice limpet mine and say, 'if Tim is telling the truth, the magnet will react with the metal plate in Tim's head and we should see Tim's head being pulled towards the magnet'.

When I move the magnet all around Tim's head, as expected nothing happens. Throwing up my hands, I exclaim, 'I rest my case, Judge'.

'Defence, deliver your case', Alan says.

'I can't', Ian says. 'He's bullshitting so well this case is indefensible'.

The jury all starts shouting, 'Guilty! Guilty! Guilty!'

Alan calls order and says, 'Tim, I have no option but to find you guilty as charged. The sentence of this court is that you are to be taken to a place known as 3P mess square where you are to be stripped naked and whipped until your bollox are well and truly blackened with boot polish by the mess members therein'.

No sooner than Alan has finished talking than the lads grab Tim and drag him off screaming to the centre of the mess where punishment will be meted out. The reasoning for the sentence is that black cats should have black balls and to get the boot polish off would be immensely painful and not something you would quickly forget.

# ELEVEN

During my time on HMS Exeter as Helicopter controller, there are several occasions when things could have gone badly wrong for the pilot. At all times, however, I remain calm and follow the procedures and managed to get the chopper back safely to the ship. Because of that, the pilots have a great deal of respect for me.

During a down time in Portland, whilst on exercise, the pilot takes me up in the dual seat on a Lynx helicopter and lets me fly for a full 15 minutes. He is so impressed with my flying ability that he recommends me for pilot training. If successful, I will be one of the new Harrier Jump Jet Pilots coming into service in the Royal Navy.

I'm over the moon at the prospect. His report, backed by my divisional officer and the Captain, is despatched to the relevant parties in the Admiralty, again, as you will see later in the book.

Fast forward to early 1982. I'm training regularly with Ian and become fitter and stronger than I have ever been in my life. And I know I'm going to need every ounce of strength I can draw from myself, as recruitment has started in earnest for the 1982 Portsmouth Field Gun Crew.

Royal Navy Field Gun is widely regarded as the

toughest competition in the world. To be selected to run for either Portsmouth, Fleet Air Arm or Devonport crews is the ultimate accolade about your physical fitness and mental strength. Believe me, this is not a place for the weak or faint of heart.

As of now, however, I'm mostly known for being an off-the-wall character, and proof in the pudding, I have been dubbed by my mates with the moniker, 'Mad Jack' (Jack being slang for sailor). This nickname has since proven ironic, as we know.

# TWELVE

The Portsmouth crew has trained for the Field Gun competition, the 'Guns and Guts' of the Royal Tournament, for almost 100 years. The crew live and train in HMS Excellent on Whale Island, situated at the beginning of the M275 Motorway in Portsmouth.

The Field Gun competitions arose post 1899 during the Boer Wars, in recognition of a heroic and physically demanding movement of Large Guns by the British Navy, in support of her Garrison in Ladysmith Africa. It is considered by some, to be the world's most dangerous sport.

Naturally, Field Gunners are a rare breed, being as they are both super fit and immune to pain. The 'Guns and Guts' competition involves a team of 18 men dragging a heavy gun and limber box (a two-wheeled cart) over an assault course at a frightening pace over a manmade obstacle course with no bodily protection, against another team.

At the end of the training period, all three crews compete against each other at the Royal Tournament at Earls court London in front of sell-out crowds, including members of the British royal family. Sadly, defence cuts in the government's military budget have seen the demise of the Royal Tournament and the Field Gun, such that this competition in this format has been committed to history.

During the run, the gun and limber, at a combined weight of 2000 pounds, must be broken down into their component parts and transported over, under and through extremely difficult obstacles, and the team who completes all three stages of the run in the fastest time wins the race. Of course, there is no shortage of characters in the Field Gun arena with a wicked sense of humour, and this fellow Jim is no exception.

To illustrate, during a training run in a previous year, one lad was unfortunate enough to have one of his fingers chopped clean off. Had they been able to find the finger, it could have been packed in ice and re-attached later at the hospital.

Instead, sadly, Jim decided to put it in his pocket and take it home to show his wife and brighten her day. When he returned it the next day to its rightful owner, the finger had died an inglorious death and was only salvageable as an example of what you should never do upon finding a chopped off finger.

On another occasion at the Royal tournament, on the home run one of the lads realised he had dropped his metal pin. He was supposed to place the pin in a hole on the Gun Axle to keep the wheel on whilst the team pulled the equipment at full tilt boogey to the finish line. Rather than risk losing the wheel and the run, he put his finger in the hole instead, and whilst the wheel turned at high speed on the axle, it was severed off. His ingenuity, therefore, saved the day and the race.

This and many other events known for their endurance and brutality have led to apropos motto of the Portsmouth crew, 'To the limit and beyond'. And 1982 is one year that will go down in history, where this Portsmouth motto takes on more than a little truth.

To be considered for selection to Portsmouth crew, you have to undertake a murderous training session under the supervision of the $1^{st}$ and $2^{nd}$ trainer and the crew's physical training instructors. The PTI's or club swingers as they are known would make Genghis Khan seem like a namby-pamby jellyfish of a wimp.

So, I receive my instructions to attend the Field Gun shed at HMS Excellent and arrive there feeling elated and pumped -- until I look round the room to see some absolute monsters with biceps bigger than Popeye on steroids. My heart sinks, but I think, fuck it, you're here now so you might as well give it your best shot even if you don't have a fighting chance.

Thousands of applicants try to run Field Gun every year for Portsmouth, but the selection process whittles them down to a sinewy 40. The A crew consists of 18 men, the majority of which were ex-field gunners who ran in previous seasons. The B crew consists of 18 men who mimic everything the A-crew does. The other four are available whenever A-crew gets injured (which happens frequently).

Everyone wants to be in A-crew, but even being part of the 40 strong is an amazing achievement that elevates you to an elite group of men who, to this day, keep alive the Field Gun memory and camaraderie.

The fitness test starts in a matted gym area complete with home-made barbells weighing about 20 kilograms and fastened together on bars that are painted blue. When the PTI blows the whistle, he screams out the exercise to be performed – yeah, baby, let the good times roll!

Sometimes he'll yell for us to use good ol' fashioned dead weights, and other times he'll yell for us to do abdominal exercises or squat thrusts or something totally punishing that would waste every muscle in your body. The gimmick is to trick your body.

The only relief comes every 20 minutes when he shouts, 'pick up the sandbags!' Well, these sandbags weighed 15 kilograms, and then what would he do to us? He'd send us off galivanting round the friggin' perimeter of the island, which measures in circumference not one foot less than a mile.

I have banked this one particular section with Pete, and I am the second guy back to the shed. A chap that's ceremoniously referred to as fly larvae, Maggot, has come in first. Obviously the bulkier, more muscular guys find the run very difficult, but this affords us lighter runners a rest period waiting for everyone to finish.

Once we are all back at our weight bar, the beasting resumes with the PTI's screaming for more effort and the 1st and 2nd trainers walking round trashing individual performances. We repeat the process three times and by the end we all look like we have spent the last hour standing fully dressed in a shower. i.e., we are drenched.

Because I think that is the end, I am surprised to see the staff setting up five blue weight bars with 50 kilograms attached to each. The PTI then declares, 'anybody who fails this next section is automatically eliminated. Is that clear?' I am utterly frazzled, spent and knackered, but I have no choice but to carry on.

The requirement is to lift the bar above your head 10 times in succession without putting the weight down or using your legs to assist in the push up. I am about to say

I'm glad we have been given the easy assessment this evening, but think better of it.

Quite a few of the lads fail this section and my heart goes out to them. The disappointment in the room is tangible. When my time comes, I get to eight repetitions when my arms refuse to move. I suck in a huge breath and scream bloody mercy whilst pushing up the last two times, before tossing the weights to the floor in sweet triumph.

Exercise session conquered, we all go next door for a cuppa whilst the staff deliberates. After what seems like an eternity, they call us back in, and in an emotionless matter-of-fact style, call out the names of those who have been successful and those who have not. I'm in, but some are not. Watching grown men cry is not easy.

I return to HMS Exeter and tell all the boys. That night much beer is drunk and even more stupidness prevails. As is normal when I'm drunk, I go to bed fully dressed and wake up with the mother of all colossal hangovers the next morning.

Meanwhile, the Field Gun staff has contacted the ship and told them I have been selected to run for Portsmouth in the 1982 Field Gun competition. Yee-ha! But to my complete horror, my Captain has sent back his reply: 'No, I can't release him. He is the ship's only helicopter controller and without him the helicopter cannot fly'.

I'm totally devastated, as years of brutal exercise and the father of all beastings is now turned into a waste. I speak to my divisional officer and ask if there is any chance of getting a HC from another ship to replace me. If and only if I can convince one of the leading hands from the radar department to do the Helicopter Controllers course, would he then entertain an application.

I have a lightbulb moment, thinking that my brother from another mother, Alan, is just the man for the job. But convincing Alan to do the course will be no easy task. I'm not asking him to shag a horror, which he would have done. No, I'm simply asking him to sit in the hottest seat in the operations room and put his career on the line every time the chopper leaves the flight deck (which is what I routinely do).

I am HC1A-qualified to control three helicopters at the same time. The course I need Alan to take only qualifies you for the HC3 level capable of controlling one helicopter at a time. Moreover, Alan is convinced from the get-go that he will never pass the course. It takes me weeks to convince him, and only after copious amounts of beer and Bacardi do I succeed.

Not to mention, there is constant peer pressure from Ian, who is pulling at his heart strings when I'm not there, and from Jean, who is laying it on Lucy to persuade Alan that this is a once in a lifetime opportunity for me. Alan finally gives in and puts in an official request to be put on the next available Helicopter Controllers course at Portland in Dorset.

# THIRTEEN

Let the good times roll.
These are indeed happy times and not long after Alan heads off to Portland for his course, Lucy is working at the Cambridge pub and Jean has gotten a job at a local night club behind the Bar. And shortly after that, I learn there is a potential job as a bouncer available at the club.

Jean arranges for me to meet at the pub with the manager and the head doorman, Ronny. Instantly, Ronny and I get on like a house on fire and I land myself a part-time job. You can never have too much money, and besides, the club has a great crew working there and we all get on like gangbusters.

Mick the cocktail barman and Ruby are a couple. Norman the owner and Lesley are a couple. Rachel is married with kids and Andrew is married. Lurch the doorman is as dim as an Irish candle and is destined to remain single. Andrew is married and later we are joined by Richard who is quite a tasty kickboxer. Otherwise, Katrina and Maria are also single.

Every night working at the club is fun with a capital F. Occasionally we have to break up a fight, but in the main the club has a peaceful party atmosphere. One day, that fun continues into the wee hours, as we often stay late after the club closes to have a few drinks and play a game of spoof, to decide who amongst us will have to pay for the curry from a local restaurant.

For those who have never played spoof, the rules are quite simple. Each player has three coins in his possession. You choose how many coins you play from (none to all three), and when you're ready, each player puts their closed hand out into the middle of the group. In sequence, everyone then guesses the total amount of coins held between the parties in their outstretched hand.

Now, the rules forbid you to call a number that has already been called. When everyone has had a guess, the hands are opened and the coins counted. The winner is the person who correctly guesses the total and is not required to take part in the next round. That continues until there is only one person left who hasn't won a round and they must pay for the meals for all those who participated or eat a phall (fat) curry in default.

This curry is so hot that it cannot be eaten without sweating like a roasting pig. I chose the phall option once and spent the next week shitting a stream of liquid so foul that it could not be wiped by toilet paper or flushed in commode. Not only that, my arse is red raw for a month. Next time, I took the easy option and paid the whole bill.

About this time, the Officer training section comes back with their response to the pilots report about me flying aircraft for the Royal Navy. Sadly, it states to the effect: 'Dear Rob, it would be unprecedented for someone to be trained as a pilot who has not had five GCSEs to include Maths and physics and any three others. We are sorry…'

I'm absolutely devastated but have to accept my fate of being a wanker at school has finally caught up with me

– not only caught up, but well and truly bit me on the arse. But the pilot didn't give up and he somehow managed to get me enrolled for one month of GCSE courses at HMS Nelson in Portsmouth education Centre.

Hallelujah, brother!

I sail through GCSE English and my spirits pick up; but physics is a killer, and I cannot for the life of me get a grip of it. But whilst I am there the police hold a seminar about leaving the services and joining them. I attend and like what I hear, committing the idea to memory as a future career option.

Indeed, my friends laughed at the thought of me becoming a cop and write a little poem, which they sang to me thusly: 'An overactive thyroid gland was inflicted on Rob since birth, No villain will be safe from him, the fastest cop on earth!'

# FOURTEEN

Alan comes through like a warrior and passes the HC course with flying colours. Therefore, I'm given permission to leave the ship and join Portsmouth Field Gun Crew -- a time of my life that I will never forget for many reasons.

One thing that stands out in my mind is that when I'm looking round the assembled crew there's a varied mix of men -- from small to tall, thin to monstrous, brains to muscles. All of them, however are mega fit and in good shape, with that that Glint of steel in their eyes telling you none of them is ever to be fucked with.

The first and second trainers are Dan and Matt. Dan is an experienced Field Gunner that is responsible for training the 'A Crew'. He has a quiet demeanour and reputation for getting things done. Matt, on the other hand, is loud and look like the screaming skull with teeth like an old piano keyboard. (One black, one white and one missing). This man has don't mess with me written all over him and nobody ever does. He oversees the 'B crew'.

When I'm selected for 'B Crew,' I think I am just born Lucky. Training starts in earnest and is based initially around fitness, stamina and strength. The PTI's send us to hell and back twice a day, with a variety of physical exercises which often conclude with most of us being either violently sick or fainting.

We have our own dedicated chefs, and it is compulsory because of the level of exertion it takes to consume between 5000 and 7000 calories a day. This regime is strictly monitored, but drinking two pints of Guinness in the Field Gun bar every night is also encouraged.

One of the most tortuous physical challenges is being put into teams and made to race along the mudflats that surround the island at low tide. It's a major feat to run in the three feet deep sloppy mud without having the added embuggerance of carrying a full -sized telegraph pole with rope handles attached. They say what doesn't break you makes you stronger. I'll drink to that!

I make some great mates in 1982 and to this day still are in touch with them. I become particularly friendly with Billy, who is a good looking muscular chap, 21 years old at the time, and engaged to be married to a young lady in the WRENS (Women's Royal Navy). We become so close he asks me to be his best man at their forthcoming wedding.

Earlier I referred to Alan and I being called Jonah, and not without good cause. For some bizarre reason, whilst I am running Field Gun, the cheeky Argentinians decide to attack the Falkland Islands, in the South Atlantic. Margaret Thatcher, in my opinion the only decent PM since the war, dispatches a military task force of ships and men to send the Argentinians packing.

Argentinians speak Spanish as their first language, and by the time this government got its act in gear, the Falklands would be Argentinian, not British! Anyway, HMS Exeter finds itself part of the task force, and Jean, Lucy and I go to Old Portsmouth where all ships entering or leaving the Harbour must pass through a small gap at the head of the estuary.

As the Exeter passes through the gap, we all wave at Alan on the upper deck standing to attention in full uniform with the rest of the ship's company. When Alan sees us, he breaks rank and shouts, "The fucking things I do for you, R Sole!' I almost piss myself laughing as memories flood back of where I had heard that before.

Training on the cinder track at Whale Island started. This is a replica of the Earls Court Arena and has an obstacle course set up for two running crews. Beginning, on the straight, the equipment is dragged down and around the corner and over the home wall.

Every piece of equipment and 18 men go over the wall before assembling the rig and breaking down the gun and limber to traverse between two man made ramps. The gap between the two ramps is for all intents and purposes a bottomless chasm and nobody or none of the equipment is allowed to drop in it. It goes without saying the heavy equipment is awkward at any time, never mind over walls and across a chasm.

The gun barrel alone weighs 900lbs or 408kgs. The gun carriage is 350lbs or 158kgs and each wheel weighs 120lbs or 55kgs. The 'speedy' and 'slow' wheels, as they are called, respectively, have to run with a wheel on their shoulder as part of the process, with concurrently inflicted pain and weeping sores on the shoulder blades after only a couple of practice runs would make most men weep.

Once over the chasm and through a gap in the enemy wall, everything is meticulously placed and the crew kneel like statues waiting for the bugler to sound the start of the run back. The run back is a reversal of the run out and concludes with the flying angel riding on top of the wire landing on the home side ramp and causing all the equipment to collapse. The sheer legs which hold the rig up weigh 200lbs each or 90kgs, and when they fall, it rocks the earth beneath them.

I get on well with Matt, the 2$^{nd}$ Trainer, and he makes me captain of the crew. I know better than to get on the wrong side of him, though, as he's got a ferocious temper and many things, he does in today's airy-fairy life would be considered bullying. I genuinely worry what servicemen in the future will be like in battle, having been molly coddled through training so as not to hurt their feelings. I wouldn't like to be part of the services today.

Matt used to carry a wooden gun spike and would think nothing of hitting us with it if we made a mistake. He even whacked one of the lads for handing him a one-inch lump of lead which had fallen from the gun carriage wheel. He cheekily said, 'Number 2 one of your fillings has dropped out'. We all wet ourselves laughing but Matt didn't see the funny side. Nobody in the crew escapes without injury, and depending on what your role is determines what part of your anatomy loses the most flesh.

Billy wins the honour of being the flying Angel for B Crew. His A Crew counterpart is a seasoned field gun veteran called Stuart who is an absolute fucking monster. As an example of Stuart's monstrosity, one night outside a bar somewhere he was trying to diffuse a fight and someone shot him in the back with a shotgun.

The blast would have killed any lesser mortal, but Stuart's muscle grouping in his back and neck saved his life despite resulting through the 1982 season in an uncontrollable twitch when trying to remain still. The judges were aware his condition and allowed for this and did not issue him any penalty points. A shrewd move by them, as I wouldn't have wanted to piss him off, either.

We start off practicing the run in small sections, but once we master the drill, we move onto the next part. One of the lads, Malcolm, has to ride across the chasm sitting on the right-hand side of the limber box. The chasm has a wire rope traversing it between the sheer legs on the home side and a ten-foot timber spar on the enemy ramp.

Everything is pulled across the chasm by the swing numbers when the word 'go!' is shouted by those whose drill it is. The barrel, carriage and limber box are hooked onto a traveller, which is a set of small metal wheels in a metal section which has a quick release hook on the bottom of it. Malcolm's drill is designed to hook the limber onto the traveller, where he reaches up with his right hand and grabs the 'outhall' rope being pulled by the swing numbers. When he shouts 'go!', he commences.

However, when Malcolm jumps on the limber, he reaches up and misses the outhall and instead grabs hold of the main wire and then shouts go. The swing numbers set off running and pulling the outhall, but the metal wheels of the traveller chop off all four fingers of Malcolm's right hand like a hot knife through butter. Malcolm does not feel a thing and we continue off the enemy ramp, re-assemble everything, then proceed right through the enemy wall as the first action fired three rounds from the gun and kneeled down.

That's when the pain hits Malcolm and he starts screaming like a banshee and leaps to get up. Matt then launches forward and hits him with the spike and yells 'stay down' until we sort it at the end of the run. Matt has no idea what's wrong with Malcolm but doesn't give a fuck and neither do we because we must finish the run completely. By then end of the race, Malcolm therefore feints from the shock that he more or less tacitly enduring.

Only then do we notice his fingers have been severed off. We are able to recover them from the centre of the chasm and place them in ice, and he and his fingers are all rushed to hospital. His fingers are ultimately returned to his hands, but they are never the same again and he is eventually invalided out of the Royal Navy. He was not the first person in this brutal competition to be injured beyond repair, as this one of the toughest and most dangerous competitions known to modern man.

We eventually get to the stage in the training where the Flying Angel has to perform the most crucial part of his drill. This is the part where he releases the wire from the top of the ten-foot spar, removing the ten-foot spar from its housing, and then riding on top of the traveller across the chasm whilst carrying the ten-foot spar and ditching it on the home side of the chasm. This is no easy feat, demanding both enormous strength and the balance of a tightrope walker.

Having dismounted the traveller onto the home ramp, an important part of the drill is to stop, wait a second, then clear the wires from the chasm as the entire rig collapses and runs over the rig and kneel for the $2^{nd}$ gun firing. Matt has us all kneeling in our respective positions, looking back towards Billy who is on the enemy ramp.

As Attempt 1, Billy releases the wire, removes the ten feet, balances on top of the traveller, and shouts 'go!' He gets about one metre and falls off into the chasm. As

Attempt 2, he gets slightly further and falls off again. And Attempt 3 falls of as soon as he starts moving. Attempt 4 -- no better.

I can see Matt getting angrier by the try, but Billy is also getting angry with himself. We are all willing him to go all the way. By Attempt 5, he gets half way across but then falls off. Matt explodes, 'the next is your last chance you useless cunt if you don't make it this time you can fuck off home and I'll get someone else to be the fucking angel'.

Everything is set up again and Matt signalled to Billy to release the wire. This time, there are no mistakes. The ten-foot spar carried by Billy soars over the chasm, and he's elated, grinning from ear to ear as he arrives. Finally expecting to be triumphant, he jumps off at the home ramp, dumps the ten-foot spar, and continues running, forgetting to stop and wait the mandatory two seconds dictated in his drill. The slip pin has released as it should have on the enemy side, but as Billy runs between the sheer legs everything collapses on top of him.

I am dumbstruck as I watch my friend get hit on the back of his head by the sheer legs falling at high speed, and there can only be one and only one outcome from this impact. When I race over to him, blood is pouring out of his ears and he is completely still.

Matt screams, 'all of you up the fucking shed now', and the staff bundles us off the track and up to the gym area. The PTI is ordered to give us a beasting which he does but all I can see is a recurring nightmarish vision of the final run. My body is doing the exercise, but my mind is elsewhere.

Eventually Matt comes in and says, 'Right, Billy's dead. Get down the track and lay the gear in. We are running again in ten minutes. Brum, you're the new B crew angel'. Brum goes white but everyone does exactly what Matt says because we all are in a state of shock. At the time, I think, what a heartless bastard, but in truth, I think if he had sent us home, we would not have come back the next day. That is the only time as far as I am aware that anyone has paid the ultimate price to be part of this amazing competition. 'To the limit and beyond' wins a prize as understatement of the year.

Because of my relationship with Billy, at the end of that awful day, I have to go with the Gunnery officer to tell Billy's fiancé what has happened. We are both in full number 1 uniform when we arrive, and I knock on the door. These were days before the advent of mobile phones, so she didn't know we were coming and shouted as she opened the door, 'where have you been, I've been worried sick'.

By the look on our faces, she realises something is majorly wrong and, after a few wobbles, collapses on the floor and starts sobbing uncontrollably. By the time I get to the floor to console her, I'm also crying. As we had entered the flat, I had noticed what was obviously her wedding dress in a cover hanging up on the back of the door. They had been engaged to be married.

We stayed about an hour then left. As a major victim of this tragic event, it's a long time before she gets her life back on track. I've since lost touch with her but have heard she is happily married to another man and living in Newcastle.

Billy's funeral is an emotional affair for all of us, with very few dry eyes in the room. When they play the 'Last Post' (a popular dirge played at military funerals) at the end of the funeral, I fall apart, sobbing. To this day, whenever I hear a bugler play the 'Last Post', I think of Billy and when I think of him, invariably tears stream down my face.

As the Field Gun season continues, the Falklands war rages on. The top brass decide that the Royal Tournament should go on to show the world that despite the fact we are at war we can still put on a display by the military at home – the British stiff upper lip and all that crap. Of course, the Falklands ruins the season for Portsmouth and Devonport, as men are suddenly drafted away from Field Gun to join ships with shortages of certain skills to head south and go to war.

Field Gun attracts harsh men and a sense of humour that most would find hard to stomach. One of the lads, Gary, had booked his wedding during the Field Gun training season. But he and his lovely bride were about to find out that this was a fatal error of judgement, because, on the Saturday of his wedding, he still has to train with us on the track until midday.

The track is covered with cinder and as a result our black boots, black trousers and Pompey blue rugby shirts all get filthy. Gary is scheduled to get betrothed at 2pm sharp at the Portsmouth registry office. As is the norm on Saturdays, we wrap up at noon and start packing all the gear away ready for Monday.

Gary is completely oblivious to what we have in mind for him until he is grabbed by a group of us and tied up. We spray his face and hair blue and hold him captive until 15 minutes to 2pm, in respect to proper Navy tradition. With his face and hair blue, and still wearing his filthy stained track gear, we unceremoniously drop him off in our lorry at the registry office at precisely 2pm, and not a minute earlier.

There is much hooting and hollering from our boys and complete and utter shock and dismay on the faces of the wedding party. No matter how game for a laugh the bride might be, I don't know anyone except us who would not think this was a bridge too far.

To continue the wedding theme, I have also been chosen by Ian from HMS Exeter to be best man at his wedding to Janice. Ian should have known better but, having kept his cards very close to his chest, he thinks there is nothing negative that I can do to negatively impact on the day.

How wrong he is, as during the evening reception, I manage to trick his brother into telling me where Ian and Janice are going to spend their wedding night. It transpires that they are staying at the best hotel in the area in the honeymoon suite which happens to be on the top floor.

Revelling in my cleverness, I bring a piece of rotten fish with me to the wedding and secret it in their soft top sportscar where it can't easily be found, knowing this to be the car they were using to go on their honeymoon. Previously, I rang the hotel purporting to be Ian and cancelled the reservation for the honeymoon suite, giving the receptionist a tirade of abuse to ensure Ian couldn't recover the situation.

At the end of the evening after the reception, Ian and Janice come out of the party and to my surprise delight jump into the sportscar bearing the smelly rotten fish. Ian has obviously decided to stay sober to maximise the fun in the bridal suite and consummate the marriage unhindered by excessive alcohol consumption, as we all could be wont to do at any normal celebration.

With all of us hooting and cheering before heading home ourselves, off they go. Now, I am staying with Jean, Alan, and Lucy on blow-up beds at Ian's mum's house, and have barely gotten asleep when we are rudely awoken at 3am by Ian. Jumping on me and punching the daylights out of me, he shouts, 'you are a fucking bastard. It was you, wasn't it?'

He only stops hitting me when I convince him I have no clue what he is talking about. When I ask him why he's home to his mum's house, he explains what has happened to him and we all sit there with mouths wide open in a state of shock and wonderment.

Apparently, they had pulled up to the hotel still wearing their wedding attire, Ian carrying Janice into the foyer and up to the reception desk to check into the bridal suite. When they told Ian the room had been cancelled by him, he went into orbit and denied ever making the call. It then transpired that the room had already been let and that there wasn't a spare room at the hotel, They had all been taken because of a local horse racing event.

Ian said Janice left the hotel crying and in an inconsolable state. Trying to get another room, they had trawled all the good local hotels and there were no rooms anyway. After two hours and in desperation, they had checked into a mediocre bed and breakfast, going to the bedroom frazzled and shattered. The mood had been totally lost.

Sitting on the bed and reflecting on what to do, they decided to cut their losses and return to his mum's house and confront me, the logical one. The smell of the fish within the heating system where I had placed it was enough to gag a maggot and they were forced to drive home with the windows open and feeling nauseous.

After my vigorous denial, I decided it would be wrong to confess right now and play the how-could-I possibly-know-where-they-were-staying card, as I had never been told where that would be. Janice's female intuition had zeroed in on me as the culprit, but without proof, they were stuffed. Back in Portsmouth, I did confess and to be fair they both said it did make the night extremely memorable, albeit for the wrong reasons.

The Field Gun season continues, and we become fitter and fitter until B Crew is good enough to race A Crew before a public audience. I will never forget marching out onto the track to 'Hearts of Oak', as you can feel the tension and the pride. I must warm up B Crew before the start of the run and quite often say, 'This one is for Billy, let's have it'. We push A Crew hard every time and they are amazing competitors.

The author in Portsmouth Field Gun crew preparing for the Royal Tournament in Memory of the B crew: Angel

# FIFTEEN

Back at home, despite his drinking and other problems, Dad's wages have allowed my parents to buy their own home for a ridiculously cheap price (at least by today's standards). At this time in Middlesbrough, you can purchase a whole street for under £100,000.

James and Gail are growing up but are having an awful time with Mum, who when pissed is immensely cruel. On one occasion, Gail had stolen some sweets, and Mum had stripped her naked despite puberty, sat her on the dining table and made her stay there with a sign round her neck saying, 'Don't talk to me, I'm a thief'. I vow that as soon as Gail and James are of legal age to leave home, I will move them in with me.

The Royal Navy is an amazing place to be, with most matelots leading a Peter Pan Life and never growing up or taking on mortgages or any kind of responsibility. I break tradition by giving 18 months' notice to leave the Navy, eventually applying to the Metropolitan Police and Hampshire Constabulary, and purchasing a house with Jean in Portsmouth.

However, I draw the line by making no promises to grow up, and quite frankly I never have to this day. You see, I believe that age is more a state of mind and a physical thing. When I do finally die, I will have no complaints. Far too many people put off living now for a variety of reasons but rarely justifiable. Too many people I know have died having done nothing. I don't want to be that shrivel old person.

Besides, I don't believe in religion or afterlife and my heart goes out to those that do. Blind faith destroys lives. In fact, I have no knowledge of anyone who has died and made contact via any medium including the church and said it's amazing here you will love it meet me in the party room with 12 virgins at your side. I think religion is the biggest con ever perpetrated on humanity by normal human beings in pursuit of money, power and control that they have not otherwise earned. I am sure the original concept was to have rules for society to abide by, but it has been distorted beyond recognition ever since.

Prior to leaving the Navy, we have an amazing circle of friends who party hard together whenever possible. Beast the Dobermann has become a full-grown beast of a dog, and because we have been surgically joined at the hip over so many moons, Alan has also put in his notice to leave. My motive for leaving the Navy is to join the MET Police, whereas Alan's has decided to become a professional windsurfing beach bum.

We spend most weekends windsurfing off Southsea beach. I have two boards and teach Alan to windsurf. It isn't long before he's leaving me for dead. I put it down to him being three stone lighter than me. He claims it's pure skill, and I'm happy to let him to maintain this delusion for once in his life. 1984 marches up quickly and the staff at Field Gun let me leave early to join the MET police on the 2$^{nd}$ of July 1984.

As an aside, Mick and Ruby have decided to get

married, and Mick's stag night is booked in Bognor Regis shortly after I have joined Hendon Police training college. I have also decided to have puppies from Beast and have booked her in with a champion Dobermann Stud on her next mating season for the princely sum of £400. We men are missing a trick here, giving our sperm away for free at the Donor clinics.

Before technically starting with the MET Police, I decide to utilise an HGV licence that I now have as a result of my end-of-service resettlement course. I get a job delivering appliances for British Gas out of their Portsmouth Depot, and the job entails loading on 15 appliances and delivering them to customers in the local area.

On my first day, I leave the yard at 8.30am and return by 1pm, enthusiastically offering to deliver more. I'm given a second load and return to the depot at 3.45pm for a 4pm finish. The next day, I am pulled over by one of the other drivers, who gives me a stern warning never to come back for a second load. He goes on to explain that the quotidian routine demands that I load up, grab a leisurely breakfast at a café, then complete the deliveries in slow time and return to the depot just before 4pm (having only made one trip).

The union will get rid of you if you start showing up the other drivers, this chap explains. 'If you are gonna be back early, park up and go to sleep'. I ignore his advice because it's never been in my nature to be a slacker. True to form, the union intervenes, and I'm handed my notice to leave surplus to requirements. Margaret Thatcher kicking the union's arses was the best thing she ever did, because it is virtually impossible to run a competitive business once you've allowed the unions to get control of the workforce.

# SIXTEEN

My joining day at Hendon goes as expected with half a dozen ex-servicemen in my intake. As I'm just 25 years young and very amiable, I gel quite quickly with a lot of the new recruits and the staff. I take temporary quarters in Hendon while Jean remains in Portsmouth, commuting home on weekends. Unfortunately, word gets back to me that she has been unfaithful with one of my Field Guns mates, but I decide to keep what I've been told to myself for the time being.

I know in my heart the relationship is over because of it, but I've always thought that it must be hard staying faithful when your partner is swanning around the Caribbean for six months at a stretch and you are in the bloom of femininity. Naval life certainly is not conducive to long term relationships or marriages, as much as the Navy would want it to be.

I remember once when one of my Navy mates consumed a skin full of beer and was able to pluck up the courage to tell his wife that he had contracted gonorrhoea, only to have the lame excuse, 'I'm sorry I won't do it ever again'. You could have blown him over at her revelation that, apparently, they had both been unfaithful.

On the weekend of Mick's stag night, me and his mates board the mini-bus and head to Bognor Pier for drinks and a bit of a dance. I say that tongue in cheek, as none of us could ever claim to have an ounce of rhythm. What we are interested in is smooching and grinding our dancer's lance against some poor woman – and that's where our abilities in dance started and ended.

But we sure know how to get pissed, and during the evening, one of our lads is crossing the dance floor with a tray of beers and suddenly keel sideways and drops beer helter skelter. He's picked up and the mess is cleared up, and because no sees exactly what happened, we assume he's mortally pissed.

Twenty minutes later, Alan and I are spread-eagle at the loo having a proper whiz when the Hulk alights in the urinal between the two of us. Not knowing who we are, he starts laughing uproariously and says, 'did you see me knock that wanker out on the dance floor, fuckin hell'. Alan and I must have read each other's minds, because we both nod, turn and smack him hard on the side of the head, dropping him to his knees like a stone.

We're not through with him, so we pick him up and slam dunk him into the urinal a couple of times for shits and giggles and good measure. There's blood and snot everywhere, but we're careful to be hygienic so when we finish him we wash our hands before we leave. A while later we notice a couple of lads carrying him out of the pier, his night being over.

The stag night now in full swing, we find ourselves drinking and mucking around on the dance floor, much to the annoyance of the locals. Being a doorman in another side of my life, I can sense that all is not well by our shenanigans, and my intuition proves spot on when we leave the pier at closing time.

As we stumble out, we are met by a gang of blokes carrying boat hooks which they emancipated from the fishing boats on the beach. Gnarly as all get out, these particular boat hooks are six-foot long poles with a nasty hook at one end. By happenstance, I spot several cops in a van and give them a shout before wading into the imminent fight: 'I'm a cop! Help!'

One of the marauders takes a vicious swing at Alan with one of the hooks. As Alan cleverly ducks and bobs his assault, this bloke cannot stop the out-of-control swinging hook, and so Alan is able to clobber him and knock him plum out. More police arrive and, barring me, they manhandle everyone into police vans. A few of our lads are injured but thankfully not badly.

The cops ask me to identify my group from each van and all of them are all released. On my return to Hendon, I report the night's events to my Sergeant. Fortunately, no-one has to attend court because all the boat hook gang plead guilty to causing an Affray and are all sentenced to eight years imprisonment for their misadventures in daring to mess with a bunch of matelots. You might consider this the first of the cat's nine lives that I've been allotted in my wondrous existence.

From there, I continue through the training programme with considerable ease, and being an ex-serviceman, find the discipline a walk in the park. Because I get on well with the instructors, that also works massively in my favour, which pertains to my next story. At Hendon, there is a tower block for the male recruits and a tower block for the females, and in the basement, there is a walkway between the two blocks. And there is a ban on men visiting the female block and vice versa.

After a heavy night in the bar, one of the girls named Tracy says she is going back to her block and with a wink and a smile hands me a slip of paper. 'I want to fuck you right now,' it says, gloriously. 'Wait 5 minutes and come to my room 3$^{rd}$ floor 311'.

What can you do, I ask myself. She had put it to me and obviously I have no choice but to comply. So I finish my pint, feign a big yawn and excuse myself from the group with a parting fib, 'got to get some rest'.

When I race back to the male block, I bump into two ex-squaddies in the lift and feel obliged to travel up one floor for purposes of pretence. When the coast it clear, I turn around, run back down the stairs all the way to the basement, and proceed through the adjoining walkways and up the lift to the 3$^{rd}$ floor.

Thankfully there is no one about, and after looking both ways, I tap at her door with my heart beating so loudly it threatens to depart my chest cavity. When she opens the door, she's donning a sexy Basque suspender and stockings. I'm over the moon with delight. Not messing round, we engage in sexual gymnastics like we're trying out for the rabbit Olympics, before collapsing on her bed.

When we wake up from a heavy, drunken slumber minutes before the eight o'clock morning parade, sheer terror sets in. I'm dressed and out of that room before you could scream, 'Holy shit!' I reverse course, taking the lift to the basement where, of course, I run full tilt boogey towards the male block, turn a corner, slams into the cleaner as she's pushing some equipment.

Screaming to holy hell, I fall spread-eagle across the floor in a huge collision, but like a man possessed pick myself up immediately and run straight back to my room where I throw on my uniform and arrive on my heels at the parade area with only seconds to spare. Tracy looks like she has been dragged through a hedge and we both exchange grins with me blowing her a kiss.

After the parade is done, Drill Sergeant Williams adds another. 'There has been a serious breach of the rules and the person responsible will be found and sacked,' he states. My heart sinks and I think the shit is going to hit the fan for sure.

He then says, 'Last night in the male lift someone decided it was a good place to take a shit. It most definitely is not, and the offending article has been removed. When we forensically identify the owner, he will, I repeat, be sacked. Whoever it was should come forward immediately."

I pretending to think, you dirty bastard, but in my heart of hearts I know who it was. That is a serviceman's idea of humour and is definitely one of the two ex-squaddies I had met earlier in the lift. Their secret is safe with me, so I breathe a sigh of relief until Sergeant Williams adds one more thing to his list.

"It has also been reported that there was a male in the female block last night. In the basement that man ran past the cleaner and frightened her so much so that she fainted'.

Sweat broke out on me as if I'd just exited a sauna bath as another instructor brought the cleaner towards us. 'Now, take your hats off, Gentlemen.

Sergeant Williams tells all of us to take our hats off. My arse is twitching uncontrollably, and I can see Tracy going pale white. I blow her another kiss and mouth, 'don't worry'. If the cleaner should identify me, there's no way I'm going to finger Tracy as the collaborator in arms. One indelible thing you learn in the services is total loyalty to your comrades in arms is non-negotiable.

The cleaner walks past all of us in turn and to my amazement she doesn't recognise me. Though I'm ecstatic, I decide it would be prudent to check and, if necessary, change my boxers ASAP. Sergeant Williams is livid that no-one has been identified. He promptly dismisses the parade with the parting shout, 'Sole meet me in my office in 5 minutes'.

Sheeet! I can feel my legs shaking as he stares me in the face in his office. 'Sole, you are mates with everyone. I want the name of the Phantom Fucker and the animal that shit in the lift by the end of the week. Their days in the police are numbered'.

'I'll do my best, sir', I say, spinning on my heels and marching out with Cheshire grin, fully realising that it's cat's life number two and only seven to spare.

For reasons known only to himself, one of the nicest guys on camp confesses to having a dump in the lift and is therefore, per the Sarge's threat, immediately dismissed. As ex-army, he would have been an awesome cop. I'm assuming he believed that a forensic examination of the offending turd would have done him in.

I must admit, I would have confessed as well, but many years later I asked a scientist if there was any forensic evidence in shit, and he said, none whatsoever. It's just shit. That may well have changed now with the huge advances in forensic detection, but it never crapped or cropped up again in any of my investigations.

In due course, I sail through my exams and am posted

to Wandsworth Police station in South London. Until I arrive, I have no clue where Wandsworth is, but am pleased to have survived Hendon and the Phantom Fucker remain exactly that – a Phantom.

Life is going on everywhere -- Gail has moved into the Portsmouth house, James' arrival is imminent, and Beast is heavily pregnant with puppies. Despite knowing it is wrong, I am still bouncing at the nightclub for cash whenever possible because I need the money and Ronny the head doorman doesn't trust anyone else. Mum and Dad are drinking themselves into oblivion every day, and their life in the north is a complete mess.

Mating beast has been an adventure. Point blank, she refuses to allow the stud Dobermann to mount her and bites him unmercifully despite the fact he is a huge, super stud champion. It takes three of us to persuade her to do what should come naturally.

First we tape her jaws shut. Then Alan holds her head from the front and strokes her constantly. I stop her back legs from moving and the breeder does the honours with the stud and forces the dog's erection into her baby-maker. I'm so glad there are no smartphones, or we would all have ended up in court for animal cruelty. I'm convinced that Beast believes Alan impregnated her because from that day forward she follows him round like a love-struck teenager.

The puppies arrives whilst I'm working in London. Together with Jean and Lucy, Alan takes charge of the entire birthing process. Out pops eight puppies but the last one she pushes to one side without even opening the birth sack. Alan must tear it open and massage its tiny body and blow on its face until it suddenly splutters to life.

Alan places number eight onto Beast's nipple and retires to bed exhausted from the night's event. The next day all the puppies are suckling on mum except for the tiny one which she has deliberately moved well away from the group and has since gone cold. Trying to revive her, he wraps her in a towel with a hot water bottle and feeds her with an eye dropper baby's milk. As a result, all the puppies survive and grow quickly, apart from number eight who remains much smaller than all the rest, sort of akin to a Dobermann-coloured sausage dog.

When I come home, Alan playfully punched me and says, 'the things I do for you R- Sole'. And we both burst out laughing.

# SEVENTEEN

Ethnically diverse with gaps in great wealth and abject poverty, Wandsworth in south London is naturally a busy police district. Before long, like a duck to water, I develop a strong policing reputation, not only as a prolific thief taker, but as a man with my own informants, which during the probationary period is virtually unheard of.

Because I've never forgotten a police officer's discretion saving my life at 16, I adopt a firm but fair attitude to policing. Even with mere traffic issues, I deal with offenders and criminals the way I would expect them to treat me were the roles reversed: tough but not too tough, in control but no knocking someone's teeth out.

It's a fact that a lot of police problems stem from recruiting youngsters with no life experience and even less communication skills, and I believe it's a testament to the way I dealt with people that, in 25 years of service, astonishingly, there has never been a single complaint registered against me. Some think that police work is only about being a hard arse, when it really is about firm compassion.

If I stop someone who may have been over the limit for drink driving, before breathalysing him, I give him an option to leave the car where it is and drop the ignition key down a roadside drain. Funny thing -- nobody has ever taken the breathalyser option. From my side, there won't be any future accident, and the worst that has happened to him, is that he might have to buy a new key rather than losing his job, his home, or even his family.

Small amounts of cannabis go down the same route and therefore enables me to get on with the business of catching real criminals and those that deserve it, and not spending four hours plus dealing with someone who will only be fined £10 at court and probably not even sent to rehab.

There can always be an exception, of course. I deviate from my rule if the person I stop is aggressive and can't be calmed down, or when he has an active criminal record. Then the opposite happens: I show him no mercy, as people who challenge the police are the authors of their own demise.

Something I learnt very early in life, is that it is hard to be horrible to someone who is being nice and maintains that position throughout the encounter. Indeed, career gangsters have learned that lesson well, and all the ones I have dealt with are always polite and a pleasure to deal with. They have learned their lesson the hard way, and now know better.

Because of my life experience and fluid communication skills, I am constantly being seconded by different squads attached to the CID if manpower is scarce. Quite early in my service, for a time I live in the police flats for single men at the rear of Putney Police station and commute home to Portsmouth when I have a few days off.

One morning I am awoken in the early hours by what sounds like a huge bomb going off. It transpires that a block of expensive private flats on Putney Hill called Manor Fields have suffered a devasting gas explosion which causes the entire three storey block to collapse into the basement. I am seconded to deal with property (cash and jewellery) and the bodies.

This is my first encounter with carnage on a large scale and brings home the nightmares that the emergency services must deal with. You develop a black sense of humour in the police, because you have too. If you fail to compartmentalise these kinds of events, and lock that box when you go home, madness and nightmares will engulf your very being.

My police colleagues heartily confirm I am a 'mad', off-the-wall character and commence to call me 'Mad Jack'. There was no counselling back then, and post-traumatic stress disorder hasn't been invented yet or is in its infancy. The complete devastation I witness at Manor Fields is mind-blowing. Nobody is coming out of there alive.

The gruesome task of recovering the dead starts in earnest with the fire brigade digging out the area by hand and ensuring it is safe for others to come forward and do whatever they have to do – i.e., for other 'responders', as they are now called.

In one bed in the basement, there is an elderly couple. Tragically, they have been decapitated by the steel girders of one of the buildings as they headed south. It's not only gruesome, but shocking beyond comprehension.

In the process of doing our excavation, we find tens of thousands of pounds in cash which must have derived from a flat whose occupants were selling drugs or laundering or engaging in other criminal activity. Not surprisingly, nobody ever claims the mounds of cash, as they would have if Johnny had just been socking it away for a rainy day.

Miraculously, one lady survives. She had been taking a bath when the explosion happened, and the entire ceiling collapsed and dropped her tub and all that jazz into the basement. I can't remember how long it took to find her, but it was days rather than hours.

Sometimes it's your turn to die and sometimes it's not. This lady was one of the lucky ones whose time clearly had not come. A reminder that you should live every day like it's your last, because one day it truly will be.

Death and horrific injuries are far too common in the life of a police officer. Coupled with the fact you see the worst in people daily, I'm surprised more cops are not permanently mentally scarred by their experiences.

# EIGHTEEN

These incidents are not chronologically accurate, but they are all incidents in which I have played a part whilst a relatively new police officer at Wandsworth... and some still haunt me to this day.

### The Putney Rapist

A series of rapes occurs in and around both Putney and Wimbledon Common in the night hours. The suspect is a young male who hides in the undergrowth close to the bus stops that surround these areas. As soon as a lone female stops and waits for a bus, he creeps out, puts a knife to her throat, pulls her back away from the road and brutally rapes them.

He leaves absolutely no clues, proving to us that he has considerable knowledge of our forensic detection capabilities. When the rapes continue, eventually we identify the perpetrator as being Mr Everald Irons. Just arresting him is not an option, however, as there are no real forensics and it's too much of a gamble to parade him before the severely traumatised victims.

So we place him under surveillance, which is not easy, bearing in mind his *modus operandi* and the general principles of surveillance. For police to be able to follow and keep an eye on someone, they must assume that there is a strong possibility that the target will see them. Also, there is a huge risk dealing with someone like this, in so much as we can't watch him 24 hours a day.

For starters, contrary to the belief that we can, what happens if the target brutally rapes someone whilst we are not following him? Because it often comes out at the subsequent enquiry that we were following him, and that we knew who he was. Then the shit well and truly hits the fan.

Once a pattern of behaviour has been established, a decision to arrest him is made. It transpires, quite unbelievably (though it does explain his knowledge of forensics), that his wife is a policewoman, and in the post-arrest enquiries, it is further established that she has doctored her diaries to give him alibis for his brutal rapes.

Why she is never charged with attempting to pervert the course of justice is a mystery to me -- a decision made that's way above my pay scale. So, in July of 1988, the fellow is convicted of six rapes (notwithstanding his wife's alibi) and he is sentenced to 18 years in prison.

Finally, women can walk safely at night in Putney and Wimbledon Common.

## The Stockwell Strangler

A series of rapes and buggery of elderly females is reported in South London. The suspect, a young male, is breaking into the houses of female pensioners, after which he murders and brutally rapes or buggers them or both. Upon finishing, he places them into bed and covers them up and leaves the scene. Thankfully, unlike the cop's husband mentioned earlier, he has no forensic awareness.

His crimes come to light on Wandsworth Patch when he breaks into a pensioner's house just off West Hill. Apparently he had entered through an already broken window covered only with hardboard. Once inside the house, he had subjected the victim to a horrific assault, brutally killed her and, whilst she was dead, sexually assaulted her. He then put her into bed and departed.

A while later, a young probationer visits the property and finds the elderly lady lying in bed assumed and assumes she has died in her sleep. Because it is cold in the house, he also fixes the hardboard to the window and makes it secure again. Only when the undertakers come do they suspect that the lady is a victim of foul play, prompting commencement of a murder investigation.

In 1986, Kenneth Erskine is arrested for this and a series of similar murders. During his interview for the Wandsworth Murder, when asked in interview about the murder, rape and buggery in West Hill, he becomes sexually aroused, and in front of everyone including his solicitor commences the act of masturbating.

Thankfully, he is convicted and committed to Broadmoor as criminally insane, where he may well never see freedom again.

## The Battersea Rapist

Wandsworth and Battersea form part of W division in the Metropolitan Police area, and it is common practice for us to help each other out with manpower for specific enquiries. On a warm summer evening, a young lady with a first floor flat decides to open her bedroom window, allowing more air to circulate.

I have no wish to frighten anyone, but I genuinely believe there are a lot of bad people out there, and all they need is an opportunity. Thus the open window constitutes an invitation card to this rapist, who quickly scales the building and slips through the window.

The victim is awoken by the weight of a large male on top of her and pressing a large knife to her throat. He commits a horrific sexual assault on her, during which she is made to perform oral sex on him. She notices his penis has many scabs on it, and although awful to visualise, this observation will play a crucial part in the evidence against one Aliyu Ceesay at his subsequent arrest.

When we've gotten him in custody, we take photos of the scabs and other evidence, and he is eventually convicted as the Battersea Rapist. Rape is a hideous crime and quite often the victims are so traumatised they struggle to maintain a normal life from that point forward. I cannot recall his sentence, but I'm sure it made double figures.

## The Murder of Christopher Wandless

Chris Wandless is a 20-year-old man who has decided to walk home through Wandsworth through to Wimbledon in the early hours of the morning after visiting his friends. As he walks down East Hill, he becomes aware of someone following him and stops at the red phone box to call his mum. He tells her that he's frightened because he thinks he's being followed.

Whilst making the call, the door is opened and he is shot twice at close range with a sawn-off shotgun. He dies instantly. A murder squad based at Earlsfield Police Station is formed and we're then dispatched to the scene. I'll never forget the look of abject terror that's been permanently etched on Christopher's face as (apparently) he was being shot. A multitude of reasons are put forward as to what had happened and why, but every lead bottoms out.

One caller identifies a suspect with an address on the Earlsfield/Wandsworth border, and we are despatched on an early morning raid to bring in the alleged suspect. At the premises, I'm met by an elderly male and directed to his son's bedroom. When we race upstairs, the bedroom has a single bed with a huge male with long blonde hair laying on it.

'Get out of bed, Ivan', I shout. 'It's the police and we need to talk to you about a murder'.

'I'm not Ivan, I'm Debbie', he replies.

That stops me in my tracks whilst my brain tries to catch up. "Oh, sorry, Debbie, can you get out of bed slowly and keep your hands where I can see them?'

This hulk of a man gets out of bed wearing a pink baby doll nighty and matching pants. I immediately realise we have been well and truly had, but continue with the search and proceed to eliminate this suspect. I have this vision of a neighbour opposite looking out of the window, pissing himself laughing at our mistake.

On the bedside table are birth control pills which have been taken up to date and photographs which even turn my stomach, and by this time, I've seen a lot so that is hard. In desperation, and having been refused transgender surgery, to prove he is serious he has taken a Wilkinson Sword razor blade and cut off his own cock and balls and meticulously photographed the procedure.

How he has not bled out and died I will never know. Needless to say, I leave sausages and plum tomatoes off my breakfast order later that day. Of course, we eliminate her off our list after ensuring that he did not commit the crime before the procedure.

The murder squad draws blanks at every turn, and we are beginning to think this one will not be solved, until we receive a call from another police station. They have a man in custody who has shot his mother with a sawn-off shotgun and is also talking about shooting a man in Wandsworth.

It transpires that the suspect - whose name escapes me - just wanted to know what it was like to hunt a human being and left home that night with the intention of stalking and killing anybody he came across. Hopefully no mother will ever again have to hear her son being shot in cold blood from a telephone booth.

# NINETEEN

The night before Christmas, Alan and Lucy are rudely awoken by what sounds like the start of World War III. In fact, it's just our Dobermann puppies launching themselves into the Christmas tree in an effort to eat the baubles, resulting in the entire tree crashing down.

Alan is the first person downstairs to find all the beautifully wrapped presents ripped to shreds and the lounge and dining room looking like a smattering of grenades went off. Thankfully, mobile phones have not been invented, or otherwise I would have received an angry call from Alan to the effect, 'The things I do for you R- Sole' – especially after they are also sorry to report that the Dobermanns pups are so huge that they've managed to eat the entire ground floor carpet and are working on the surrounding woodwork.

Now back home in Portsmouth, it's New Year's Eve 1984/5. Against my better judgement, I agree to work the door of Ronny's club for purely monetary reasons – yes, I need the money. After what's been a great night, and after all the punters have gone, the owner allows the staff to remain at the cocktail bar and drink for free.

We start drinking and playing spoof and this time the group decides the loser must do a forfeit. The owner Norman loses first and the girls decide he has to go into the gent's toilet, come out buck naked, and then streak around the entire club and back into the toilets. Like a trooper, he runs the gamut and with all the girls laughing hilariously as they are chasing him with their boobs hanging loose.

Next to lose is Katrina. She's a very pretty petite girl with disproportionately huge firm breasts, so the group wants her to put on quite the display. They – both the men and the women amongst us - decide that she will be made to remove her shirt and bra and allow all the boys to kiss her perky jewels.

When she hears the sentence, she runs off, as she does not want any part of this display.

'Rob, get her back', Norman says.

I chase after her, pick her up, and spin her around upside down and proceed to walk her back to the cocktail bar. Unbeknown to me, she has no knickers on, and lo and behold, her beaver immediately goes on full display in full view of everyone except me. Fair play to her, she doesn't bat an eyelid, and when I stand her upright, she releases her amazing breasts ala Marilyn Monroe and all the lads take turns copping a nuzzle.

Feeling we have to one up the last sentence, we play on and Norman loses again. Hell bent on revenge, Katrina suggests that the forfeit should be that she put Norman's cock in her mouth, and of course being drunken sailors all clap and cheer. To be honest, I'm sure that Norman won't mind, either. However, this is where Lesley, Norman's better half, wants none of it and yells, 'fuck off, Katrina, you are not sucking my boyfriend's cock'.

Naturally, we respond by booing and cheering, but Katrina dives forward and starts attacking Norman's trousers and zipper. Lesley steps forward and slaps Katrina hard round the face and commences a hair-pulling cat fight. Ronny and I instinctively part them as they kick and scream, and Norman declares, 'take Katrina outside, she needs to go home'. The boys collectively muscle her out of the club and send her off packing.

The party is not over, but we continue drinking at the bar in a much more subdued atmosphere than that previously evoked by forfeit. Eventually, we all go home mortally pissed in the early hours of the morning. A couple of days later, I return to work in London, but what none of us know is that Katrina had gone into the local police station and reported us for indecently assaulting her.

Because she was so pissed- arse drunk, the local cops hadn't taken her seriously until she said one of the guys - Rob Sole - is a copper in the Met Police. That got their attention fast, and they started taking the pissed witness/victim with renewed vigour.

You need to know a bit more context to this story. I think it is fair to say that Hampshire Constabulary has a hatred for the Metropolitan Police, and vice- versa. HC thinks we are a bunch of corrupt, arrogant, flash wankers, and we, on the other hand, think HC are a load of lazy, useless, carrot-crunching dickheads. You cannot tarnish everyone with the same brush, but from personal experience, I can attest that Hampshire are the laziest force I have ever dealt with. Just my opinion, for what it's worth.

Of course, there are a few exceptions to this observation, and I will explain my justification for this general statement in due course. Now, unbeknown to me at the time, the spoof crew are subjected to dawn raids by police for indecently assaulting Katrina, and the Hampshire Constabulary sends a telex to the London Metropolitan Police demanding that I be arrested and transferred to Portsmouth Police Station.

I'm in uniform for an early shift, 6am to 2pm, when my relief inspector tells me to report immediately to the office of Superintendent Bona (excuse the relevant pun, but that is his God-given name). I report forthwith to his office, completely clueless mind you as to the purpose of our meeting. He sits me down and says, 'PC Sole, the Hampshire Constabularies has asked me for an explanation for your behaviour as to one Katrina Smith'.

'Sir, it is a complete load of bollox', I begin by saying. 'She was completely up for everything and all that happened was part of a game of Spoof'. I proceed to tell him the entire story as he stares at me sternly throughout my harangue. I can see my career disappearing before my very eyes and facing a firing squad for what was just good and consensual fun, at the time.

When I finish talking, he stands up, looks me straight in the eye, and says, 'I don't think it's a load of bollox at all, PC Sole'. Then he pauses, and I feel the colour drain from my face and my leg started twitching uncontrollably. 'Sounds like a load of fannies', and he bursts out laughing. When he stops, he says, 'you are one mad colourful character, PC Sole, and I want to party with you'.

When I realise I can believe my ears, I slowly start to relax and start laughing at myself. He shakes my hand and gives me the telex request and says, 'we are not arresting you to get the jollies off for these wankers at Hampshire.

Go home and get changed and get the train to Portsmouth and report to Detective Chief Inspector Akerman, ASAP'.

When I thank him and walk out, I can hear him laughing out loud all the way down the hallway. I head to Portsmouth, arriving late afternoon and making an appointment to see DCI Akerman the next day. That night, Katrina comes to see me and apologises for the mess she's gotten me in. She assures me she would not have attended court anyway, as what they had written was not what she had said. In other words, she thought they were trying to stitch me up.

At the appointed time, I attend Portsmouth Police Station, where I am promptly arrested and taken to an interview room and dealt with by DCI Akerman. When I immediately informed him what Katrina has told me, his demeanour changes dramatically. He asks me to lay out what happened, which I do, and then he interviews me contemporaneously to make sure all the relevant facts come out.

At the conclusion, he says he will prepare a report suggesting no further action and advises me to temper my behaviour and be careful about the company I keep now I am a Police Officer. In short, he's a complete gent, and I can't thank him enough for the stance he has taken. As a result of my interview, no-one is charged with anything, and rightly so, in my opinion, but it could have ended so differently.

For a second, I actually think about changing my behaviour – but I decide against it I'm having too much fun. Three of my nine lives is well and truly gone.

# TWENTY

Life four is not long to follow, when I again - foolishly - agree to work the door at Ronny's place because he is short staffed. Ronny and I work well together, because he is frightened of nobody and walks into fights as casually as I walk into the supermarket. But maybe this is not a good thing.

It is a Saturday night and Ronny, kickboxer Richard, and I are all on the door. For most of the evening, it's perfectly peaceful. Then up the stairs towards us comes a guy we know is a handful, and he also is pissed drunk, which makes for a dicey situation.

When we decide against letting him in, he kicks off straight away trying to thump me and Ronny, who are the ones closest to him. To defend ourselves, we just push him back away from the door. There is nothing big or clever in hitting drunks, and we have a reputation for not assaulting anyone unless it is unavoidable. As a result, local gangsters rarely give us grief and respect us for that.

Unfortunately, on this occasion we push him a bit too hard, and he falls down the stairs and breaks his leg. An ambulance is called and he is taken away to the local hospital. We think no more of it until the club closes at 2am and the police arrive, arresting all of us for Grievous Bodily Harm.

As we are sat in the back of the van, I mouth to the boys, leaning on my police training, 'don't say a word, fellas'.

We are taken to Portsmouth Police Station and they lock us in separate cells to do the 'he said this, he said that', on us. Because I am due back at work on the Sunday night, I again see my police career swan-diving toward the floor at breakneck speed.

The night CID crew interviews us, and I say to them, 'It was a straightforward self-defence. He attacked us, we pushed him away, and because he was pissed, he accidently fell down the stairs'. They inform us that they will leave us to the day staff as to how to proceed.

I am a great believer in fate, and what will be will be. At 6am, the dayshift cell block staff come on, and when one of them comes to check on us, I notice he has a tattoo saying, 'The sweetest Girl I ever kissed was another man's wife. My Mother'. Bingo, I'm thinking, this guy must be ex-Navy.

Right away we start reminiscing and swapping sea stories, and I'm thinking, in for a penny, in for a pound, so I declare to him I am a serving cop and due on night duty at 10pm that day. He says, 'Fuck me, why didn't you say so earlier?'

He disappears from view and comes back 30 minutes later and opens the cells and lets us all out. He tells us the guy at the hospital has refused to co-operate and won't make a statement, so we were free to go. I could have kissed him, I am so elated, so we all get out of there as quickly as possible before anyone can change their minds.

Outside we're all hugging and jumping around like school kids, but I inform Ronny and Richard right there and then, 'Boys, from now on, you are on your own. Don't ever call me again, because I will be telling you to take a fuck-off pill regardless of the wages'. We part company and live to fight another day, but that is my final night on the door – with another of my nine lives spent.

I decide to sell my house in Portsmouth and buy a flat in Carshalton Beeches, Surrey. This has the knock-on effect of causing Alan and Lucy to buy their first home in Portsmouth, and Gail and James, who have been in Portsmouth, to source accommodations for themselves.

All the puppies are sold for £400 each except for the Sausage dog. Alan decides to keep her/him, and because Alan is a massive 'Star Wars' fan they decide to call her Vader. They say nature is cruel, and that may be true, but I figure Beast discarded Vader for good reason. Vader was born with a complete mismatch of internal organs and had been dealt with both a penis and a vagina, and apparently Beast had sensed that.

Throughout Vader's life, he/she was constantly ill with different digestive problems, and although Alan and Lucy loved him/her dearly, I'm sure it was a relief for both when she went into a mad running session in the back garden of their flat and dropped down dead of heart failure. She was definitely a huge drain on their finances, with massive vets bills coming when Alan was working as a poorly paid HGV driver.

Once everything is complete, Jean, Beast and I moved into the flat we have purchased, but it is fair to say we both realise quite quickly that our relationship has run its course, with bickering and arguing becoming a regular occurrence. As life is wont to do, when things aren't going well, a new woman starts working at Wandsworth and she turns my head.

I decide to pursue her, along with a few other eligible males, so I inform Jean our relationship isn't working. We agree to call a halt to it and Jean moves back to Portsmouth and I stay in the flat with Beast. I pay Jean a cash settlement to end the relationship cleanly, and I have remained friends with her and her new family ever since.

# TWENTY-ONE

Seven years my junior, Denise is an attractive woman working as an admin clerk to which a bunch of fellow cops at Wandsworth including me have taken a fancy. But she's now embroiled in a relationship with her childhood sweetheart, George, and so has deliberately chosen to rebuff all advances, including my own.

Throughout the year, Accommodation Block at Putney has a function area where they hold disco parties. On one of these nights, I am there having drinks when Denise arrives with a group of other girls. I decide not to chase her and instead am content with watching other guys try and fail to get her to dance.

Towards the end of the evening, I notice her and her friend looking straight at me. I can feel movement in my loins, and as if by magic, a slow dance track comes on. No pun intended, practically pole-vault towards her and take her hand and pull her onto the dancefloor in a flash and with a large smile.

It's brutally obvious to her that I'm donning a raging hard-on, because every time she pulls herself back a bit, I pull her back in close and thereby give her a big poke. Sometimes beating about the bush doesn't help, and this is definitely one of those times.

In a way, I'm glad she doesn't offer to come home with

me that night because, being honest, by the time the smooch has finished so have I. An urgent change of pants is required, but my Dancers Lance clearly impressed Denise, as that night she has me drop her home to where she lives with her parents.

When her dad opens the door, he beckons her inside the safe confines of the house before I am even able to kiss her goodnight. He must have been standing within a foot of the door waiting for her to get home. Despite driving, I'm semi-pissed as was the reality of many cops back then, since in those days cops would never arrest another cop for drink driving (nowadays they go out of their way to do exactly that).

Clearly, I had done something right as the next day at work she agreed to go out with me on a second date. Why then did she remain a mystery to me? Because she was 18 years old, very pretty and extremely shy, whereas I am the polar opposite: loud, cheeky, inappropriate and full of myself. Maybe there is some truth in the adage, opposites attract.

As relationship gathers pace, it is obvious that going to her parent's house is strictly off the menu, so at every opportunity we go to my flat in Carshalton. We must have been noisy in the bedroom, lounge and kitchen, because frequently at emotional moments the neighbours would bang on anything they had at their disposal -- walls, floor or ceiling.

Denise would curl up sheepishly and I would scream something like, 'shut your pie holes and get a life!' Fortunately, Denise gets on well with Beast, but on one occasion, she becomes a bit too involved. We are enjoying some afternoon delight, and mid-way through the engagement I feel her start licking on my arse.

'How the fuck is Denise doing that?' I think, then I suddenly spin round and scream out, 'Beast!' Denise jumps out of her skin and I burst out laughing at the realisation that it was Beast all along.

The moment of course is lost instantly, bringing another adage to mind. It has been said that having sex is like using a bank account. As soon as the man withdraws, he loses all interest. Me personally I love a cuddle as close together as possible and prefer falling asleep interlocked with my partner. Needless to say, that does not happen here.

Denise has one major flaw which impacts our relationship. She is insanely jealous which, for an affable fellow like me, is not compatible. I think it will mellow with time, but the truth is it never does; it only gets worse. Despite that, we are in love and get married in 1988.

It goes without saying that my best man must be Alan, and obviously Lucy comes with him. Denise and all the bridesmaids looked stunning, Alan and I wear top hats and tails, and the ceremony is amazing. Despite being estranged, both my mum and dad come, and I give the family strict instructions to keep an eye on them and control their consumption of drink.

The reception dinner and drinks go down well, and then Alan stands up to deliver his speech. 'I don't know Denise very well', he begins, 'but I know Rob too well as the chairman of the Portsmouth area mooning society'. (Fortunately or unfortunately, as the case may be, whenever I get drunk, I'm known – indeed, renowned - for shining my arse in the most inappropriate places, and to this day, that bizarre behaviour has been unstoppable despite my arse now looking like it needs a good ironing.)

Alan continues, 'So it is only fair that I should start my speech with a big moon beam'. He then proceeds to get on his chair, turn toward the diners, drop his pants and expose his tattooed bare arse to everyone in the room. Everyone goes deathly quiet and looks to Denise for her reaction. I break the silence by saying, 'and as you can clearly see, he hasn't cleaned his teeth'.

Denise's 70-year old nan, Dolly, has been sitting at the front with her mouth hanging open staring at Alan's scruffy arse, but she suddenly bursts out laughing with just gusto that she splutters and spits her false teeth out into another guest's pint. The room erupts, and by the time Alan has finished talking, everyone's jaws are aching from laughter.

Despite my dad's earnings, he hasn't contributed at all to the wedding, so when Alan finishes, I stand up and point to my Dad, saying, 'my dad would like to thank you all for coming and has kindly offered to buy every one of you a drink, so please join him at the bar whilst we get the room ready for the evening party'.

Dad's face is a picture of veiled horror, as he can't show his surprise because everyone is clapping and rooting him on and he's too big a bullshitter to say that he can't afford the bill. I don't know what that bill turned out to be, but it gives me a great deal of satisfaction to see him put his hand in his pocket and buy drinks for someone other than himself.

The evening reception is a roaring success, apart from Denise's aunty Brenda falling over whilst dancing drunk to 'Rock Around the Clock', injuring her back, and having to be escorted to the hospital by ambulance. Denise and I leave in the bridal car to a lovely hotel in Croydon, and have a debaucherous night of sex and champagne, and in that order.

The next morning when we check out the bill, it shows two bottles of Moet and a packet of paracetamols, as we are both hanging. As we got older, I used to jokingly take paracetamols to bed in the evening for Denise. If she declined them, that meant she didn't have a headache and I would say, 'great, get your panties off and brace yourself'. Who says men don't do foreplay?

We go on our honeymoon to Kavos in Corfu, which at the time is an unspoilt, beautiful resort with Benitses up the coast (it's an 18-30 something shag-fest resort). Denise throws the wedding ring back at me three times during the honeymoon, accusing me of fancying other women on the beach and in the bar. The only way I could have avoided an argument was to spend the entire fortnight looking at my feet.

I'm not prepared to do that and decide the best strategy is just to ignore this unprovoked paranoid behaviour. Conversation and sound reasoning definitely don't work, as Denise is extremely short-sighted with a minus 7.5 prescription that some people say is the only reason she fancied me at the start. Truth be told, she typically wears strong contact lenses when not on the beach and can see better than you and I.

Many times in our lives together, I would say to her, 'how come you can't see what you are looking at, but you can see exactly what my eyes are looking at?'

Maybe I have been witness to a modern day miracle this whole time!

SECRET AGENT MAN

AKA, DANGER MAN

'Every government has its Secret Service branch: America, CIA; France, Deuxieme Bureau; England, MI5. NATO also has its own. A messy job? Well that's when they usually call on me, or someone like me. Oh yes: my name is Rob, R Sole'.

- Cheeky take on John Drake's 'Danger Man'

# ONE

Life five starts in earnest. I'm selected for the CID, sent on the detectives course at Hendon, and posted to Chiswick Police station as a fledgling Detective Constable.

As a varied patch, Chiswick has extreme wealth and extreme poverty in close proximity to each other – drugs dealers or C-suite executives, blue collar verses white collar, wages as against salaries and dividends. The jurisdiction includes all of Brentford, Isleworth, and Twickenham Rugby grounds.

My reputation as a thief taker has preceded me arriving at Chiswick, and I am quickly seconded to the Local Crime Squad responsible for targeting the burglars, street robbers and drug dealers. It is at Chiswick that I meet one of my favourite criminals. His name is David, and he's an amazing fraudster.

David has patented a system of stealing major amounts of high value goods from major UK retailers. His trick is that he plays on the greed and ego of the people he cons. Arrested by pure fluke and bad luck, he has ventured into a jeweller's shop and taken a look at the expensive watches. As part of his modus operandi, he flirts with the staff, getting as much detail about a particular watch as he can, and then leaving seamlessly asks for the name of the manager.

Out he goes to a phone box and rings the jeweller from whose shop he has just visited. 'Hi, its Fendi Timepieces here', he says. 'We have misplaced your account number with us. Can you read it back to me'.

The staff always oblige, and then he ends the call and rings Fendi Timepieces. 'Hi, it's Mr Wilson from XYZ jewellery shop. We have had an urgent order in from Saudi Arabia for 30 of your Fendi timepieces valued at £1500 each'.

Of course, the jeweller is drooling on himself now.

"Please, can you put a rush order through on our account number 12345 and we will send a courier to collect them in 30 minutes."

The supplier happily obliges, and David despatches a courier on a motorcycle to collect his order and deliver them back to him in Chiswick, outside a closed industrial unit. The plan goes like clockwork and David sits there happy in the knowledge that, within the hour, he will take possession of £45,000 worth of quality watches.

Unfortunately for him, a million-to-one freak incident occurs, and the manager of XYZ jewellers rings and makes the same exact order. Police are called, a trap is set, and David is arrested.

Fortunately, he and I get on like long lost friends. He confesses to a multitude of other similar crimes, including nicking 40-foot lorries full of Champagne, children's toys and beauty products.

His coup d'état is that he went into a limousine hire company purporting to be a BBC reporter, gave a BBC purchase account number, and told the company he was doing an expose on hotels around the M25. He spent days being chauffeured from one hotel to the next eating and drinking like a king, then adding insult to injury with another simple scam.

In the morning before departure, he leaves the hotel and then rings reception. 'I'm a guest', he says, ' and I've asked for a valuable parcel to be delivered which may arrive while I'm out. Can you pay the courier for it and add it to my account? I'll square it with you when I check out'.

He then gives a wrapped-up telephone directory to the courier and tells him to get £500 for it from the delivery address and bring the cash back to him. Of course, the courier does as he is told, getting £500 from the unknowing hotel clerk and making David £500 richer. I have to admire the absolute cheek and cleverness of this man.

When I charge him, he says he has been doing this for years and had never once been given a long sentence. 'I could probably do with being inside for a rest', he hilariously says. I prepare all the paperwork and send the prison to which he has been remanded an order to produce him for further interviews.

I roar with laughter when the prison apologises and says he is no longer with them, as they have apparently released him to attend his mum's funeral. As he never comes back, when I enquire further, I learn that his mum died over ten years ago.

I have to confess, I'm not overly disappointed. I take my hat off to his chutzpah and ingenuity.

# TWO

Violent deaths are something a police officer must live with. In my service, I see some horrific ones. Some involve murders, as I have related, some involve car chases, and some involve suicides.

There's a young lad about 18 years old who steals motorbikes and then puts on a public display so that we give chase to him. But our cars are no match for his stolen superbikes. To rub it in, he always slows down and goad us on, before pulling a wheelie and rip-roaring off again.

If Karma is a bitch, then it definitely comes to roost for this tearaway. As we chase him at speeds in excess of 100 MPH, he goes round a bend and out of view, whereupon we hear a horrific bang. Turns out, our motorcycle thief has run into a transit van.

But that's not all. The petrol tank on the bike has exploded from under the van, engulfing the poor bike in flames. There is absolutely nothing we can do but stand and watch. I do think, note to self: cancel the barbecue planned for this weekend. Not to be crass.

There also is a group of young lads that steal high-powered sports cars – again, for the purpose of being deliberately chased by police, sort of like joyriding on steroids. On this particular occasion, these four marauders steal a convertible Porsche and are driving at breakneck speed with the roof down to get away from us. They roll the car going to fast around a tight bend, and all of them are decapitated. We find the bodies still in the car, but the heads scattered at various points along the roadway.

On another occasions, I'm en route to Southwark Crown Court and standing on the platform at the Elephant and Castle station. I always stand with my back against the wall in tube stations, and here's why:

First, the multitude of pickpockets that work the tube steal from the pockets of the crowds that push towards the track edge as the train approaches. You don't even feel them as they brush up against you and sleight your wallet or purse or whatever is in your jacket.

Secondly, whilst I was working at Putney, a day release patient from a mental institution ran forward and pushed an unsuspecting commuter into the path of the oncoming train. The fall killed her outright. Call me paranoid, but don't want that happening to me.

On this occasion, my attention is drawn to a woman close to the platform edge wearing a thick fur coat. I think, fuck me, it's a scorching summer's day; she must be roasting in that coat. I hear the train approaching, look at her, look back towards the train, and then look back to her again, sensing something.

Suddenly, she dives headlong into the path of the train and is chopped in half at the torso. Stunned, I see the train grinding to a stop as people start screaming and scattering. Being a detective, rather than move away I instinctively move towards the train, and within minutes, the platform is deserted apart from me and someone else who is trying to comfort the driver.

I run over to them and ask if I can help. This guy is

shaking uncontrollably but says he's okay. We wait for what seems like an eternity for the ambulance and fire crews arrive. One medic come up and says, 'I'll get under the train and see what I can do'. I say, 'don't bother, mate', I say, pointing toward the train. 'Unless you can reattach the head to that body, it won't do any good'.

For at least 20 years, that vision has haunted me. And whenever I am driving long distance and want to slip into autopilot, the image of the woman in the fur coat always jumps in front of my car, causing me to break hard and get my shite together. Thankfully, as a result, I have never crashed, though on one occasion I did do a full 360-degree spin on the motorway. An urgent coffee break followed a change of boxer shorts.

A vivid memory which remains with me now that was neither suicide nor accident. I receive a call to visit a property of an elderly woman who has called in and asked for the police, but they have been unable to ascertain why. When I arrive at her address, she invites me in. After some small talk, she points to her ceiling fan, explaining that there is water coming down the ceiling light from the flat above, landing on her dining table.

I knock at the door of the above flat, and though the lights are on, no one answer. I return to the lady and assure her that I will sort it and then return I return upstairs and knock harder on the door. Still no answer, I open the letterbox and peek inside. The foulest smell hits me full throttle in the face, and I immediately realise someone is very ripely dead.

I break in and enter the lounge, only to see an elderly man sat in his chair close to an electric fire which is full on. His cats have eaten his face and eyes, and the water dripping down to the woman's house is this man's body fluids seeping through the floor.

I don't know how long he had been there in this state, but it looks like the electric fire has literally cooked his lower body. This man has family, so as I sit waiting for the undertakers to arrive. Mental note to self: never sit by an electric fireplace for warmth whilst courting the holy ghost.

# THREE

Denise, her insane jealousy unabated, continues to accuse me of fucking every woman that I work with and our mutual friends' wives and partners as well. To her, I must be Eros, Himeros, and Pothos, the gods of love, passion, sexual desire and promiscuity – all rolled into one.

The irony for me is that I'm not and never have been that kind of guy. As a married man, I would rather slide down a razor blade using my balls as brakes than have an affair. I have always said men who have affairs are either too lazy too wank or too spineless to walk from the relationship they are in.

Yet, to this day, I'm shocked at the number of people I know who can't stand the relationship they are in, but do not have the balls to call it a draw and start again, presumably, mainly, for financial reasons. I live by the saying that we are here for a good time, not a long time, and every day you are not happy is a day wasted and which can never be replaced.

Therefore, I only have two speeds, 100mph or asleep. The day I can't live life at full tilt boogey will be the saddest day of my life, and probably the last.

Meanwhile, back at the ranch, a rather distressed young lady comes in to the station and says that she has been raped. A black man close to Chiswick Park tube station committed the dastardly deed, she says.

A rape squad is formed, we get her detailed version of what happened, and she is subjected to a forensic examination by a trained specialist. Her graphic description of what happened portends that this man needs to be caught yesterday, so we go into overdrive working long hours and leaving no stone unturned.

We retrace her movements and look at hundreds of hours of CCTV footage in hopes of identifying the scoundrel. We also carry out house to house enquiries and stop and search anyone who fits the victim's description. But we come up totally emptyhanded, finding diddle squat, nothing.

Giving it some very hard thought, I take the risky position of saying to the boss, 'well, you know, she might be lying. There's no other explanation'.

Not long afterward, we receive a call from the forensic science laboratory. 'Houston, we have a problem', they report. 'This victim has ten different semen samples inside her, with ten different DNA results'.

'What the fuck!' I exclaim. We bring her immediately into the station and is sat at a chair in the interview room. 'We think you are lying', the interrogating detective says. 'You have DNA from ten different blokes inside you, ma'am'.

Rather quickly, she breaks down and confesses to making the whole Black Rapist story up. In truth, she was out in the town and met a couple of squaddies from Chelsea Barracks. They managed to sneak her into the barracks and take her up to their sleeping quarters, where she willingly participated in a no-holds and no-orifices barred gang bang.

The next day, she feels extremely dirty and decides for reasons only known to herself to cry rape. This is not the only fake rape allegation I deal with, but this ranks in the top three most serious entrees -- and they always leave me with a foul taste in my mouth.

Of course, this does untold damage to men's reputations and to the community in general. Because we must have stopped every black man in the area that week, quite often it was highly resented. It also impacts on the credibility of genuine victims who have been brave enough to come forward and report what for them has been a harrowing, life-changing experience.

Of course, we have to interview the squaddies, and even without the sex side of the story, they have committed a serious breach of the rules by sneaking her into the barracks. They all risk losing their jobs for that alone. Not to mention, all the Army lads must be interviewed with a senior army officer present.

In one of the interviews, one lad is faced with the allegation that he engaged in vaginal sex with the alleged victim and then spun her over and buggered her. To our astonishment, he says, proud as punchy, 'yes, I did that'. It is pointed out to him that Buggery with a woman or man, ever since the time of Oscar Wilde, has been a criminal offence in merry ol England, so he had to be further cautioned.

At this moment, the senior officer turns and pauses the tape of the interview. Then he says, 'are you saying - did I hear you right - anal sex with a woman is a crime?'

'Yes it is', we uniformly reply.

'My God,' he exclaims, 'don't tell my ex-wife that'.

It is hard not to burst out laughing, as being inappropriate at times like this would be massively frowned on.

On the other hand, I know several men who have been charged with rape after having consensual sex. So be careful. My advice to the youth of today, is if you are not absolutely flame-proof, do not have sex with strangers. If a stranger is prepared to have sex with you, then you are not the first and you may end up with more than you wished for, for any number of reasons – venereal disease, spurious charges of rape, pregnancy, what have you.

Obviously not hearing my advice, one man comes in swearing that he's the one who has been raped, not the woman. Men being raped is not something that gets regularly reported. His story is that he met a woman in a pub for the first time and after drinks she invited him back to her house. At the house, she led him up to the bedroom.

They strip off, and after some foreplay, she ask him if she can tie him to the bed, face down. Once tied up, the woman's husband jumped out of the wardrobe wearing a Batman outfit and buggers this chap. He is eventually released and report what happened.

I have to say if this: had that happened to me, I would have taken it on the chin and gone back another day wearing a balaclava and hospitalised the pair of them. But clearly, as a police officer, you cannot advocate summary justice, so the suspects were duly arrested.

Predictably, they both said everything was consensual. So it was two against one, and the chances of securing a conviction were too low to proceed. To be fair, the victim had already been humiliated enough without letting it happen again at a public trial.

# FOUR

In the main, my nickname of Mad Jack relates to my off-the-wall humour and tendency to engage in activities that most people would consider extremely dangerous, like bungee jumping, parachute jumping or motorcycling. I do not consider myself a hard man, but I am rarely frightened by anyone or anything. And there can be frightening side of me, which only occasionally comes out as I possess an extremely long fuse and high tolerance for danger.

As I have a strong sense of family, that fuse can be tempted with family, because to me loyalty is non-negotiable. Therefore, my bad side is not so much a madness that infers being 'out of control', but it is a cold-hearted, dispassionate ability to do in anyone who interferes with the wellbeing of someone I love. Of course, it would be a very serious breach, not some relatively minor matter. But I would have no hesitation putting any transgressor in a box for good.

The first time this happens is when Alan's brother Brett goes for a drink close to the family home. He is an extremely good looking yet mild mannered young man who would not say boo to a goose. And at five-foot, seven inches and eight stone dripping wet, he couldn't fight his way out of a wet paper bag. (Sorry, Brett.)

So, Brett walks into a local pub on the 10$^{th}$ of May 1990 minding his own business, whereupon a big fat football hooligan decides he doesn't like the look of ol' Brett. Without any provocation, the hooligan beats Brett to a literal pulp, hitting him so many times in the face he is barely recognisable. Soon thereafter, Brett dies from his injuries.

As soon as Alan tells me about the killing, my mind goes into revenge mode and I mentally started plotting this hooligan's demise. Of course, there will be a trial for what he has done, and I may have to wait a while, but I have the patience of a saint and do not need to be angry to continue what I've put my mind to do.

Alan's family are in a total state of shock. I cannot imagine what it must be like as a parent to attend your child's funeral from a beating in a bar, and hopefully I never will. To this day, Alan's mum still sleeps with a lock of Brett's hair and a photo of Brett under her pillow. Alan's dad aged 20 years overnight and not one day has passed where he did not blame himself for failing to protect his son.

I think a conviction for manslaughter at the very least is a forgone conclusion, but I have spent enough time working with the judicial system to know that the law can be a farce. Juries are often either stupid or bias or bent or all three. Only a barrister turned lawmaker would say it is acceptable to have people with criminal convictions on a jury, and yet police officers are banned from the jury because they create the appearance of bias.

Criminal barristers prostitute themselves to the highest bidder and regularly build defences for their clients based around false or sketch evidence which they don't believe for one second. In my opinion, the right of silence is NOT enshrined in law to protect the innocent as it only gives the guilty something to hide behind and to ensure their barristers (which many judges once were) of their ability to command huge fees.

Criminal trials are not a search for the truth, but a game of poker between the prosecution and the defence barristers, in a game where the prosecution must show his hand first. The right of silence puts innocent people at risk of being convicted on a regular basis, not the other way round. In my experience, most innocent people want to shout it out loud, and only don't do so if some solicitor convinces them otherwise (because there is money in them there hills).

The man who beat Brett to death is charged and remanded in custody awaiting trial. I am cool with that because I know what I could do if this were a movie. I might stash an old pistol with a full magazine of bullets in a sealed bag and bury it in the rear alleyway where I live. Then I might research the area on the pretext of visiting Alan's family, and while I'm there, look for safe places to carry out, purely biblically speaking, the eye-for-an-eye. When I actually visit Alan's mum and dad, they have been altered dramatically. Brett's murder has had a devastating effect on them both.

They have never recovered from the actions of the pond-scum who beat their son to death. But eventually he goes to trial and uses farcical self-defence story that causes a jury to find him not guilty because the prosecution cannot prove the crime beyond a doubt. The jury never new Brett, because if they did, they would have laughed this defence straight out of court.

I have heard barristers and judges say it is better that 100 guilty people get away with murder than one be wrongly convicted. What a crock of shit. Interestingly, when a member of a magistrate's family is the victim of a serious assault, his attitude changes dramatically, and he wants the suspect hung out to dry.

When Brett's killer is released, I start conceiving the movie where I, hypothetically speaking, make final plans to put an end to this turd's life. But in my story, Alan himself would cause a halt to my intentions because he is worried that the family of the killer will blame his family and start exacting some form of revenge on them. As hard as it is to accept, I respect that decision.

Knowing now how much Brett's death has affected Alan's parents, I cannot wait for the movie to happen, with perhaps a different ending.

# FIVE

Justice, who's kidding who? To answer my scepticism, two cases spring immediately to mind (though there are many more).

A man I am dealing with at the Old Bailey tells his barrister that, provided the Judge reduces his sentence to under ten years, he will plead guilty and not make the prosecution try the case. His attorney even has a discussion about the prospects of this plea with the prosecuting barrister in my presence.

We go into court and the defence barrister puts his client's offer to the Judge. The Judge says no way is he going to guarantee that the sentence will be under ten years, as the defendant enjoys a previous conviction for Armed Robbery. He is definitely looking at double figures.

The jury is then sworn in and the defence barrister on behalf of his client accuses the police of fitting him up with the Armed Robbery charges. The defendant meanwhile hides behind the right of silence and does not get in the witness box. He is duly acquitted by the jury and set free to rob again.

I would like to say this sort of thing is rare, but my police service is literally littered with similar incidents where the system has shown it is not fit for purpose and needs a complete overhaul. More examples come to mind:

At Chiswick, I deal with a rape on a down syndrome female who has been out drinking and is befriended by a seasoned local criminal. She alleges that he offered to walk her home, and, on the way, he attacked and raped her. She is extremely distressed, and whilst giving her statement, bursts into tears many times.

I arrest the suspect, but I know if he says the sex was consensual, because of the circumstances, it will be very difficult to prove rape beyond a reasonable doubt. His solicitor advises him to remain silent, which he does, and he is consequently charged with rape and remanded to custody.

Over two years later, he appears at the Old Bailey and the victim is called in to give evidence. The Judge stops the trial because, in his opinion, the victim is not a competent witness. I am heavily criticised for not making the same assumption. However, that diagnosis is not something I feel qualified to make, as I believe she has been raped as described by her in minute detail.

Though I take the bollocking on the chin, the defendant is released immediately. Outside the court, he shouts at me, 'You are a fucking wanker. I knew I would get off and that retard wouldn't be any good in court'.

Not responding, I turn away and smile as the thought has just crossed my mind, that he has just done over two years in prison for remaining silent. If he had spoken at the interview, the case may never have gone to trial.

The law will always remain in favour of the suspect, not the victims, because the law makers are all ex-barristers and judges, and they will never bring in laws which foreclose the extortionate wages the next generation of barristers will be poised to make. At least, in my opinion, it's the old boys network protecting the new boy's network.

When I joined the police in 1984, I took all my cases extremely seriously and thought of acquittals as personal failures. As I get older, I realise the judicial system is just a game and nobody other than the police rarely give a toss about the victim and the impact on their lives.

Strangely, or maybe predictably, all victims dramatically change their views on crime and punishment when they are directly affected. Death, mayhem and robbery tend to have a sobering effect on anyone, a kind of 'welcome to the real world, baby'.

There is of course a victim support system in place now, but the acquittals of guilty people will continue unabated until the jury system is abolished and the burden of proof is reduced to what it is in the civil court, which works on the balance of probabilities. Also, in my further opinion, as grizzled as it may be, there should no right of silence in criminal or civil cases.

# SIX

In 1990, Denise falls pregnant, and it is one of the best days of my life nine months later when I'm present for the birth of my eldest daughter, Louise, on the 31$^{st}$ of October. It may have been Halloween, but she looks like an angel, and I cry uncontrollably when she enters the world.

# SEVEN

Whilst working at Chiswick, the Detective Inspector in charge recommends me for two of the most demanding but prestigious positions that it is possible to achieve as a detective.

The first is for a five-year posting to SO8, Scotland Yard's elite crime fighting unit called 'The Flying Squad', or, as villains call it, ''The Sweeney'. The Flying Squad deals solely with Armed Robbery on Security Vehicles, Banks, Building Societies and Jewellers.

The second is to SO10, as a level one Undercover Operative. The word undercover police officer is widely used to describe police officers working whilst not wearing the uniform. Nothing could be further from the truth. A better description is an officer who adopts a fictitious identity with a view to infiltrating organised criminals.

This can involve meeting with organised criminals in character, or actually living amongst them. For policemen and women, both of these roles for different reasons are hugely sought after, and the selection process is fiercely competitive.

In 1991, though I have been a police officer for seven years, it is unheard of to be posted to these units when so young in service. I go through the selection process and interviews for both jobs and pass with flying colours. And I'm ecstatic.

By contrast, Denise is equally unimpressed, for no other reason than SO8 has its own female groupies, some of whom she knows, and she also knows that driving around to banks and building societies to take statements will put me in touch with a lot of females.

She has as much knowledge as me about undercover work, but it sounds a bit flash and difficult to monitor, so she makes it known to me that she is extremely unhappy about my selection. To be fair to Denise, looking back, we have just had a new baby.

So, on the one hand, she would have preferred me to have found a nice little 9am to 5pm job. In my defence, on the other hand, I am 100% committed to everything I do, including work, relationships and parenting, and I try my best to juggle them all effectively to give maximum attention to each.

This doesn't always work out, but in the main, I would say that I have an interesting work life, and my family has a loving, committed partner/dad. It is normal for example, once breast feeding stops, for me to do the feeding at night regardless of what time I have to be at work in the morning.

I'm lucky that I can survive on five hours sleep a night, waking up if a pin is dropped and then falling back asleep within five minutes of feeding the baby. So I make it work, juggling the juggle with fierce determination and devotion at every step of the way.

In early 1992, I go on what is the only recognised undercover course in the United Kingdom, controlled by Scotland Yard and shrouded in secrecy. We make an inviolate promise never to disclose the format of the course or identify each other, and although I will talk about specific undercover jobs I have worked on in this book, I have no intention of disclosing anything that would run afoul of this mandate or be of any use to someone actively engaged in crime.

Truth is, the only way you can guarantee not being caught by an undercover deployment is to retire early from criminal activity early like Donald Sutherland tried to go in the movie, 'The Italian Job'. Except often there is the one final job, and then we nail them.

Everything from here on relating to undercover work is already in the public domain. If there is one thing villains do well whilst in prison, it is to discuss and dissect what brought about their demise, and then try to prevent their cohorts in crime falling into the same trap. I say this with a strong degree of confidence and from personal experience.

Level one undercover work must be fully authorised and is not to be confused with street-level gramme drug buying, eco-warrior and football intelligence gathering. The latter two have been responsible for a huge amount of damage to the reputation of undercover policing generally.

The only qualities you need to qualify for football hooligan intelligence gathering are tattoos and a love of football. The football hooligan infiltrators so lacked the detective qualities necessary as to make a mockery of their first court trial that they were disbanded. To be an eco-warrior undercover, you just need to look scruffy and not wash very often (and not get the target's pregnant).

I understand the rules may have changed now, but on

the level one course we are told in no uncertain terms that having sex with anyone whilst deployed in an undercover role is deemed tantamount to rape, and we will be dealt with accordingly. The rationale for that is simple. Women are not consenting to sexual intercourse with who you really are. Essentially, it's a fraud on the woman.

Getting through the course is immensely difficult, with a lot of the students pulling out because they are unable to take the pressure, or because they realise this job is not for the fainthearted and making a mistake could seriously damage their health. However, one of my personal biggest fears performing this role is not that the villains might think I was a cop, but that they will think I'm a grass, i.e., an informer. And believe me, that can come with deadly consequences.

Within days of the course finishing, my phone rings and it's SO10 giving me my first job. Every job has an operational commander, and I meet mine in due course. He briefs me about what the operation is looking to achieve, and I confirm that I am happy to take it on. He leaves me with some homework.

There is a saying, 'Fail to prepare, then prepare to fail'. This is especially true for undercover deployments. On my first assignment, they want me to buy three kilos of heroin from as yet unidentified gangsters from East London. He says a grasser will introduce me to the gangsters and tell them I am someone they can trust and do business with.

Referencing of each other is a crucial part of criminal activity and is very often the criminals Achilles Heel. In the Krays era, for example, undercover buying would have been much more difficult than today, but drug use has destroyed the loyalty that criminals once had for each other through a rigorous allegiance to omerta. Nowadays, nobody can 100% trust anyone any more, because cash and the next deal are far more important than loyalty – range of the moment concerns, greed, what have you.

I have never seen a kilo of heroin as of this point in time, let alone tested the drug, so I hotfoot it to the police lab and ask a scientist to show me what I need to know. Basically, he teaches me how to burn the heroine to test for quality. You get really intense smoke coming off the foil when the powder turns to liquid – the slang term being 'chasing the dragon'. Obviously, the lab won't allow me to inject heroine into my veins to test it.

Next I visit a quiet pub on the Southbank and give the bar staff a fake name and a fake life story to go along with it. Of course, I already possess the same false identification should anyone need to check. I go back the next day and continue the conversation, being totally cool and chill like I imagine gangsters do.

By the time I leave, I know the names of the bar staff and they know me as Bazza, the shandy drinking doorman. Back then, we didn't have mobile phones, so everyone used pagers. For the youngsters reading this book, a pager is a small digital screen that rings a number and leaves a short message for you to contact the caller.

The informant has been given my pager number and the barest of details about me, including my description. It's worthy of note that at the time I have a short ponytail. A couple of days later, my pager jumps to life with a message to ring a certain London number.

I go to a call box and ring the number. The man who picks up confirms that he is in a call box, too, and that it is safe to talk. He asks me to come to a pub in Hackney that evening. I say I'm working down the Southbank but can meet him in a certain pub that I suggest at 7pm (this way I know the layout of the pub).

He agrees to come to me and meet there, which I think is a bit odd, because most villains are more comfortable in their own manor and domain, where they can be in control at all times. (In a way, it's a battle to control the playing field.) I decide to deliberately arrive late and when I walk into the pub I say hiya to Sue the barmaid.

Sue smiles and says, 'Hi, Bazza, your usual shandy (a mix of lager and lemonade, a diabetic cocktail for those who have never drank it before)?' I give her a huge beaming smile but not for the reason she thinks. 'Yes, thanks darling'.

I pay for my drink and sit idly at the bar. A Turkish guy walks up to me and introduces himself as Mehmet. We move away from the bar and sit down. 'Man', he says, 'as soon as you walked in, I knew you were a drug dealer'.

Clearly, even criminals stereotype other people.

We sit and chat and he confirms something I already know. By his scruffy appearance and smell, I can tell he doesn't have control of the heroin; that it's another mate of his. When he agrees to take me to him, we jump in his car and start heading south towards Clapham. My adrenaline is already pumping.

I quickly form the opinion that the intelligence on this job is crap, but hey ho, let's see where we go. There is no surveillance accompanying me, as I've convinced my boss not to use it until I have a measure of the people we're dealing with. That is a huge gamble for the operational team – that I'm going along - but I am confident from years of working the door that I can talk my way out of trouble. Moreover, surveillance is far more likely to compromise me.

To my horror, we start driving into Wandsworth. He says, 'not far now', and pulls up outside the Spotted Dog Pub on Garratt Lane and asks me to wait in the car whilst he legs it into the pub. My heart starts pounding harder, as I have been involved on drugs raids at this very place. Everyone knows me inside, so I'm a tad worried of what may come.

Looking around, I spot a local cannabis dealer named Jimmy, who thankfully cannot see me inside the car. I know I can't get out with Jimmy here, and wonder who the fuck Mehmet is going to bring back to the car. By now, I can feel the sweat running down my back, but decide that remaining pat and sitting in the car is my only option. I certainly can't get out and run away.

Mehmet returns with another Turkish dude named Turgay, whom I recognise but fortunately have not interacted or dealt with when in uniform. He gets in the back seat and we drove off, stopping at a callbox with Turgay getting out to make a call then and then returning to the back seat. He apologises and says the guy who has the gear can't meet today.

We swap pager numbers and I agree to meet Turgay again when he is ready. We drop Turgay at the Spotted Dog and Mehmet drops me back on the Southbank. This is my first undercover outing, and I learn that what has happened here is quite commonplace.

People with absolutely no control of the drugs offer them for sale to make a small mark-up profit. They have been asked by friends of friends, and this is something that affords us opportunities to infiltrate without using informants. I could say that that becomes my life of danger, but compared to some of the other things I'm asked to do, it's actually much safer.

Turgay messages me a couple of weeks later and we arranged to meet at my local pub on the Southbank. In the interim, I have continued drinking there and become more and more friendly with the staff and some of the regulars. I don't deliberately try to warm up to the regulars, but I do tend to attract strangers who want to share their life stories with me.

In preparation for this meeting, I have also convinced the Operational Commander to have a second undercover cop and £50,000 available at the ready. The other guy has agreed to be in a car around the corner from the pub with the money.

When Turgay arrives, we have a drink and he says, 'I'm sure I know you, but I can't place where from'. I stifle a grin and say, 'probably done some business with you or someone you know in the past'. What I can't say is that I have raided his local pub a couple of times as a uniformed cop.

He agrees that it is probably a business deal where he knew me from. On the way out, I make a point of saying goodbye to a few people and using their names. 'See ya later, Bazza', they all reply, reaffirming my standing as a local.

Outside the pub, I tell Turgay I have something I want to show him and take him to the car containing my mate. When we get into the back seat and I show him the cash, his eyes come out on stalks. 'We are ready to go whenever you are', I say. 'Just wanted you to know we're serious'.

He suggests we bring the money with us to Hackney to meet the next man. But him suggesting this tells us that he's not a regular at this level of criminality because, if he were, this kind of thing would never happen. Too many criminals make a living robbing each other at gunpoint, so it is a rule of self- preservation that the cash and the drugs never meet.

I tell him, 'mate, that's not going to happen'.

'Okay, cool', he says.

'My mate Stew will come with you and meet your mate and he's gonna want a sample and he will test it, okay mate?'

Stew gets in Turgay's car and continues to Hackney, and I retrieve and return the cash to the operational team. At Hackney Stew and Turgay, we meet the next man in the food chain, who is Turkish but calls himself Andy. Similar to Turgay, he has someone else to call.

Things pick up when two huge Turkish guys turn up. We can tell by their demeanour that they are hard bangin' gangsters and not to be messed with. Turgay pretends he has done business with Stew before, and that Stew is loaded with cash (that he has seen the £100,000 himself). Andy confirms that as true.

Turgay and Andy then reference him as a criminal, saying they have done business with him many times, and I can only assume greed has taken away good sense from Turgay. Turgay is effectively signing himself up to get badly hurt when and if these guys go down.

The huge Turks don't want to talk in front of Turgay and Andy and dismiss them from his company. And once Turgay and Andy have gone, the Turks became threatening with Stew, warning him they are part of the

Turkish Mafia and that if anything goes wrong he's a dead man.

Stew is an experienced undercover agent and holds his ground. When he does, they think he is the real item and quickly mellow out. They then give Stew a sample and say they will allow him to test the main parcel of 3kilos of quality heroin that day -- and that they will call him in a couple of days to take delivery. They want £21,000 per kilo and will not budge on the price. They exchange pager numbers and part company.

For reasons I fail to comprehend, the police in the UK are not all routinely armed like most other countries – the U.S., Australia, all of Europe. The olden days of Dixon of Dock Green should have been committed to history a long time ago, but it hasn't been. In contrast, many criminals are armed to the teeth, giving the unarmed police a decided and very obvious disadvantage.

Shootings and stabbings in all major cities are commonplace, both in the UK and abroad. Consequently, if there is no intelligence that the people you are targeting are currently armed, then the chances of getting armed officers immediately deployed in the UK are remote.

To be fair, there are more armed response vehicles nowadays, but they are as much use as a one-legged man at an arse-kicking party if someone pulls a gun on a beat cop (or any other unarmed cop for that matter). By the time armed officers fight their way through the traffic, you are as dead as a Dodo.

In my opinion, with the increased volume of criminals carrying concealed weapons, it is only a matter of time before a huge lawsuit hits the metropolitan police for failing to arm its cops. Indeed, there are places in London where even the cops are frightened to patrol -- and that cannot be right under any governmental system that purports to protect its citizenry.

Case in point, the Turks contact Stew and arrange to meet and supply the three kilos of heroin. The meeting point is agreed upon, and Stew takes with him another undercover officer to test the gear. Unarmed surveillance has been authorised, with more undercovers now on hand.

True to form, the Turks take the drugs tester on a merry dance around London to shake off any surveillance team that might be following them. Better to be safe than sorry is the watchword of any good criminal. Confident they are not being followed, they stop in a car park and go to an empty car and retrieve the heroin for testing.

Once weighed and tested, our undercover agent gives the signal for the team to arrest the suspects. The arrest team surges forward, only to turn around and run away. It turns out that both Turks have produced Uzi submachine guns on lanyards draped around their necks (but until now hidden under their coats).

One quick burst and everyone drops to the floor or dives for cover. They take the drugs, get back in their car, and drive off at breakneck speed. Thankfully, they don't shoot the buying undercover agent, but that is not always the case. Unlike the book *The Infiltrators*, in which two undercover cops get shot on a drugs-buying operation in Birmingham, this time we live to fight another day.

I have achieved my objective in the operation, and word filters back to SO10 that my performance was good and credible with the criminals. I have been asked many times what makes a good undercover operative, and the answer is simple: you must possess the ability to communicate with and be liked by everyone you meet, regardless of age, race or creed.

Fortunately, I have a natural ability to compartmentalise my life. That allows me to have numerous jobs with different names and histories, including different accents – all running at the same time. Having additional skills helps, but there is nothing that can't be taught during the learning process. On the other hand, if you can't communicate well, you are never going to make it undercover. After completing the National Undercover Course, some people get a lot of work (like me) and some deploy once and can't cut the mustard, so are never called again.

Quickly, my next job comes through to buy £100,000 of counterfeit £50 notes from a team of Irishmen from Bethnal Green. I am introduced to them by an informant in a pub called the Blind Beggar. The pub has been made famous by the Krays, when Ronnie Kray shot George Cornell dead on the 9th of March 1966.

In the pub, I meet three of the Irishmen, and after a couple of beers, we leave and jump into their car, which is an old Ford Escort. We are all big lumps and look ridiculous crammed tight into the car like the kids did in phone booths in America. If we don't get stopped by the cops, I will be more than surprised, for we have up-to-no-good written all over us.

I have agreed to pay £25,000 for the notes, which they have represented to be of an amazing quality with a large number of different serial numbers in the batch. I am sat in the back seat and the driver meanders sedately out of London through the Blackwall Tunnel and onto the A2 towards Kent.

Throughout the journey, the man in the front passenger seat is spinning around and looking constantly behind us. I say, 'mate, you okay? You're making me nervous'.

'I can smell the pigs from a hundred miles away, and I'm making sure we are not being followed, okay?'

When I look in the rear-view mirror, every car behind us constitutes the surveillance team.

'Nice one', I say, stifling a smirk. He must be looking for a convoy of marked cars, I think.

We pull off at the Black Prince interchange and drive to the car park of the Black Prince Hotel, closely followed by a car with a couple chaps from the surveillance team. They go straight out of their car and into the hotel, disappearing while we sit in the car for ten minutes watching for the police.

Thankfully, nobody else comes in, and we sat and talk about football until the main man with the bright ginger hair says, 'I'm happy, come on mate'.

As we're walking away from the hotel, we're stopped by a car in a side street about 1000 yards away. A chap opens the boot to this car and pulls out a substantial parcel wrapped in brown paper and sealed with yards of packing tape. Apparently, that's the money, so I say, 'can I have a look then?'

'No', he says. 'This isn't it. This is just a parcel of telephone directories. If the cops are following us', he chuckles, 'any minute now they will jump all over us and find squat'.

As my arse starts twitching, I am praying that the operational commander does not call a strike until I give the signal, which of course I have not yet done. Thankfully, he's a seasoned veteran and knows to wait.

We return to the car park and the ginger man sorts me into another car that's parked in the lot. He then produces a holdall with a substantial amount of counterfeit £50 notes in it, all of exceptional quality and all in £5000 bundles.

I start counting the bundles, hoping the team in the hotel can see me. When I give them the signal, within 30 seconds all hell breaks loose and the four of us are dragged from our respective vehicles and unceremoniously slam-dunked on the ground, face down.

The ginger Irishman mouths to me, 'don't say a word'.

We are all arrested and taken individually to separate police stations. Once out of view, my handcuffs are taken off me and I'm congratulated on a job well done. When the counterfeit money is officially counted, there are only £88,000. This proves there is absolutely no honour amongst thieves, notwithstanding the lore perpetuated by the movies.

When undercover officers give evidence, they do so from behind a screen that blocks everyone from seeing them except the jury and the judge. When this case goes to trial, all these rag muffins are convicted and sentenced to four years imprisonment.

During the trial, one of the defendants puts forward an argument that I wasn't the man he met. The Judge asks for clarification, and the defendant says, 'The man I met had a South London accent and swore a lot and this bloke hasn't sworn once giving evidence'.

I confirm to the court I am the man and that I'm using my real voice in the courtroom. At that point, the defendant says, 'It is definitely not the man, coz the man I met wore trainers and he's got shoes on'.

I almost burst out laughing. The knucklehead could obviously see my feet under the screen. Of course, the Judge dismisses his point and tells the jury to ignore what this moron has to say on the subject, as if I wouldn't be inclined to want a change of shoes for court.

# EIGHT

To increase my skills profile, SO10 has organised for me and two other undercover officers to be trained in the use of a multitude of firearms and explosives. Accordingly, we attend the SAS headquarters at Stirling Lines in Hereford.

In the canteen at lunchtime, I am shocked at how ordinary most of the special forces staff looks. They could be people walking in right off the street, regular blokes to a tee. That's because most foreign special forces teams are full on meatheads with biceps stacked on their biceps. None of our lot looks like bodybuilders.

One day, I ask what the criteria is to get in the SAS – Britain's elite special forces unit. The instructors say there are a couple of tests you have to take. Neil and Mack, the mates doing training with me, both decline, but being as mad as a fish, I say I'm up for it.

We go across to the swimming pool, which has a big circular tube sticking out of the top of it about sixty-feet high. I strip down to my boxers and am taken up to the top of the pool tower and look down at the distant water below – like diving down a funnel into a thimble of water.

The instructor explains that jumping down the sheer drop tube, which doesn't look wide enough at the bottom to fit through unscathed, gets rid of a lot of applicants. He asks me if I want to do it, and of course I say yes and proceed to step onto the edge of the platform that gives vertigo its name.

He then declares that he's forgotten to add something and shouts to his colleague, 'We are ready turn! Turn off the lights!'

I'm suddenly faced with having to plunge into complete darkness when he shouts, 'Go!'

Upon launching myself off the precipice, I am falling, falling, falling endlessly. I can feel the wind rushing and rippling by me in a centrifugal force that ends when I hit the water so hard with my feet that I feel I've been smacked hard with a baseball bat.

Not unexpectedly, I love it, so I'm anxious to continue on to test number two. However, I don't want to spoil the surprise for any potential recruits who might read the book, but let's just say it involves cutting a parachute free before it sweeps you off a cliff after landing. Spoiler alert, because this very test has been shown in the TV show SAS Rogue Heroes.

As we continue our training, we go on to blow up cars and buildings and use a plethora of guns from around the world that might presuppose a small arsenal is at our beck and call at times – living the dream of 007 on steroids without the added attraction of Pussy Galore.

At the culmination of the course, we all go into Hereford for a curry and a shed load of beers. I genuinely ask the instructor, 'is it possible to tell which of the Army guys is in the SAS and which are not?'

His reply makes me smile when he replies, 'Mate, all those who aren't in the SAS will be telling the girls they are, and all the guys who are in the SAS will be denying it'.

After all this, my reputation gets chiselled in tablets of stone, and the next time I venture into Scotland Yard, the bossman announces for one and all to hear when I walk into the office, 'here he is, SO10's own, Mr "Barking Mad"'.

# NINE

In mid-1992, I'm told to report to the Flying Squad head office at Scotland Yard to meet the boss and start my five-year posting. I'm posted to the Barnes office under the boss, Colin.

Because I'm also an undercover operative, I've been given the name 'Duvet' by my colleagues. Everyone on the Squad has a nickname, some complimentary, some not. My name I suppose would have been 'Blanket' or 'Counterpane' back in the day.

Two of the lads who work together are known as 'Shotgun and Thrush' because one is a smooth bore and the other an irritating cunt. A lad who has no mates at home is appropriately called Lonely, and a heavy smoker has been dubbed 'Beagle'.

These are a hard bunch of men who pull no punches, are completely professional and, once they have you on their radar, you are going to jail for a long time. The Flying Squad has the reputation of being one of the premier detective agencies in the world, and I would wholeheartedly agree with that assessment.

Stories of extreme bravery are commonplace, and having a sense of humour is an absolute must. A legend called Dave who works at another office is reputed to be almost as mad as me. When he had a case at the Old Bailey, the defence Barrister said to him, 'I put it to you that you called my client a cunt'.

'Yes sir, and he is', he said, though everyone in the courtroom was expecting him to vehemently deny it. The Judge was shocked. 'You had better explain yourself officer', he said. 'I'm not happy with that answer'.

Ol' Dave replied, 'Well then your Honour, anyone who does a burglary and steals two gold-plated Purdy Shotguns jointly valued at £20,000 and then saws the barrels off, rendering them worthless, and then uses one to rob a post office for £50 – well, could you please give your learned explanation as to why that man is NOT a cunt?'

The jury bursts out laughing and the Judge, God bless him, tells the jury to do the impossible and dismiss Dave's story from their minds.

Another detective gets his jollies off by saying to the suspect, 'I'm arresting you for knocking down the walls of Jericho'. Later, at the trial of that particular defendant, the defence Barrister says to this detective, 'why did you arrest my client?'

'Armed Robbery, sir', he responds.

And the barrister says, 'That's not true, is it, officer? Because my client distinctly remembers you arresting him for criminal damage to someone's garden wall'.

The penny drops with us immediately and we almost wet ourselves laughing.

At one time, Armed Robbery was a proper gangster's crime, committed by the top end of the food chain amongst the criminal underworld, and there was an unwritten code not to shoot anyone. Unfortunately, drugs have changed all that and now a lot of robberies are committed by junkies who have managed to get hold of a firearm.

Firearms are more readily available than most senior police officers would like to admit. You can buy a sawn-off shotgun for £250 and a handgun with bullets for £400 – the cost of a cab ride to and from and a meal for four at a fancy London eatery (with wine and pudding thrown in, of course).

The price increases with the quality of the weapon and its experience. Whether or not the weapon has been used in a crime really matters -- nobody wants to be caught with a gun that has a history of murder and mayhem. With bad luck, forensics could connect the last man handling the weapon to a crime even he did not commit.

I have bought many guns during my undercover career, but one of the funniest robberies I've ever dealt with is at a post office. The suspect, Albert, has approached the cashier carrying a handgun and donning a plastic carrier bag with eyeholes over his head.

'This is a robbery', he says, and no sooner than he says this is the bag is sucked into his mouth. Dropping his gun, he falls to the floor choking, almost suffocating himself. Believe it or not, the post office staff must then give him first aid. At court, I am compelled to admit that Albert is no threat to society whatsoever.

In days gone by, the armed robbers were the elite of the criminal underworld -- hard men and committed professionals with a good and learned knowledge of police tactics. One of my favourites is a west London man called George, and if George put as much effort into honest work as he applied to crime, he would be a wealthy man.

When living at a Hayes Middlesex council flat, George

gets out of bed at 4am every day to drive around the streets of London, making sure he isn't being followed by his arch enemy, the Flying Squad.

His practice is to buy a car for a couple of hundred pounds, not register it in his name, and then set off for a three-hour road rally around West London, quite often disappearing up his own arse. He and all his mates are fully aware that police use tracking devices to follow surveillance aware targets.

One of his favourite tricks is to drive into Hammersmith and then drive out at a high speed onto the A4, going through every red light and speed camera on that road. Believe me, there are a lot of them, and a reckless motorist could be banned for life just going to work in the morning.

He then stops near Heathrow and looks back, watching the sky light up for the flashes from the speed cameras after the surveillance tracking team comes through them and after him. George's knowledge of security vehicles routes and times of drop offs would put a computer to shame. He would regularly observe a security vehicle making a drop in Wembley high street, and then be in front of that vehicle at every drop on its route back to base.

Once George selects his target, he is like a lion stalking his prey and preparing for the kill. Our enquiries and observations note that, whenever he is close to committing a robbery, he also stops shaving to alter his appearance with a growth of facial hair; and we take full advantage of this knowledge.

On many days, our observation post says, 'Standby! Standby! George is out of the house towards the car and he is clean shaven'. The surveillance commander then immediately calls in, 'Okay, boys, stand down back to Barnes. Nothing's happening for at least three days'.

When we return to base, I always smile at the vision of George driving round London like a maniac, shaking off a surveillance team that isn't actually there because he's unwittingly tipped them off by using a Bic.

Quite often when we are following him, he stops his car in a road with width restrictors, gets out and then runs back down the line of cars shouting fuck off copper to every driver. This level of paranoia is counterproductive, as more often than not he's simply screaming at bemused motorists going about their daily lives. Some phone the police, so we get an update of where he is and what car he's currently driving.

George eventually comes out with facial hair, so we follow him to the intended target of his next attack, which is Lloyds Bank in the High Street at Hayes. They say preparation prevents piss poor performance, and George is the epitome of meticulousness in this department.

He places four stolen Subaru Impreza autos round the intended target at 12 o'clock, 3 o'clock, 6 o'clock and 9 o'clock. If things go awry for any reason, he has four separate avenues of escape. Unfortunately for him, we know George loves a Subaru, and during the night, we search the streets and find all four and place static observation posts containing officers accordingly.

The night before the robbery, typically he places the handguns in litter bins closest to the bank, and then spends the next hours praying that the bin men don't show up in his absence. True to form, on the day in question, he's out of the house at 4am, into the car and off for his anti-surveillance drive around town.

We leave him to it as we have the bank covered from every angle. A mouse couldn't escape from there without us handcuffing and charging him with violating the Rats and Mice Destruction Act 1919 (a real offence in the UK).

The security van is due at 11am, and as if by magic, George and his mate Andy walk around the corner at 10.45am and take up positions about 30 metres apart and on either side of the bank.

Unfortunately, because years of bitter experience has taught the Flying Squad that the law is an Ass with a capital A, the time to put a stop to the crime is a decision which requires balls of steel. Too early and you have blown the operation for nothing; too late and you run the risk of a security guard or member of the public being shot.

Had I been in charge, I would have let the offence unfold, applying the thought process that if we aren't observing the subjects, it would happen anyway. Whereas, to call the arrest early would blow the operation out of the water and make the subjects ten times harder to catch in the future. Even with the best will in the world, you cannot follow every active criminal 24 hours a day, seven days a week, contrary to popular belief.

As we watch and wait, Beagle goes into overdrive, and I'm surprised he can see George and Andy through the cigarette smoke. The tension is tangible. We have every possible scenario covered, and there are armed cops everywhere in unmarked cars. It's a strange feeling, because the targets are thinking any minute now we will be rich, and we are thinking, any minute now you are going to jail for a long time.

I have seen some extremely hard men fall over and

lose control of all their bodily functions, so I wonder what will happen here. Suddenly, they steam in and attack the security van, and out of nowhere, we overpower them with far superior numbers and fire power. From a mega high to a low low, in the blink of an eye these guys are foiled and arrested.

It's not as if robbing a security vehicle or bank earns you a lot of money, either. The maximum the guard carries in the box is £15,000, and that sum is protected with anti-theft devices. Quite often, the vehicles carry a dummy box containing nothing, to fool would-be robbers. I have seen armed robberies committed with a box containing a mere £3000 in coins.

Hardly worth a 15-year prison sentence if caught. In fact, this is one crime now where the risks and jail terms are just not worth it for the possible reward. That is why a lot of the old school armed robbers have moved into the drugs arena, where risks are much lower and rewards much higher.

# TEN

There are some top tier armed robbers who try and take the whole security vehicle, but with advances in technology, that is becoming increasingly difficult. There was a team who stole an entire van some years ago in East London, but when they opened it at their lock-up garage, it contained £3 million in coins (virtually worthless unless you want to carry around £50 bags to go to an expensive meal).

Crooks can be clever, no doubt about it, but often not clever enough. They were all arrested when we identified an amusement arcade who was banking excessive amounts of coinage daily. That should have been one of those wipe-your-mouth and walk-away jobs, but as is often the case with criminals, greed gets the better of them and good sense flies out of the window.

That could have never been said about George. He had eyes like a hawk, and no matter how close he got to the prize, he was focussed on everything going on around him, where most get tunnel vision and only see the end result and certain wealth. This is true at Lloyds Bank at Hayes.

The van arrives and starts carrying out the delivery. I have no idea what George has decided should be the strike box, but he obviously is waiting for something to trigger movement. He and Andy have been seated, but now they are standing. Unfortunately for us, a woman walks up and sits at the bus stop close to George.

That spooks him, so he signals Andy to forget it and mouths, 'police'. They both walk off in separate directions. She had nothing to do with us and, yet we are gutted. Still, we maintain observation on the delivery until it's away safely, before standing down and returning to Barnes.

Life on the Flying Squad is very similar to life for the armed robber. Months of drudgery and hard work, for 30 seconds of adrenaline overload.

Later that day, there is a robbery on another van which we are sure is George and Andy, but we can't prove it beyond a reasonable doubt. It's just a strong suspicion, so we put George on the back burner and concentrate on Andy, who has also joined another little firm of armed robbers.

This firm are all arrested robbing business premises in Brentford for computer chips. Long prison terms follow, and West London security van robberies dip for a while, as we've pulled these rascals off the streets until someone else takes their place.

As a side issue, whilst we are working on George, I have a bit of a run in with one of the Squad drivers, Simon. Although he is married with children, he is effeminate to the degree that he goes out of his way to drop his teammates in the shit with the bosses. He's also meticulously tidy, eats nothing but health food, and brush his teeth ten times a day.

He grasses me up one day to Vince the detective inspector in charge of the surveillance team for leaving my car window open in the police yard, saying because there is a briefing sheet in it, I have caused a security risk. I take the bollocking that follows on the chin, but vow to have my revenge on this little twerp.

My opportunity arises several days later when Simon leaves his car window open and briefing sheet on the seat. It's not in my make-up to snitch to the boss, so I take his tooth brush out and, witnessed by others, clean the crack of my arse with it and then put it back where he has left it.

We almost wet ourselves laughing when he returns from the canteen, having eaten his lunch and wanting to brush his teeth. I hold off telling him until his retirement party at the police sports club, Imber Court. Despite the passing of time, he knows that I am telling the truth and vomits everywhere.

My forays into the undercover world continue, and I quickly develop a reputation for being able to win over even the most difficult criminals. Undercover policing historically uses what we call the buy-bust scenario, where a police informant introduces an undercover cop into the gang at a particular level.

That undercover cop then introduces other undercover cops and they all eventually orchestrate the purchase of large quantities of drugs, or some other commodity, and the people present on the day of the trade get royally busted.

'Referencing' is a crucial part of any criminal business, so most high-level criminals will not deal with anybody who does not come fully 'referenced' from somebody they trust implicitly.

In the undercover gangster movie 'Donnie Brasco', the

wiseguy played by Al Pacino introduces the undercover cop played by Depp, as 'a friend of mine'. Meaning, he vouches for him under penalty of being wacked.

Typically, savvy attorneys realise that the police will never expose their sources of information and so they set in motion a hunt-the-informant exercise, with a view to forcing us into a corner -- either identify the informant or drop the case.

This is at best unethical, in my opinion, but to be fair, most criminal law barristers and solicitors think that ethics is a county to the Northeast of London where the Buffalo roam. Quite often, we drop a case simply to protect the informant, with the result that guilty men go free.

One of my early undercover jobs is buying guns from a career East London gangster. He is offering for sale a sawn-off shotgun with ammunition, and after we make contact with him, he asks me to come to his house. This is quite unusual and quite unsettling. Going to the abode of thieving, murdering schmuck cannot be good for one's health, and most criminals are extremely keen to keep their work and home lives separate.

My antennae way up, I arrive at the agreed time and am just about to speak in the house when this guy whispers, 'don't talk here, the house may be bugged'.

Having gone out to his car, he repeats, 'We can't talk in there, it may be bugged'.

I then jest, 'don't talk here, the lamp posts may be bugged'. I laugh and say, 'we wouldn't go to those lengths to catch you'.

'What did you say?" he says, the suddenness of how he says it getting my attention.

I realise I have fucked up royally and try to cover my butt by saying, 'they wouldn't go to those lengths to catch you, would they?'

'They fucking would', he says. 'I've seen it on the telly'.

I breathe a sigh of relief that he didn't hear my first reply and made a mental note to self. Note: You will never be that lucky again. Think before you speak!

We then go and stand in the middle of a field and discuss
 the purchase of guns and prices. As I'm recording the conversation, I know the irony will blow his mind when the prosecution plays it back at court. £250 is the price that I pay for a sawn-off shotgun from this dude.

Not long after that, he is arrested for Armed Robbery on a security van, and because he is already looking at a long term of imprisonment, we do not pursue or disclose the undercover operation out of concern that we will blow our network and ability to get referenced.

On another occasion, we have information that a team of career gangsters is planning to break into the vault at a bank in Earls Court by taking control of a flat next door. They plan to hold the occupant hostage and break through the adjoining wall to access the bank and its money.

I'm asked if I am prepared to attempt a cold infiltration into the gang, as they this particular gang are considered untouchable. I agree and the operation is commenced. They are regulars at a South London wine bar, so I start frequenting the place on weekends – not a bad gig and beats munching crisps in a days' long stake-out.

For weeks, they completely ignore me as I chat with other regulars. I have the wine bar in stitches telling jokes and outrageous stories, but on more than one occasion, I catch them earwigging my conversations and eventually the main subject bursts out laughing at my joke.

From a table, this same guy says, 'do you fancy joining our card game?'

I admit I'm shit at cards, but he says, 'not to worry, it's only a laugh and only bet what you know you can afford to lose'.

I agree to join the group, and because this particular guy has called me in, everyone else immediately accepts me. I'm still subject to a subtle interrogation, however, to ascertain whether I'm straight or bent (honest or dishonest).

Because gangsters love to brag about their criminal exploits, the evening is filled with drinking, playing cards and telling war stories, most of which have definitely had a sudsy wash and a polish. I tell them I'm a boffin around scanners and regularly monitor police radio chat. As my visits continue, I quickly am accepted as a regular and often sit with the main players of the gang.

The planned job is gathering momentum, and the questions I am being asked lead me to believe they intend to use my electronic scanning knowledge at some time in the near future. One evening, I arrive at the wine bar and there is a table and chairs set outside the front, adjoining the main road.

It isn't a warm evening, and nobody is using them. I have a couple of drinks inside, and the main man arrives. He buys me a drink and then says, 'let's sit outside and chat privately'. Obviously the bar has put a table out specially for him. We spend 30 minutes outside talking about nothing of any note before he declares he's cold and we go back inside.

Unbeknown to me, a corrupt police officer on the gang's payroll has driven past in his car and had a good look at me. I continue drinking and leave that night blissfully unaware. On my next visit, when I arrive the gang is all there. The main man buys me a drink and then says, 'we are not sure whether to call you Gary (the name I have given them) or Rob Sole'.

You could have knocked me over with a feather, but I hold it together, somehow not squirming too much. 'If you want to use a nom de plume, that is a matter for you, but there is nothing happening now or in the future', I say. 'I haven't got a Scooby-Doo what you are talking about'.

He smiles and give me a hug. I stay drinking at the bar, and when they move away, I'm not invited. The other customers continue chatting to me, and at a convenient time, I get up and leave. This is a check-your-boxers time because, what that disgusting piece of shit masquerading as a police officer had done, could have caused my untimely death.

Fortunately, these are old school gangsters with a never-harm-the-police mentality. That ethos is rare in today's world, particularly amongst the Yardies, Russian, East European and Turkish Gangsters, who don't give a flyin' crap if they behead and enshrine you in Madame Tussauds Wax Museum, or tie you buck naked to the London Eye and spin the wheel.

I report back to the operational commander what has happened, and my deployments are rightly terminated, with an enquiry commenced to identify the bent cop. I don't know if that enquiry was successful, and the team knows better than to tell me who it is. Rest assured, if I had found out, he would have been a dead man walking with his nut sack on fire from that day forward.

# ELEVEN

There is no way I can continue staying at the house. At the time, I am living with my wife and young daughter in London, knowing that my family could be the subject of a violent attack by disgruntled criminals at any moment. I convince my wife without telling her the real reason that now would be a good time to move.

We have one daughter approaching school age and another baby on the way. We have been in constant contact with Alan and Lucy, who are now living in Naval Married accommodation, as Alan has re-joined the Navy unhappy working long hours for no money as a lorry driver.

We visit Alan and Lucy for the weekend, and without any prompting by me, Denise says, 'why don't we move here; it's beautiful'. I knew as soon as it was Denise's idea, it was a done deal. Women rule the world, and any man who says otherwise is deluded.

I remember meeting one of London's top gangsters on a job. We get on well, and one day I meet him in the Turkish sector of Green Lanes. He arrives with two minders, and I flick him hard on the nose and say, 'you're fucking late'.

When the minders step aggressively forward, he laughingly says, 'back off boys, I like this guy'.

He puts his arm around my shoulder and we walk away from the minders. Out of earshot, he says, "Sorry, Steve, my Missus thinks I'm having an affair and she wouldn't let me out of the house until I convinced her I was meeting you'.

'Tell me about it', I say, and we both have a hearty laugh and re-join the minders.

Mind you, this guy has a reputation for being one of the most dangerous hard men in London. 'If you repeat to anyone what I just said, I'll fucking kill you', he says and flicks me harder on the nose, and we both burst out laughing.

I inform boss Colin that, because of what has happened with the bent copper ratting on me, I'm moving well out of town and will not be putting my new address on record. He agrees and sanctions the move. So we sell our house and move to Portsmouth. From that day forward, for 15 years, I commute to London and back for work, a small price to pay to sleep comfortably at night.

My undercover activities continue, and it is not uncommon for me to have up to four jobs on the go in different parts of the country. That annoys the life out of Colin the boss at Barnes, because he knows if push comes to shove, SO10 has precedence on what I do from day to day.

Colin does say that he would never accept another undercover officer on the squad. 'I'll be pleased when you fuck off somewhere else, Duvet', and though we get on well, he wants me 100%. One man down on the Flying Squad is one too many.

# TWELVE

A seasoned armed robber called Dave is known for being extremely violent, even when it isn't necessary. Because of the randomness of his violence, he has made a fearsome reputation amongst his fellow criminals. One day whilst she is shopping, Dave accosts one of the wives of a Squad member and says, 'I've been following you; I know your address; and if your husband and his mates don't stop nicking me, I'm gonna come to your house and stick my sawn off (shotgun) up your nose and blow your fucking head off.

Naturally, she was absolutely petrified and distraught -- and what woman or man wouldn't be. Her husband isn't overly impressed, either. Fortunately, it never comes to pass, because a couple of days later, two men wearing Balaclavas and wielding baseball bats visit Dave at his home address and beat him within an inch of his life.

I have no idea who they are, but it was a while before Dave could walk or talk, and even longer before he dares leave home, never mind getting involved in any criminality. We assume he has ripped off one drug dealer to many, and who says karma is not a bitch. It definitely is for Dave, as he's shot dead by uniformed armed police who chance upon him committing an Armed Robbery not far from Hammersmith Bridge at an off- licence premises where the contents of the till was only £300 (so he effectively died for £300).

I don't expect many people to have mourned his passing. Ironically, the police officer who shot him went through hell and back for doing so. Further proof, in my opinion, that society today has a fucked- up sense of what is wrong and right. Sadly, the opinion of armchair experts is far more important than the people who live life at the sharp end of the shaft and must make split-second life or death decisions.

Justice is often an illusion caused by too much alcohol or drugs. I say that because my time at Barnes is littered with ridiculous acquittals at court. Some defences are so outrageous that they even surprise the criminals who get away with them.

Maurice and Slippery, career armed robbers, are an odd pairing because Maurice is widely known in criminal circles as one of the first ever super grasses, back in the day. It would be a brave or foolish man who jumps into bed with Maurice on a criminal venture, but Slippery does do.

When we are sat in the office at Barnes, we receive a call that a black guy is acting suspiciously outside a post office in Shepherds Bush, and that a security vehicle has been dispatched and it soon to arrive. That's not a call we could ignore, so we cobble together a team that's armed up and we hot foot it to the scene and secure ourselves at the post office in question.

It just happens to be that at our observation point is a couple of Barnes most comical characters, and they commence talking about events in front of them. They both have awful eyesight -- one from natural deterioration with age, and the other from detached retinas, a by-product of his boxing days. It's definitely the blind leading the partially sighted.

The black guy stays sat on the wall, and as the security vehicle arrives, he stands up and walks away, continuing down the road until we lost sight of him. The decision is taken to stay until the delivery is complete, and thankfully, we do. Whilst the delivery is in progress, the alarm at the post office bursts into life, the radio crackles, and Skinny screams the immortal words, 'I think one's gone off!' Clearly this is code for, 'I think a robbery is happening'.

Out of the post office at breakneck speed comes two white guys running at full tilt, and they hop into a car and away they go. A chase ensues around Shepherd's Bush, during which Maurice jumps out of his car and points a 357 Magnum at us and starts pulling the trigger indiscriminately. Bearing in mind, this is the most powerful handgun in the world, as used by none other than Clint Eastwood in the Dirty Harry movies. If it had hit anybody in any part of the body, dying would almost be a welcome certainty.

Fortunately for us, there is either a fault in the gun or operator error, and the hammer does not hit the cartridge hard enough to detonate the charge and send the bullet on its journey. This is known as a light strike and can be caused by the user snatching at the trigger rather than pulling it correctly.

Eventually, we corner Maurice and Slippery, and when we do, they gave up. As is often the case at this level, they exercise their right to silence but then are duly charged and remanded in custody awaiting trial.

At the Old Bailey, they put forward the ludicrous defence that Maurice is a police informant, and the Flying Squad has asked him to take part in a training exercise, during which Maurice and Slippery are to commit an Armed Robbery at a post office and we would give chase. Shots are to be fired by us and then they would be arrested, taken to a local police station, and we would all debrief the exercise before popping over to the pub for a couple of brewskis.

Naturally, the jury believes this plausible but really implausible defence and they are both acquitted. Twelve good men of our peers is truly a laughable statement for today's society. I'm not sure whether today's juries are stupid, weak-willed, anti-police, or a combination of all three – but whatever it is, they buy b.s. like this by the wheelbarrow full.

It is a little-known fact that you can have a number of criminal convictions for dishonesty and still serve on a jury. However, having served a prison sentence is one of the few things that bars you from taking your place on a jury when called. Bearing in mind you only need three people of the twelve refusing to convict, and the person charged walks free.

Most members of the public today, because of speed cameras and other minor breaches of the law, have a less than favourable opinion of the police, and that probably impacts on and spills over to the conviction rate for major crimes. When I was younger, I was proud to tell people I was in the police, but as times have changed and people's attitudes towards the police have deteriorated, I have long since given up admitting to being a cop.

Another gang from Mitcham are searched after an

Armed Robbery. Millions in cash, burnt money bags and handguns are found. Their defence is the Flying Squad committed the robbery and then planted everything on them. As preposterous as it sounds, the jury acquitted them all, believing that could have happened – when it couldn't, not in a million years.

What right minded detective (or anyone for that matter) would get clean away with a million-pound Armed Robbery, and then, rather than keep the money, plant it on someone else on the hundred-to-one chance he might get a conviction. The only winners in the legal system are the defence barristers and solicitors and the criminals who line their coffers.

One of my most satisfying jobs is buying guns from a Gloucester-based professional comedian. He is funny as all get out but clearly should have stuck to comedy. For purely monetary reasons, i.e., greed, he has set himself up as a gun dealer to the criminal underworld. Call him crazy.

Though he most likely didn't intend it or maybe didn't even see it coming, his weapons are responsible for the shootings of people in Liverpool and Manchester. Busting him and locking him up is definitely going to save a lot of lives and perhaps inject a dark humour into the penal system.

When I am introduced to him, he offers to sell me whatever weapons I want. We're talking big canons -- pump action sawn- off shotguns and brand-new boxed handguns, for extremely good prices. I put feelers out in London and contact him by phone with an order. To avoid phone tap problems, we would use the codeword Trousers for Shotguns and shorts for handguns.

Not long after I return to London, I ring him and place an order for trousers. 'Do you want the trousers sawn-off or full length', he says.

Bursting out laughing at the metaphor, I say, 'are we using a code or not.' He laughs, and he says he will call me back.

At our next meeting, I tell him henceforth sawn-offs will be referred to as Corbett's, after the comedian Ronnie. Over time, I buy a number of guns from him, and he is eventually arrested and charged. His defence is that I was an Intimidating Character, and that he only supplied the firearms because he was frightened of me.

Boo!

Thankfully, and ironically given my confidence in them, juries sometimes are a lot less gullible in Gloucester than London, and he is convicted and sent to prison despite being an old man and getting a glowing reference from the comedian, Stan Boardman. This brings to mind the saying (in a German accent), 'Ze who laughs last, zlaughs longest'.

Denise, Louise and I move to Portsmouth, and in September of 1994, we give birth to Ella Chiv Chiv Sole (Chiv Chiv is baby chick in Turkish). Now, our family is complete. Only fools brings more children into the world than they can afford.

Life in Portsmouth is idyllic, as compared to the hustle and bustle of London. We even get to know our neighbours. Where we live, we can leave the car unlocked overnight and pushbikes in the garden without being nicked and fenced or sold as parts. That takes some serous getting used to.

# THIRTEEN

Hampshire Police, don't make me laugh.
Not long after moving to Portsmouth, I have my first of many poor experiences with Hampshire constabulary. Denise and I with our children decide to go to Bournemouth for the day with my sister Gail and her family. We travel in convoy in separate cars.

Since joining the police, I have had a number of off-duty arrests, and even with the family, still have eyes like a hawk as to what's going on around me. Gail is about 500 yards in front of us, when my attention is drawn to a car that's swerving from the outside lane to the hard shoulder and screeches to a halt.

I slow right down and watch in my rear-view mirror. As the driver get out, He runs around and pull the front seat passenger out, thump him, and then picks him up and throw him over a 20-foot steep embankment, before getting back in the car and speeding off.

Gail and her family continue onto Bournemouth, completely oblivious. I let the car overtake me, then start discreetly following it and giving a commentary to the Hampshire constabulary control centre on my mobile.

In London, you would hear sirens and activity within minutes. Not here. I follow him for about 20 minutes with not a cop in sight. He eventually realises that he is being followed, however, as we travel down quiet country lanes where we are easily spotted.

Suddenly, he stops his car and jumps out, and by then, I'm also starting to run towards him. Seeing me, he turns and runs, and at a mini roundabout, he jumps on the back of a flatbed lorry and the driver speeds off. I flag down a car and instruct the driver to follow the lorry.

After a while, he jumps off the lorry and starts to run across a cricket field. I take off after him, and he must have thought, who the fuck is this guy? He runs into a gypsy camp, and once safely inside, flips me the bird. I decide not to go any closer, but continue talking to Hampshire control.

I hope you are starting to understand why Met Police cops think they (Hampshire cops) are lazy carrot crunchers.

I wait for what seems like an eternity, when suddenly the gate opens and my suspect (together with another male) head off out of view in a vehicle. I get the registration number and start walking back to my car, mega unhappy. By some miracle, uniformed officers spot them and rightly make the arrest.

I'm asked to go to Bitterne Police Station where I make a statement and give it to the officer that has arrested the suspect. 'Do you know who that guy is?' he says. 'His name is Joey, and he is one of the hardest men in Hampshire. The local police have strict instructions not to go near him unless they are mob handed.

'Yeah', I say nonchalantly.

'Are you bloody mad then?' he says.

'Yes, I am, and that's why my nickname is Mad Jack'.

One more question, he says. 'When the car was stolen,

was it east or west of the Hamble River?'

'East'.

'Great, I can go home. This is a Fareham case, so can you take your statement to the Fareham police station?'

'You could have knocked me over with a feather. 'No I can't, you fucking lazy cheeky bastard. You need to fuck off before I slap you'.

Then I walk out to where my family is waiting and drive home with my blood boiling.

Joey is never charged with any crime. And unlike Metropolitan Police protocol, I don't receive any recognition for conduct above and beyond the call of duty – though clearly it was.

# FOURTEEN

Who wants to live forever?
We regularly go out drinking with Alan and Lucy and Steve and Melanie. Lucy considers Melanie her best friend and vice versa. They are extremely close. We all party hard, and on the face of it, we are extremely happy as couples.

Nobody knows what goes on behind closed doors, of course, and it transpires that Lucy is drinking heavily all the time. Alan isn't happy with that, but he is back in the Navy and not at home all the time, so he is powerless to stop it.

Over time as a couple, they start to drift apart, and instead of addressing their problems together, both commence having affairs. Alan with a woman called Maria, and Lucy with a guy called Paddy. Alan and Lucy have a daughter, Linda. As is often the case, the last person to know that their partner is having an affair is the aggrieved party.

We all hope that both affairs will peter out without ever being discovered. Sadly, that turns out not to be the case. Alan and Lucy have a huge bust-up and Alan moves out of the marital home. They both continue seeing their paramours, but neither is truly happy.

Things come to a head when Lucy finds out that Steve

and Melanie have been out for a drink with Alan and Maria. Lucy is heartbroken. To her, Melanie doing that is a complete betrayal of their friendship. So she comes around our house and pours her heart out, sobbing uncontrollably.

We try to get her to stay overnight, but she won't and leaves for home at about 10pm. She has blood pressure issues and has been prescribed Beta blockers and warned to curb her drinking. Lucy is a headstrong woman, however, and wild horses can't make her stop drinking Bacardi.

That night, the $30^{th}/31^{st}$ of August 1995, apparently Lucy has taken a cocktail of Beta blockers and booze whilst home alone. In the early hours of the morning, she contacts Melanie and says she's going to commit suicide.

'Fuck off, Lucy, your pissed', Melanie says and puts the phone down.

Hours later, Lucy rings Alan and tells him what she has done. He drives to the marital home and rushes her straight to hospital in his car. Despite frantic efforts by the medical team, she dies on the operating table.

The shockwaves, when the news breaks that she has committed suicide, goes far and wide, and there's an immense outpouring of grief. Without doubt, she was a larger-than-life, beautiful woman that everyone loved.

Alan literally falls apart in front of me. I am seriously worried about his mental stability for a long time. As is often the case when a young person dies in tragic circumstances, a quest by family and friends is undertaken to blame somebody else; and at times, this gets out of control.

Thankfully, time is a great healer, and everybody

accepts that this was just a tragic accident, a cry for help which had fatal consequences that went unanswered. None of us will ever forget her. She leaves behind a husband, a daughter, family and too many friends to count.

I'm sure that whatever happens after death, if there is a party going on, Lucy will be right smack in the thick of it. I have seen far too many deaths and been to more funerals than I would like to, but Lucy's is by far the most emotionally charged.

The opening song is 'Who Wants to Live Forever', by Queen.

I write and give the eulogy, but seeing the words on the paper is almost impossible because of the tears streaming down my face. As I look around the crematorium, there's not a dry eye in the room.

The closing song is 'Why?', by Annie Lennox, and again the words are so poignant that everyone falls apart.

To this day, I can't listen to either song without crying.

Alan and Linda move in with Denise, our children and I until they have recovered enough to start again on their own. Linda still carries the scars from that fateful night, and probably always will.

# FIFTEEN

The best thing about being on the Flying Squad is every day is different.

One afternoon, a group of us are sitting in the office when a call comes in, saying, 'Armed Robbery in Progress, Putney high street. Male armed with a sawn-off shotgun'.

Putney is a mile from the office, so we hightail it to Putney armed to the gills with firearms. We end up chasing the man, with the non-armed cops backing away to leave us to it. Eventually, he heads across a bridge running over the River Thames and heading towards Fulham.

That's a huge mistake, as cops from the Fulham side are coming the other way. Realising he's trapped, he stops running, spins round, and drop to his knees. Then, shocking all of us, he positions the barrels of the gun into his mouth, sucks on it, and pull the trigger. You've never seen the head and skull exploding and then imploding in slow motion, oddly, and you never ever want to.

Because of my covert role, I am told to get away before the press and all the television stations arrive to capture the spectacle that could have been beheadings at the Roman Colosseum. I am with him later when his mum arrives to see him.

He looked nothing like the boy and man she knew, and I try to dissuade her from witnesses his corpse. She insists, and then says, 'That is not my baby. Where you have put my baby'. Crying uncontrollably, she starts slapping me hard around the face, but I just stand there and take it.

There is nothing I could do or say that would make this God-forsaken sight any easier for her. It transpires that he had been released from a long prison sentence recently and had vowed he would never go back inside again.

# SIXTEEN

In memory of Paul Clarke.

My Flying Squad days are coming to a close, but I have been selected for the Regional Crime Squad, another prestigious post dealing with major criminals on a regional level. Because I am living in Portsmouth, my bossman Paul at the Southampton office calls me in to a meeting.

During that meeting, he asks me to join him at the Southampton office and try and inject some life into it. With the exception of half a dozen guys, he says the whole lot are a bunch of lazy incompetents who much prefer getting pissed to working for a living.

At the time, they hadn't had a decent seizure of drugs or charged any major criminals in a Blue Moon. The Met didn't have a good reputation in Hampshire Constabulary, and this office is predominately a Hampshire team with a smattering of Dorset Constabulary.

Needless to say, when I accept this position and report to duty, I am treated like a pariah. They have never controlled an undercover operation from the Southampton office, but I convince them that this is an amazing tactic in our armoury. That the opportunity exists to deploy these undercover tactics on a few of their listed Operations.

Martin, Paul and Maurita are three keen, competent detectives who have been investigating a team of lorry hijackers. These blokes – the hijackers - have committed a large number of high value lorry thefts, quite often with the driver being a victim who collaborates with them and is paid as soon the heat died down.

I convince them to introduce an undercover cop to be the lorry driver who is willing to cooperate in the robbery for a payoff. This tactic is allowed and there are even precedents in law to support what we are doing.

It works this way: An informant introduces a driver to them who offers to have a lorry loaded with spirits and valued at £250,000 stolen from him. As soon as the hook has been laid, they pick it up and run away with it.

Greed is the enemy of all criminals, and they speak freely to the undercover cop about other jobs that they have done and how successful they have been at stealing high value loads.

On the day in question, they meet to finalise the plan, and the main man, Dave, laughs, 'We are bang in trouble if you are the regional crime squad'.

'The undercover cop says, 'I am,' pausing for a second and before bursting out laughing, to which they all merrily join in.

The undercover cop is directed to a service off the M4 called Sylvia's Cafe and told to park up and lock his lorry and go for dinner for one hour. He's already given them a spare key, and as soon as he takes off, one of their team wearing a disguise (due to security cameras) jumps in the lorry and drives it straight out of the services, followed by our surveillance team.

The lorry is driven to a lock-up in Wiltshire controlled

by the gang, and a frantic unloading commenced. Our operational commander calls in the arrest, and within minutes, the police have surrounded the place and arrested the gang members.

They plead guilty at court to a number of lorry thefts and all receive hefty sentences. I did hope they would go to trial so the recording could be played of them laughing about the prospect of the undercover driver being on the regional crime squad, which they found hilarious. If only they had realised in time that they were psychic.

From my military service, I had a Class 2 HGV licence, and being on the regional crime squad it makes good sense to develop that skill further. So I do so, and go on to pass my Articulated Lorry Licence and also attain the Certificate of Professional Competence to run both national and international haulage companies.

Except for the anti-terrorist squad, the police conduct all of their operations on a shoestring budget. It's a sad fact of the times that budget control is far more important than locking up criminals. Most managers are promoted on how much money they save, as opposed to how many major criminals they have locked up.

That, coupled with the completely risk adverse policies that are now in place together with the spineless managers, and I'll be surprised if undercover work even exists in 20 years' time. That will be a crying shame, as it is without doubt one of the most successful tools in the fight to combat organised crime.

I said earlier, I went on the only recognised undercover course in the UK, but I stand corrected... because there is another one.

# SEVENTEEN

## All the Gear and No Idea

Because none of the staff of Her Majesties Customs and Excise are good enough to pass the SO10 course, they design and hold their own training course. As a result, the Beta Projects is born. The Beta Projects is a small team of about eight officers with an unlimited budget and broad jurisdiction to take control of any seized boat, plane, train or automobile.

Whilst SO10 scratches around for pence under the cushion, Beta Projects have it all. The phrase, 'all the gear but no idea', therefore springs to mind.

Customs' idea of a successful undercover operation is to intercept a parcel of cocaine that has been posted and swap it for baby's milk. Then they deliver it to the intended recipient dressed as a postman. Major credit is given to their undercover operative when the guilty party is arrested, and he hasn't realised the postman was from law enforcement.

If only undercover work were as simple as donning a postman's uniform and delivering a parcel. I must say at this point that they do have one good man who is ex-special forces and affectionately known as Captain Barbosa. He is a legend for many reasons and rightly so.

Captain Barbosa's only shortcomings are that he can't

hear -- he's as deaf as a post from being involved in too many gun battles in his military life. And he has little experience with criminal investigations and procedures relating to law. Consequently, he has limited experience giving evidence at Crown Court against top defence barristers, and they routinely tear him a new arsehole in need of huge amounts of paper.

Unfortunately, source protection has never been a customs strong point, and high-level informants have been literally fried alive and been left with no option but to go into witness protection or spend the rest of their lives looking over their shoulders.

In 1996, Beta Projects covert unit is asked by a criminal group to meet a yacht in the Bay of Biscay and transfer a large amount of cannabis, end destination the United Kingdom. From the start to finish, it is badly handled. They choose a tugboat suitable for inshore work only, called Adherence, and cunningly disguise it by changing its name to Adherence 2.

The Bay of Biscay is notoriously rough, and in the wintertime - October to March - much worse. The experience of the skipper - and I use the term loosely, as he has never been in the Navy – has been mainly around yachts. If he had an ounce of common sense, he would not have set off on this journey in this boat at this time of year.

This is before the days of Captain Barbosa, as he was an accomplished boat captain. Now, even though they call themselves undercover operatives, you could write their undercover experiences on a postage stamp with a pickaxe. They are, at best, professional legend developers.

More by good luck than judgement, the skipper makes

his way to the rendezvous point with the yacht, and transports the cannabis from boat to boat using a small dinghy. The weather worsens, of course, and the strong wind pushing against a climbing sea start to make life extremely uncomfortable. With 145 big bales of cannabis onboard the tug, they leave the yacht and head back to merry ol' England.

On the 25$^{th}$ of October 1996, because of a following sea, and possibly the weight of the cannabis in the rear hold, the low freeboard of the tug starts to take on water (because this design only has about two feet above the water line). It's only a matter of time before the tug perilously sinks, cannabis and all.

They could easily have all died, but they are rescued by a ship called 'The Horncliffe', and live to tell the tale. Well, actually, they don't tell the tale in typical HM Customs and Excise fashion, because they break all the rules by failing to report the accident.

When what has truly happened eventually comes out, they try to hide behind the secrecy of the covert operation. The complete disregard of the law shown by HM Custom and Excise is incredulous. Something the police would never do, and if they did, would never get away with.

# EIGHTEEN

### RTT: Routes, Tits and Trucks

Within days of passing my Class 1 HGV licence, I am given a job to drive to southern Spain and pick up three tonnes of cannabis. I meet one of the subjects at Thurrock services in a lorry owned by the police covert unit. He comes out into the Lorry Park and asks me to move the lorry from one bay to another further back, which involve simple reversing manoeuvres.

He is sufficiently satisfied that I am a lorry driver, and he gives me my instructions and destination, which is close to Malaga Airport. We part company, and I am amazed that me doing a simple reverse procedure was sufficient from a credibility point of view to satisfy him that I am a bona fide lorry driver. But experience has taught me that it is never this simple and can only go downhill from here.

A couple of days later, I set off with a full load of red wine to be delivered to southern Spain. Empty lorries do not travel backwards and forwards across the channel, because it is not financially viable to do so, and we have to be able to stand scrutiny from a routine customs check.

Covered for that event, I head off to Dover to catch the ferry. On arrival, I join a queue for my pre-booked sailing, amongst hundreds of other lorries. Even this is a massive learning curve. When I arrive at the head of the queue, I am signalled forward by a traffic marshal.

I am about to drive up the ramp, and the marshal stop. 'Spin round mate and reverse up, you're the last on'.

I absolutely crap myself and can instantly feel beads of sweat rolling down my back. I start the manoeuvre but notice there is only room for a cigarette paper either side of the lorry at my allocated spot. This manoeuvre would have been difficult going forwards, let alone going backwards.

I can see complete carnage if I get this wrong and decide to approach another driver, candidly telling him this was my first ever drive. Like a superstar, he steps up and parks the lorry on the ferry without the width of a single playing card to space.

Props to all the lorry drivers I've ever met; they go out of their way to help another truck driver. My troubles, however, are far from over, and once parked on the ferry, the deck crew approaches me. 'We are expecting rough weather,' a chap says. 'Pass me your "Towing bracket".

For starters, I don't have a clue what he is talking about. 'Sorry, mate, I haven't got one', I say.

Thereupon he makes me sign a disclaimer affirming that if the holding chains rip my bumpers off, it is my fault for not having the right equipment. I get out of the lorry like a condemned man half expecting to find parts of my lorry all over the deck when the channel crossing was over.

From my years in the Navy, I know how fierce the sea can be, and I only hope I will have a driveable lorry to come back to. Because truck drivers have their own canteen, I head there for a well-earned cuppa and a truck driver's Fat Boy's Breakfast. A heart attack on a plate if ever I've seen one.

I get my food and sit down at a table with the other truckers. One of them says, 'you're the FH man, aren't you?'

'No, no, God no', I say.

'Yes you are; you are the Volvo FH 12'.

There the penny drops, as he's identified the make of truck I am driving. I feel such a Pratt, because I have no idea what model of truck that I'm even in. Note to self, just because you have passed your test does not make you a truck driver.

The entire crossing is spent talking about trucks, routes and tits. In fact, that is all truck drivers talk about, and if I am to be successful in this arena, I will need an intimate knowledge of all three of those subjects.

On disembarking the ferry at Calais, I head through France to Malaga. An excellent journey compared to the UK, where motors are made to drive roads that are massively overcrowded and poorly maintained. I start to appreciate where our EU contribution disappears to: providing France and Spain with quality road networks.

On arrival at Malaga, my phone sparks to life and an Englishmen directs me to an industrial area. There I'm met by another Englishman, who takes the truck and instructs me to go and get food and he'll be back in an hour.

I do as told, and in an hour, the truck is given back to me 3 tonnes heavier. At the next services, I stop to have a look at my load and notice that all they have done is thrown the bales of cannabis amongst the return loads. Clearly, so few trucks are checked at Dover that the criminals feel no compulsion to hide their gear properly.

Driving through France and Spain is a huge education for me, with British truckers preferring certain service areas, generally the ones where ladies of the night ply their trade, walking the line of trucks and offering a good time for peanut money.

Condoms are not required but a willingness to stir some other drivers' porridge definitely is. I have always admired prostitutes, because it truly is the only service industry where the customer always comes first.

I have a trouble-free run back to Calais through some spectacular scenery. The roads are high quality and virtually traffic free, and I breeze through customs on the French and English side. And I totally understand why: the volume of traffic is intense. You would have to be bloody unlucky to be stopped and searched.

I drive to Thurrock services, where a surveillance team is waiting. Next I call my UK contact, and he directs me to an industrial area in Essex. There I'm met by another man who I follow to an empty lock-up. When the cannabis is off-loaded, I leave. Later I receive a call from an elated operational commander, who reports that nine arrests have been made, including some major players.

They all plead guilty in court and my role is never declared, successfully remaining part of the sensitive documents bundle.

First port of call for me is our office, which is responsible for coordinating undercover deployments. Key to this coordination, is making sure our drivers don't get caught with their pants down on any future operations -- and I don't mean with the ladies of the night.

Thankfully our control centre for undercover

operations is run by experienced detectives. Convincing them to make our haulage capability far more resilient than it is, is not difficult.

As I said earlier, everything in the police is achieved with a shoestring budget. So what I have in mind is not going to be cheap, and because of that, will take time and patience.

To combat major crime on a national level, the six offices of the regional crime squad are amalgamated to become the National Crime Squad in 1998. Thereafter, I am selected to join the full-time undercover unit based in London. This means that instead of doing both overt and covert work, I will now be focussing only on covert work.

Undercover officers have to attend regular appointments with a mental health professional to ensure they don't start believing their own legends and lose sight of reality. This has happened, and some have fallen into the trap of using controlled drugs to enhance their credibility amongst the criminals they are trading with.

Always ending in tears, this has been the downfall of some good operatives. I spend a lot of my time with the criminals at the top end of the food chain, and most of them live by the motto, 'Never get high on your own supply'.

They often consider class A drug users as a liability, because using gear makes people loose-lipped and more prone to having encounters with the police. Someone who is regularly getting nicked and high is far more likely to turn and become an informant.

Without doubt, informants are the life blood of any law enforcement team, and Class A drug users are a regular source of good information. In my opinion, Class A drug use has completely destroyed the old school loyalty that used to exist amongst career criminals. By Class A drugs, I mean crack cocaine, cocaine and the Big H, heroin.

I have never understood the reluctance to legalise drug use. When I joined the police in 1984, cocaine was £100 plus per gramme; now you can get a gramme of cocaine for £30.That proves the supply is far greater than it ever was, and that law enforcement has failed miserably to stem the flood of drugs that arrive daily by land, sea and air.

Look at Cocaine. A kilo of coke as pure as the driven snow is about 85 percent pure and in Columbia costs about £1500. By the time it reaches the United Kingdom, it costs between £32,000 and £36,000, and if it is coming via Holland, the channel crossing costs another £2000 per Kilo.

By the time it hits street level, that kilo is cut to pieces -- as it makes for huge profits in the realm of £200,000. The illegality of it is what makes it lucrative to the dealers, distributors and sellers. If cocaine were controlled like tobacco and available without massive profit margins, who would bother to import it?

Governments always argue that to legalise it would mean more people would use it. From my experience, just the opposite is true. Most people who don't use it now, don't use it because they don't need it or want it. The fact it is illegal does not feature in their thought processes because, unlike other violent crimes against person or property, they consider it a victimless crime.

Everyone knows the chances of being caught in simple possession is about one thousand times less than being caught speeding. You have to be bloody unlucky, reckless or stupid to get caught speeding, and still everybody speeds. Unless there is some new technology that I'm not aware of, police do not have a camera which can detect drugs on someone as they walk down the street.

I always used to smile when users would say what great gear they are using. Truth is, most street level seizures are only 11 to 20 percent cocaine and the remainder of whatever mixing agent that's been included. With cocaine, that is often the dentists numbing agent Novocaine (I once imported five tonnes of Novocaine by lorry for a northern gang and they were doing that monthly), or powdered baby's milk.

So, all you users out there you're probably getting high on babies' milk, which is £10 for a 500 gramme tin in Asda. I am convinced for most people it is a psychological high rather than anything the cut-to-pieces drug has to offer. There are some drug dealers who don't cut the gear and sell it as pure as it was when it left its source country, but in 17 years undercover, I have only met three!

Looking at it harshly, if you drink heavily, you deserve to die of liver disease. If you smoke heavily, you deserve to die of lung cancer. If you use drugs and they kill you, that's your fault. We are all big enough to accept responsibility for the things we do.

Point I'm making is, we don't need the government telling us it's illegal to use one drug but not another. The hypocrisy of the lawmakers is ridiculous, especially when many elected or appointed officials think it's cool to confess to being an abuser of alcohol or drugs when trying to find favour with the electorate.

# NINETEEN

## Corruption at its Worst

On 13th November 1999, Lennox Lewis is fighting Evander Holyfield for the heavyweight title of the world at the Thomas and Mack centre in Las Vegas. If there is one thing a lot of major criminals are interested in, it's the noble art of boxing.

Information is coming in that this fight is going to attract gangsters from all over the UK, thus making it an opportunity to go and mingle and be amongst them. Referencing is vitally important to undercover operatives, and a lot of referencing and deals are struck at major events like this.

The entire gang of a South London firm is going, all those who are the subject of a National Crime Squad operation being run out of the Swanley Branch office. A decision is made to send two undercover operatives out there to attempt a cold infiltration.

The two chosen, of which I am one, are considered to be amongst the top ten of operatives in the United Kingdom, particularly in relation to cold infiltrations. However, it is always much easier to use an informant to introduce the operative, giving him or her instant credibility.

Sadly, dishonest barristers and a justice system that's

badly weighted in favour of the criminal, make that more and more difficult. Frankly, it puts a lot of informants' lives in danger, and the police always protect their sources to the bitter end. That cannot be said of our Customs counterparts, who burn informants alive regularly rather than risk losing a conviction.

We book ourselves onto the same flight to Vegas and into the same hotel as the gang. That way, we'll save costs without any surveillance cover. Once on the flight, we realise the gang leaders have moved seats to the opposite end of the plane to where the underlings are sat. I remember thinking, that's odd, but then dismissing it from the front of my mind.

Once in Vegas, it becomes apparent that the entire gang have switched hotels. I'm starting to get a bad feeling about this, because that will cost them a shed load of money. Not to mention, we hit the town and visit a number of bars and casinos as part of our cover.

We have money to gamble, but strangely, it doesn't sit well with me gambling, even though I'm not losing my own money. My mum always said you never see a bookmaker arriving on a pushbike, which is true, and true gamblers never lose, they always win or break even, which is false.

As Steve Wynn say, 'bet long enough, and the house ALWAYS wins. I've not seen a gambler beat that house consistently in 40 years'.

Looking at the way Vegas has developed, and the bucket loads of money people are losing in front of me, I find the last statement – that true gamblers never lose - incredulous. In the same week as the fight, a major football match (not American football) is also taking place. So all the hotels set up huge screens to enable the thousands of British fans to watch the game.

After the game, my mate and I walk out of the hotel to get a taxi. As we wing our way to the queue, I hear someone shouting 'Al', a name I'm using on another active undercover operation. I never use my own name or the same name on separate jobs. It gets too confusing.

At one time, I have five active operations with different names and legends running at the same time. It used to drive my wife wild as the five separate phones on our bedroom windowsill used to spring into life at the most inappropriate times.

I had to put a lock on the bedroom door to stop the kids walking in and thinking they were being helpful and answering them. Criminals have no concept of a decent time, and as far as they are concerned, they can call you 24 hours a day, seven days a week -- and they regularly do!

Hearing my Al named shouted, I look round and spot a gang leader from another operation. This guy is involved in drug smuggling, bringing a tonne of cannabis a month into the UK by lorry. I walk over to him and we embrace like long lost mates. I introduce him to my pal, and we all agree to have a go on the rollercoaster at the top of the Stratosphere Hotel, and then get down to the Chicken Ranch and fuck some whores.

We jump into two taxis -- me, my pal and the gang leader in the back, and one of his underlings in the front passenger seat. The gang leader - Paul – is smashed on booze and cocaine and, to put it mildly, is being extremely obnoxious and loud. That's ripe coming from me, as I've never been accused of being quiet.

The guy in the front is trying unsuccessfully to get Paul's attention and makes the fatal mistake of calling him a cunt. Paul thereupon drags him by the hair backwards across the front seat and bites off a chunk of his nose and spits it into the foot well. Paul's mouth is covered in blood and the lad himself is disfigured and bleeding profusely.

The Vegas cabbie is mortified and stops the car. Paul tells him to fuck off and front-seat mate gets out and runs off howling in pain. The driver is none to happy but decide to keep stum and takes us to the hotel, followed by the other cab.

My mind is racing. But much as I like the adrenaline of being on the roof of the Stratosphere Hotel with a guy who has just disfigured his mate for life, is rapidly losing its appeal. We get out of the cab, Paul puts his arm around my shoulder, and we head for the roof, laughing and joking as if nothing has happened.

My mate is pasty on a good day, but there is not a drop of blood left in his face. He is as white as a ghost. I try to reassure him with a smile, but it doesn't do the trick. I have a vision of his arse twitching uncontrollably and me thinking thank fuck I'm as mad as a box of frogs.

On the roof, we are met by a member of the hotel staff who says, 'sorry, the ride is closed for an hour because of strong winds. Please get a drink at the bar and come back'.

Paul and his boys are up for that, but I says we have a business meeting and can't hang about. We hug and part company, and there is a loud Marp sound from both of us as we descend in the lift to terra firma.

We have tickets for the fight, and on the day thereof, meet outside the Arena with Frank Bruno, who is with Chris Eubank. An odd couple, you might think, but they clearly got on well. Despite Chris Eubanks public persona and outrageous clothing, he is a very likeable, chatty guy. We have a good laugh with both of them and take advantage of the photo opportunity.

Inside the arena, the atmosphere is electric. From our seats, we look round and see all the gangs from London, Liverpool, Manchester and the North-East, some of whom I know personally. If the devil could cast his net over this lot, the arena would have been emptied, particularly the expensive seats with a clear view

Once the boxing has finished, we mooch off to a casino and by pure accident bump into the entire South London gang the subject of the operation. They are chatty, but at the same time, very guarded, and the hairs on the back of my neck are standing at attention.

After about 30 minutes, we leave them gambling and report back that something isn't right. We return to the UK as planned, and a week later are called into a meeting at a hotel to discuss the operation. It transpires that a corrupt police officer has again tipped them off about the undercover sting, but he didn't know who was going to try and infiltrate them during their Vegas trip, so they had been ignoring anybody they didn't actually know.

I don't know if the bent cop has ever been identified. In a way, I'm glad, because shooting bent cops could easily have become a full-time occupation for me. I'm 64 years old now, and if anybody in authority has the balls to order the shooting of corrupt law enforcement officers, I will apply for the job in a heartbeat.

# TWENTY

## Maverick Meets Goose

In 2000, I'm invited with a group of other undercover operatives to a briefing for a sensitive job. There I meet a man called Tony who has the same magnetic charm as Alan. Tony is late arriving because he uncharacteristically (lol) is speeding and damaged his BMW going over the top of a roundabout instead of the prescribed route around it.

As soon as I start talking to Tony, I know we will be friends for life. He has a maverick personality, and because of that, most undercover cops are frightened of working with him; me, I'm attracted to him, because I can relate to maverick and see that as a massive plus, not a negative.

Tony is extremely good looking, fit as a butcher's dog, charming, funny, has a law degree, plays guitar and sings better than a lot of popstars. His only problem is that every woman he meets wants to fuck him, and fending them off diplomatically caused issues.

I make the decision right then and there that in the future every undercover deployment I'm sent on is going to be with him on it, if humanly possible. I forgot to add, he is also an accomplished boxer, and it would be a foolish man who decided to test his ability.

One particular incident springs to mind. When he is in an up-market bar, he accidentally bumps into a gangster with his six foot, muscle-bound minder, and spills his drink. Tony apologises profusely but that isn't good enough, and the foolish gangster shows off and tells the minder to take Tony outside and teach him a lesson.

Tony and the minder go out into the car park, and whilst facing each other, Tony places an imaginary gum shield in his mouth, taps an imaginary bell, and says, 'DING, DING'. He then proceeds to knock seven shades of shit out of the minder, who within minutes is spark out on the floor and probably thinking of a new career.

Tony then walks back into the bar. When the gangster sees him, he goes white and probably shits himself. Tony walks up to him and gives him an Archie (Rockenrolla) slap in front of everyone there before heading home. It will be a while before that guy will be larging it up in that bar again.

Back home, my mum and dad continue drinking like their lives depend on it. My mum is living now in a house owned by my brother James and my dad is living in a flea ridden bedsit in the same town. Doctors have told my dad, 'stop drinking or die'. His response: 'If I have to stop drinking, I would rather die'.

Before his adult life of drinking, he was a good looking, six foot two, fit looking man. By 2001, he is an eight-stone shadow of his former self who could easily pass for a tramp if encountered on a street. He was going to write a book about how he turned £5 million in real estate into £5 cash, but he never got around to it.

Contact between me and my dad at best is sporadic. In the early days, I try desperately to stop him drinking, but eventually give it up as a lost cause. Neither of my children ever met him. On the 18th of August, I am in Gatwick airport with my family heading off on our summer holiday, when I receive a call from my sister Elizabeth. She informs me dad is in hospital and will be dead within 48 hours. He has asked to see me before he dies.

I told Elizabeth to tell him to fuck off. He has never cared before and now it is too late. I don't tell Denise and the kids, and instead we go on a holiday. Elizabeth phones me later and says he has died. I keep that to myself as well during the holiday, until we get back home.

The funeral is a pitiful affair with only mum and five of his children present. Alcoholics have no real friends.

# TWENTY-ONE

## Spineless Leadership

There have been a number of studies conducted to identify Special Forces potential recruits. They look back in history at battles and have identified that only a miniscule percentage of the world's population are capable of killing someone without the killing having a very detrimental effect on their emotional well-being.

In the days of muskets and gun powder, it was found that most of the soldiers in battle had stood up, not pulled the trigger, then kneeled down and reloaded again, repeating the procedure without firing a bullet until the barrel was jammed with gun powder wadding and bullets.

Of the small percentage that can kill, they are split into three groups. The first are completely insane and life has no value for them. The second are people who kill in a moment of extreme anger, but would never do it again. And the third can kill in an unemotional, precise fashion and forget about it five minutes later. They can flit between normal family life and controlled killing without batting an eyelid.

I have been placed into that group.

There is a psychological profile test to identify these people, and in the height of the suicide bombing problems, I am selected as part of Operation Kratos to be available to kill suicide bombers. That is done by walking up to them, and, from point blank range, firing two bullets into their brain stem. As part of the training, we are forced to watch footage of Al Qaeda beheading hostages (including some prominent British citizens whose names will remain anonymous). The thought process being we would not hesitate to kill them on any active operation in the future.

Generally, I would have absolutely no hesitation in doing that. Unfortunately, whenever there is a firearm shooting, the abundance of armchair experts in this country start a witch hunt to show that the police are out of control and shoot people for no apparent reason or even just for the fun of it. I even had a black man I know trying to convince me that the police are deliberately shooting black people to reduce the numbers of black people in London.

Come on now, I ask you, how many bullets would that take? I can assure you the combined United Kingdom police forces do not even hold enough bullets to do that, this is at best a ridiculous statement but one which is shared by a lot of his friends on social media.

The Jean Charles De Menezes shooting in 2005 is a case in point. I was not on that job, but in my experienced opinion, the men who shot him were heroes not villains to be castigated by the media and other ill-informed individuals across the political spectrum.

I accept that it is an awful tragedy, but that is exactly what it was. If the government had any balls at all the real terrorist who lived in the block of flats and had arrived in the country hell bent on creating carnage with a suicide vest and who John Charles De Menezes was mistaken for, would have had a 3am visit from well trained men, been assassinated, and then been buried at sea never to be seen again.

Trying to work within a legal framework to stop terrorism is about as effective as buying a chocolate fire guard. I laugh every time I see on television the media screaming, how did he manage to commit the atrocity when he was on the MI5 watch list. It takes a team of at least ten men with vehicles to follow one person. That's how.

So that would be 30 surveillance officers to cover a 24-hour period for every single person on the MI5 watch list. There are hundreds of terrorists in the UK on the watch list, so MI5 would need thirty men per suspected terrorist. The police would have to increase its surveillance-trained staff 10,000-fold to keep track on all of them, which is never going to happen for budget reasons alone.

Come on, peeps, smell the coffee! You also need to remember that you have to follow people from the back; you can't do that from in front unless you have psychic powers and eyes in the back of your head.

Apart from the officer who sees him come out of the block, no-one else sees his face until after he was dead. The order to kill him was taken by the command structure, and to walk up next to somebody you believe is a suicide bomber likely to be wearing an explosive vest – takes balls of steel that almost no one has. The author and a small group of others the exception to the rule

If the terrorist detonates the bomb as you approach, you and all the passengers are as dead as Dillinger with him, and you'll all be going to heaven to get served the virgin platter together. And it is common for suicide bombers to have a pressure-release trigger in their clammy hands, so if their hand opens for any reason for just a split second, the bomb detonates and its good night, Vienna.

I am also selected to be an armed courier for kidnap and extortion offences. For this I am required to deliver the ransom money to the criminals for them to release the hostage. There is quite a good example of this in one of the Dirty Harry movies played by Clint Eastwood.

Again, drugs have changed the landscape with this offence, and nowadays, most kidnappings revolve around one drug gang ripping off another drug gang for either money, drugs or both. The aggrieved gang then kidnap an innocent family member of the other gang and starts making demands for the return of whatever was stolen, in exchange for the family member's life.

Cheekily, the original thieves phone police to get the family member back and set the wheels in motion for us to deploy a courier. Quite often, the fact it is a drug rip off comes out in the subsequent investigations, and the original thieves decline to give evidence. Hundreds of thousands of pounds of public money wasted inadvertently working for a drugs gang.

Could only happen in England.

Most genuine kidnappings end with the criminals being arrested and locked up for substantial terms of imprisonment. Of course, the smarter guys have written kidnappings off as a way to make money. Whilst working undercover, I am shocked at the number of criminals who sell a kilo of cocaine and then don balaclavas steal it back at the point of a gun.

Many villains have been maimed or killed for doing

this, but it is still quite prevalent. The crew in the Range Rover murdered in Essex and immortalised in the film 'Rise of the Foot Soldier', were known in criminal circles for doing this. I have no sympathy for those that get hurt living on the edge of crime and drugs, because if you can't take the heat, don't light a Bic to your arse.

The explosion in the illegal movement of people from Europe into the UK must be dealt with. Remember the deaths of the Chinese immigrants in containers? Fortunately, container technology is now available that allows Customs officials to easily identify if there are humans onboard at all of the major ports in the UK.

Traffickers charge huge amounts to traffic people from all over the world into England which, ironically, is widely spoken of by migrants as 'the land of milk and honey'. Get to England and you will be given housing and money and far greater benefits than anywhere else in the world, supported by the British taxpayer.

The word refugee has been abused beyond recognition. Our immigration policies are as much use as a one-legged man at an arse-kicking party. Only a clown would think they are all heading here because we are nicer people than the Germans, French and Dutch, all of whose countries they step foot on before arriving safely in merry ol' England.

In fact, the traffickers charge a huge extra premium to get across the English Channel to our divine nation. Yet our immigration teams are demoralised and completely impotent. Look at the size of the land mass alone of France and Germany compared to England, which is bursting at the seams. You could never argue that we have plenty of room – but hey, just keep them coming!

Unfortunately, we deem it racist to try and stem immigration, and our politically correct politicians spouting what they think people want to hear, don't even know how to slow the flow, never mind cap the problem. It is often said we are a multi-cultural society, but I couldn't disagree more.

We have huge areas where people of a particular culture are huddled together, never dare mixing with other cultures other than in the workplace. If you don't believe me, go to Southall in London or Brixton for the afternoon.

To me, multi-culturism means we all live and socialise together in interactive harmony. That is just not happening – and, in my opinion, never will. Birds of a feather stick together, me thinks. That, coupled with politicians like Diane Abbot pushing their own agenda and stirring up racial hatred, and you know what? I can see this getting gradually worse until an explosion of violence occurs which will shake this country to 8 points on the Richter scale.

P.S. I'm not a fan of Enoch Powell, and I am definitely not a racist. Nowadays, telling it as it is tantamount to being a racist when it is not: facts are facts, even when denied. As the late great and banished Oscar Wilde once said in De Profundis, 'To regret one's own experiences is to arrest one's own development. To deny one's own experiences is to put a lie to the lips of one's own life. It is no less than a denial of the soul'.

The worst you could say is I dislike most people engaged in criminal activity equally regardless of skin colour – blue thieves, green aliens, purple robbers alike - and the same is true for 99% of the police force. A few bad apples have been allowed to ruin the whole bunch, as the saying goes.

The Macpherson Report is the biggest crock of shite ever written. It found what it wanted to find. Every culture prefers its own culture; that doesn't make you a racist. Most police officers deal with you the way you interact with them. If you are rude and aggressive, they will treat you accordingly. If you are having problems with the police, you need to look inward not outward. To lay the blame where it should be laid and solve the problem.

I would like to see the day when all police are armed. That will be the day that criminals take notice. Firmly but fairly, I say, that's what needs to happen with police behaviour, without all the nonsense today's police have to put up with. Because now, criminals think they can assault the police with impunity.

Annnddd… I blame the massive rise in shootings and stabbings in the major cities on a complete breakdown of family values. There's too many young men and old boys roaming the streets who have never had a father image in their lives, much less the discipline that comes with it.

# TWENTY-TWO

## European Cooperation

Besides other skills, I am a qualified boat captain. I can skipper a power boat or yacht up to 20 metres in length and 200 gross tonnes in weight. So it turns out that the Epping office of the National Crime Squad is running an operation, codename 'Franc', into a gang of Turkish smugglers. As a result, the Turk's attempted to get people into Dover and other ports by lorry are being thwarted at every turn.

However, evidence is being gathered to convict the drivers but not the main organisers. The payment for successfully smuggling people from Europe into England is £2000 per person, so that provides enough incentive to keep the driver's in constant demand, with no slowdown in sight unless we nab the organisers.

An informant is prepared to introduce me too the main honchos, and he is happy to do so because the Turks barely know him and it won't put him at too much risk. A meeting is arranged for me to meet the Turks at Port Solent Marina in Portsmouth, an area of which I have intimate knowledge from my boating days.

At the meeting, I introduce myself as Jay, and within minutes, I have them eating out of my hands. The main man never speaks a word in English and leaves everything to his second in command, a man named Hidir. However, it is obvious the main man understands English well, because when I discuss the terms of our engagement and how it would work in detail, the second in command always look at his boss for approval. The boss then nods and agrees without any need for interpretation or further explanation.

That proves to be quite a shrewd move on his part.

They agree for me to rent a 40-foot Gin Palace pleasure power boat capable of carrying 20 illegal immigrants across the channel, and they further agree to pay up front for the that and for my expenses. These power boats don't do miles to the gallon, they do gallons to the mile, so this is not a cheap way to smuggle people.

There is another criminal I know who is making similar trips in a large Rigid Hull inflatable speed boat. If he gets a sniff of law enforcement, at gun point, he makes the smugglees jump overboard in the Channel and makes good his escape. I often wonder if he ever misreads the approaching boat, particularly at night, and then throws the victims overboard where they drown with no one ever knowing.

The initial meeting is a complete success and I agreed to meet them in a couple of weeks' time in Ramsgate Marina to finalise plans. The pickup will take place in the port of Blankenberge in Belgium, a short hop over the Channel. Large pleasure power boats are fun in calm seas, but in rough waters they are hopeless. Travelling in strong winds and heavy seas is definitely not their forte.

We part company and I report back to the operational team, who are ecstatic. They have been after these guys for a long time. I then set about sourcing a boat and a crew, which is no easy task. These boats are expensive to rent and I only know of one other undercover operative who has ever been on a boat, never mind having any seamanship skills.

The sea can be a very unfriendly place, and definitely not for the faint hearted or those with no sea legs. If you have ever been on a big ship and felt a bit poorly, magnify those feelings 20 times over on a small pleasure craft, and you enter the right zone.

I manage to secure a boat for £1000 per day and start to pull together a 4-man crew just to get the boat from Plymouth to Ramsgate. I have an ex-Navy engineer and two complete novices, one of whom has done some day fishing trips, but that is all. When they join me at the boat in Plymouth, it looks more like a doorman's convention than a boat trip for yachties. I can't help but laugh.

Time is tight so we have half a day learning about our 40-foot Princess pleasure boat before loading up and preparing to leave harbour. I give them all some instruction in rope handling and the procedure for leaving a jetty. I mean, these guys are novices.

Engines on and we are away. Two of us on the boat and two on the jetty ready to release the fore spring and back spring. The back spring is then released and Charlie jumps onboard . I then drive forwards, putting pressure on the fore spring and pulling the bow into the jetty. The stern then starts to drift further and further from the jetty.

As soon as the angle is good enough to reverse out of our berth, I tell Paul to release the fore spring and jump aboard. He releases the rope but doesn't have the urgency about him to jump. That urgency comes with experience, and consequently, he mis-times it completely and ends up hanging from the guardrails with his legs dangling in the water.

The other lads are pissing themselves laughing until I yell, 'Get hold of him and get him out!' The other boaters in the marina must have thought we were a bunch of drunken halfwits.

Paul is pulled in and unceremoniously dumped on the deck and we leave harbour in the equivalent of the walk of shame. The weather forecast isn't ideal for this kind of boat, but at £1000 a day the pressure is on for me to get the job moving quickly. Fortunately, I have enough experience not to put us in danger. I'm constantly monitoring the weather constantly and the boat owner has every conceivable extra, including a good quality radar system.

For me and Sam it is like being back in the Navy, but for Charlie and Paul, it is fast becoming their worst nightmare. The sea is moderately rough, and they are sat at the back of the boat looking green and projectile vomiting into a bucket every inch of the way. They are neither useful nor ornament so I decide to pull into Weymouth to refuel and drop them off.

Around Portland Bill, at certain tide times, because of the shape of the land mass and the way the tide runs, it can be extremely rough, with masses of water meeting each other. This one is called the Portland Races. The Nautical Almanac (a must have book on any boat) advises to stay well south of Portland Bill in strong winds against strong tide times.

I haven't planned to stop at Portland, and to save time, decide to skirt as close to the Races as I safely can in this boat. As we get closer, it get rougher and rougher, and I can see them all looking at me for reassurance. And I can see they are very worried, so I turn the boat away and head due south until the waves are smaller and they all visibly relax.

I have never seen two happier men than Charlie and Paul when the water flattens off, as we approach Weymouth Marina. I decide we will stay overnight, have a good meal and a couple of beers, and venture forth tomorrow.

The plan is that Sam and I will head off alone towards Ramsgate. Charlie and Paul need no persuasion to accept that decision. The next day is a boaties' dream: bright sunshine, calm seas, and no wind. We make good ground and eventually pull into Portsmouth Gunwharf Quays Marina.

We takes the opportunity to have a nice meal and soak up the ambience at this beautiful outlet, full of shopping, bars and restaurants. The next day visibility is restricted because of fog, but we can see far enough to be safe and my Naval skills with radar make for a safe albeit slow passage to Brighton. At Brighton Marina, we refuel and continue on to Ramsgate.

On the journey up, the Turks have been in touch, and once berthed in Ramsgate Marina, I call them. They say they will come to Ramsgate to see us tomorrow. Charley and I clean the boat and enjoyed the weather, which is glorious. Apparently, the operational Commander from Epping is getting it in the ear about the cost of the boat, and the National Crime Squad bosses are pushing him to get things moving. So the pressure is on, notwithstanding the weather.

Meanwhile, the Commander is trying to liaise with the

Belgian authorities, who are far from helpful with our fight to disrupt organised crime. They are tergiversating over whether or not they will allow us to pick up the immigrants in Belgium, and refuse to officially sanction it, which throes a big bad fly in the ointment.

European cooperation, yes, but only when it suits the host country. We always have to jump through hoops to get things done in Europe. As is often the case, the police are happy for us to proceed but the government officials are the ones who are uncooperative.

The next day the main Turk sends his boys down to look at the boat and finalise plans. Soon, we will be collecting 22 immigrants who must have at least paid £2000 per head for the channel crossing (total of £44,000). My payment on satisfactory landing of these emigrants into the UK is £44,000 plus expenses. Not bad for a week's work.

This is another area where anyone considering working for criminals needs to be careful. It is not uncommon, once you have landed the people, drugs, and/or commodities, for the villains to disappear into the sunset and never pay you. Your average Joe is not in a position to chase the debt, and even if he were, he could end up getting badly hurt or killed if he tried.

The criminals always make promises to pay within a week of the job being done, but quite often this never happens. The cheque is always in the post – you know, I won't come in your mouth and other such lies spring to mind.

The Turks are massively impressed with the boat, and we go back to London to update the boss. I have demanded £22,000 up front before we leave to England,

and the remainder on arrival in the UK AND before the illegal immigrants even leave the boat. Those terms are hard fought but agreed.

The Turks contact me and say the refugees are already in Belgium and can be in the marina area at Blankenberge within 24 hours. I tell the operational Commander, and hear that frantic communications back and forth with the Belgians have continued.

By now, the Turks are ringing me daily and asking when I am leaving. I blame the weather, not feeling well, family problems and every other bullshit story I can think up, which quite frankly starts to wear thin. Then, to my rescue, unwittingly comes British Customs. They definitely wouldn't help us by choice, but yeah, unwittingly.

It was Friday, and into Ramsgate harbour comes the Customs boat that patrols the channel regularly. A mini warship, grey in colour, it is called a Customs Cutter. I immediately ring the Turks and tell them I can't leave and come back whilst this boat is here. They clearly don't believe me, and one of them jumps in his car and drives straight down to see me.

When he arrives, the entire crew from the Cutter are disembarking with their bags for either a weekend at home or a crew change. Either way, I know they are here until Monday. On the jetty, I exchange some pleasantries with them as they pass my boat.

They don't give us a second look because we are polite, chatty and look like what we are purporting to be. Being polite with law enforcement puts them off guard and reduces the chance of you being nicked or warranting further attention by 90%. A thought worth remembering if you are criminally active or feel the police are persecuting you for race or gender reasons. Kindness will go a long way.

I tell Serden (another gopher for the main man) that I will call him as soon as they leave, and he goes back to London a happy guy. Charlie and I go home for the weekend. Family time is precious commodity when you work undercover, so I always go home at every opportunity I can get.

Charlie returns Monday and the Cutter is gone, so I ring the Turks and tell them, 'We are ready to go, the customs boat had gone to sea'.

There is a limit to how much you can stall a criminal organisation, but the Belgians are still playing, silly buggers. The operational commander rings me and gives it the okay, but we have to take an interpreter onboard and we have to issue each illegal immigrant a life jacket and give them a full onboard safety briefing.

You can't make this shit up! What criminal enterprise gives out safety briefings to the people they are trafficking and makes sure they all have a Department of Trade authorised life jackets. Actually, the life jackets aren't a problem; you can hire them for £25 a week. But getting them will have to be somebody else's job. I have enough on my plate.

Wind forward to 2023 with the boat loads of migrants coming over with each wearing a shiny new expensive life Jacket. These are not issued by criminal people smugglers who really don't give a toss whether they drown in the channel or make it all the way. They have been paid and there is no refund policy. The whole thing smacks of government controlled migration with people or agents performing similar roles to mine but without the intention of prosecuting the original organisers

I point blank refuse to take anyone with me who is not a trained undercover operative. I have no clue who is going to be on the other side, or what level of interrogation we might get from the criminals or law enforcement at the Belgian Port. Undercover work and health and safety are, by the very nature of the beast, not compatible. Only government officials who couldn't knock a wank out would be putting ridiculous ideas like this up.

The SAS motto is, 'who dares, wins'. Anybody who doesn't live by that philosophy should not be allowed anywhere near an undercover deployment or the decision processes around it.

I tell the Operational Commander that I can give a safety briefing in a way all nationalities would understand, as air hostesses do on planes. He calls me back the very same day. 'okay, let's do it, is all he says.

The Turks are bringing the up-front money down and the plan is to leave at first light Tuesday. When they arrive and pay the money, I tell them to have the people near the marina tomorrow. 'They should be ready to come onboard two at a time at midnight when everything should be quiet and dark', I say. They tell me I will be contacted on my mobile after 6pm.

Tuesday morning bright and early we leave Ramsgate and set off across the channel with the intention of collecting a full load of 22 illegals. Not long after, the operational Commander rings me. Fortunately, we are still close enough to land to even have a signal.

'Come back, Jay', he says. 'The Belgian government

has said if we pick them up and leave the port of Blankenberge into the channel, we have to keep the migrants and support them in England.

So, ostensibly cooperating governments who could have taken out the organisers on both sides of the channel, can't get their acts together and sort it out. Is it any wonder the migrant crisis is a mess in both the UK and Europe? Really, the person who makes this ridiculous 11$^{th}$ hour decision needs to be taken out and given an ottoman slap.

When we return to Ramsgate, I ring the Turks and tell them the Customs Cutter is hanging around in the Channel and I'm not happy about that. We agree to meet up to return the upfront money, and at that point, the Turks and the head honcho are arrested for Conspiracy to People Traffic, and are charged accordingly. And Charlie and I return the boat to its rightful owner.

At their Crown Court hearing, Serden and Hidir (two of the Turks) plead guilty and are remanded in custody. The head honcho pleads not guilty and elect trial. Despite him speaking fluent English, at great expense the court provides an interpreter and, on his behalf, his Barrister argues his case. He elects not to give evidence, urging that the prosecution cannot prove its case beyond a reasonable doubt.

His Barrister manages to convince the jury that he thought that I was smuggling a boat load of tobacco for him. He is duly acquitted of Conspiracy to People Traffic. British justice at its finest! Another quality jury who would much rather acquit than convict, and unfortunately this is the norm.

There are a lot of police officers who have literally given up and have been nicknamed uniform carriers. I could never do that, but I totally understand why it is happening more and more these days. You get no more money for working long, hard hours banging your head against a brick wall, than you do if you do the bare minimum daily and spend every night at home in the bosom of your family.

# TWENTY-THREE

## Drugs, Guns, and Rock and Roll

In 2003, I sign up to work on two long term operations at the same time --one investigating a drugs and guns supply in Essex, and the other involving an untouchable family involved in a major drugs supply. I nickname the latter, 'The Midlands Mafia'.

On the Essex job, I go by Jack, and on The Midlands Mafia Job, I go under the name Gary. Needless to say, my newfound friend, Tony the multi-hyphenate, will feature heavily on both jobs when the time is right.

The Essex job.

Essex has always had a reputation for drugs, guns and violence, probably because a lot of East End villains move themselves out of London to Essex as they become more successful. Essex has more than its fair share of beautiful women and that could also be because of the adage, most women prefer a bad boy. One thing is for sure: you don't need to look to hard in Essex if you want a gun or cocaine... or a bad boy.

In my experienced opinion, as I've suggested already, a good infiltration is an unstoppable tool in the fight against organised crime. All you need is a good intelligence background, patience and the right persona to deploy (the right person being a courageous risktaker).

Having been dragged up in an extremely rough area of the north, I can relate to all the people who live on a council estate in Essex, which is the central starting point of the pyramid supplying cocaine and guns of every description. Initially, I am drafted into the job on my own and rent myself a council flat.

That is quite easy when it's an estate nobody wants to live in, and there is no shortage of them in the U.K. For months I go about my business like any other wanker resident. My next door neighbour is a heroin addict and above me is a violent alcoholic with an equally alcoholic wife.

They play loud seventies music until three or four am every night. After four nights, I knock on their door and ask them to keep it down a bit, and introduce myself as their neighbour. 'It's bloody impossible to sleep, you know, so could you please keep the volume down?'

Their promise lasts one night, but only because I can hear them knocking lumps out of each other in a violent argument. The policeman in me has to do something, but calling the police isn't an option. So I knock on the door and the fellow opens it with his wife behind him.

'What the fuck is going on here, I'm trying to sleep', I say.

He tries pathetically to thump me, but I move quickly and slap him hard enough around the face that he falls to the floor. 'This is the very last time I'm gonna come up here and be nice with you', I say. 'The next time I will rip your fucking head off and shit down your neck. I don't want to hear any noise at all after midnight, do you understand?'

That's what it takes for peace and quiet to prevail for

me and the other poor residents who have been made to put up with this antisocial behaviour far too long already.

I start visiting the local pub and bookmakers and generally keep myself to myself and don't make too much noise. When I first walk into the pub, it goes completely silent and I half expect to see tumbleweeds blowing through the bar like the old American west bar in the 'O.K. Corral'.

I speak to the barmaid and she asks me harmless questions about myself. I can tell the other people in here are hanging on my answers as well. I tell her my name is Jack, I've split with my wife and lost everything in the divorce case, and that my life has taken a temporary nosedive for me. I tell her where I'm living, and that occasionally, I drive for my mate's haulage company.

In the bookies, nobody speaks to me. There's a man in there every day called Terry who holds court amongst the other punters. I can see in my peripheral vision that he's been staring at me quite a lot, and I deliberately have not made eye contact with him yet.

I put my bets on, eat a sandwich, drink a cup of tea, watch a few races and leave. For months, I continue on at the bookies, always minding my own business. I even take my two German shepherds with me and walk them in the park on the estate at night.

Slowly people start talking to me and I open up enough to build a picture of myself that implies I'm up to no good, without being too specific. One lunchtime, I park an articulated lorry outside the pub, walk in, have a couple of pints, and then leave. It isn't long before everybody in the pub is chatting with me and everyone in the bookies with the exception of Terry.

One of the chaps in the bookies tells me Terry is a main player. If I need any Charlie (cocaine), Terry is the man to talk to. 'Thanks, but I'm sorted for Charlie if I need any', I say.

As I walk out, I notice that same chap has gone over and is now talking to Terry.

On my next visit, the same chap is there but Terry isn't. I'd told this chap earlier that I had 500 cases of beer for sale at £5 a case, and he comes over to me and says, 'I'll have two case of beer'.

I laugh and say, 'sorry, mate, the minimum order is 50 cases'.

A couple of day later, I'm in the bookies and Terry walks straight up to me and says, 'I've been told you have some beer for sale at £5 a case. My mate would like 50 cases'.

I smile to myself because 50 cases is all I had. We agree I will deliver them to the off licence that's nearby and Terry will pay me. When I deliver the cases Terry pays me as represented, our friendship is sealed. He tells me he is the man for Charlie locally, it is good quality, and he would extend me mates' rates. I tell him I'm already hooked up in that regard, but thank him for the offer anyway.

Once well established in the Essex bookies and the pub, I expand to another pub which is known for drugs supply and firearms. It is frequented by a lot of gypsies who live nearby. The landlady is a lovely woman called Estelle, but on my first visit it is apparent she not controlling the pub (the clients are).

In here, the atmosphere is different. I am immediately asked by one of the lads who I am and what brought me to the pub.

'That's my business, isn't it, mate?' I say. 'But if you must know, I've come here for a quiet pint because where I normally go on the other side of the estate it's full of fucking idiots'.

That answer is accepted. I proceed to have a couple of pints and speak to the landlady, who in the politest possible way gives me the third degree. I am more forthcoming with her, giving her my history including the bookies, the pub, the alcoholic neighbour, and my mate Terry the coke dealer. She already knows of Terry, and I am confident the entire story will be repeated to anyone that mattered in her pub.

Now is a good time to bring Tony into the operation. Because we get on like a house on fire and are laughing and joking, people start to gravitate around the pool table. We play winner stays on, and as a result, we get to know a few of the regulars. Blending in is the name of the game.

A couple of weeks later there is a party night for one of the local gypsies, and Estelle invites us along. The pub is rammed, and we have a fantastic night. Clearly, word has gotten around about us, and my story to Estelle has come back to me time and gain via the regulars.

The main man of the gypsies eyes us with some suspicion, but I would not have expected anything less; they tend to be very insular anyway. Cocaine use is going on in the pub in open view, and one girl's gets her tits out, so a couple of the guys can snort cocaine off her bodacious mammaries.

Two women hit on Tony, including Ms Bodacious. She tries to push Tony into the lady's toilet, but he resists. She's quite resilient, so she speaks frankly. 'Come and fuck me or be forever known as gay boy'.

Tony laughs. 'That's right, I'm gay', and a group of girls started chanting, 'gay boy, gay boy', and everyone joins in laughing. Then, as if on cue, everyone starts singing 'is this the way to Amarillo', by Tony Christie. Tony and I start singing loudly and doing some actions and the whole pub joins in. At the end of the evening, we are invited to stay late drinking and getting a late-night curry delivered.

That night we are introduced to a guy called Damien. He offers Tony cocaine at £50 a gramme and says it's 80% pure. Tony agrees and the wrap changes hands in the toilet. It turns out to be 24% pure. The next time Tony sees Damien, he says, 'that gear was shit'.

Damien apologised and says he'll make sure that doesn't happen again. Tony and I continue regularly visiting the pub, playing pool and chatting to Estelle. On one occasion, the boss of the gypsies comes in. He's called Mitchell, and we speak to him.

He hates people calling them gypsies and identifies his group as 'Showmen'. His wife is a lovely woman, and talking to them opens up a new perspective on the people living on the local site. Mitchell and Tony get on particularly well.

Damien continues offering cocaine to Tony and Tony agrees to buy an ounce, but he specified the purity has to be good this time. Damien initially wants £1200, but after a bit of haggling, he agrees to £1100 for the ounce. Tony is then taken to another pub, where he meets Darren and John.

John is a lively character, funny and good company, and we became good friends with him. It's a shame he is criminally active, because he is a guy we could both relate to, and in any other world, we would have been good mates. John and

Damien leave Tony and Darren in the pub to go and collect the ounce of cocaine. When they return, the deal is done and Tony leaves. The cocaine is 26 grammes instead of 28 (short by two grammes) and it is only 20% pure. Probably John and Damien have nicked a gramme each. As I say, there is no loyalty in the drugs world.

John has a good job as a container repair manager at the docks with a company car. He mentions he has some sawn-off shotguns for sale, so Tony introduces him to me. I meet John at the pub and we go to his car at the docks. He then direct me to an empty container which, with the door closed, is pitch black.

Suddenly he open the door and fires the weapon. The noise is deafening, and I shit myself, literally. I had a vision of the shot ripping into me as it bounced off the container wall. John is laughing hysterically, and when he opens the door fully, I can see that he has fired at a piece of wood propped up against the back wall of the container.

There is a neat single hole right through it. He has used a cartridge with a single, large ball bearing in it and he could easily have killed one of us as it ricocheted around the container. I have to laugh, as I thought this guy was as mad as me; so my guess is, we're gonna get on.

I buy the gun off him, we return to the estate, and we part company. But before we do, John says he also has a sniper rifle with ammunition for sale which can kill a man over a mile away because it has a telescopic sight and a silencer attached. I says I'm interested, and he says he can get it from his mate Simon at the farm.

Simon is represented as the main man in the area for cocaine. John says Tony can have as much as he wants to sell, even kilos. I ask John to introduce Tony to Simon. I also introduce Tony to Terry and Tony buys 4 grammes of cocaine off him at the bookies for £30 a gramme.

This time it's 35% pure – the highest purity yet for the Essex buys. Damien introduces Tony to another drug dealer called Nathan, and Tony starts doing business with him as well. We make Estelle's pub our home base, and over time, Tony becomes very friendly with Mitchell and his cousin Henry. All is hunky dory.

Henry is an extremely hard man, and on one occasion at the pub, arrives after closing totally pissed. Estelle refuses to let him in, so he punches through a wire reinforced glass door panel. To get through that must have been some hit, and we both decide we wouldn't like to be on the receiving end of a punch from Henry.

Tony continues buying cocaine from John and quite often he would bring the drugs to my flat. John takes me to where the sniper rifle is stored on behalf of the owner, and we also pick up ammunition for it. John is an accomplished engineer, and at the flat, decided the silencer and telescopic sight need some work on it. He says he'll show the owner Simon his find and will get a reduction on the price.

He leaves the flat with it and I stay at home. As is often the way, John is subjected to a routine stop by uniform cops for drink driving and is arrested when they find the sniper rifle in his car. I am blissfully unaware of this development and receive a call from John as soon as he is released from custody.

I can tell by the tone of his voice that he is mega pissed

off. 'Where are you, Jack', he says.

'I'm at the flat'.

'Wait there, I'm on my way over'.

Whilst I'm waiting, the operational Commander phones me and tells me what has happened with the gun. I tell him John is on his way over to my flat. He advises me to get away from there, 'and fast'.

'This isn't an option', I say. 'I'll have to deal with whatever comes up'.

When he says okay, I am pleased for once to have a boss with some backbone who believes in Tony and me and our abilities to do what we are being paid to do. Less experienced undercover operatives would have fled, signalling the demise of the whole operation.

When John arrives, he is drinking from a full bottle of Smirnoff and I can readily see he is angry as a hornet. Tepidly, we get in his car, and then he drives off at 100 miles per hour in a 30mph residential area. When he hits the speed humps, I fly out of my seat and smash my sunglasses on the car roof; that's how fast we're going.

He insists we share the vodka, and within 15 minutes, we have drunk half a bottle. Meanwhile, he has been looking in the rear-view mirrors constantly, and he eventually slows to within the speed limit and starts making calls.

He says to somebody, 'yes, I've got it with me. I will be with you in 30 minutes'.

The next call is guarded, but he does ask, 'are you ready to do this?'.

My mind is racing, but I think, whatever he has planned, I will have to deal with.

We stop outside a gun shop that sells shotguns. John

tells me to wait in the car, that he has to pick something up. I wait for what seems like an eternity before he returns to the car with what looks like a long gun in a cover. He then turn the car round and says, 'we are going home. You have passed the test. You're not a grass. If you were, you would have legged it from the car'.

He then goes on to explain about being arrested with the gun and accept that it must have been a routine stop. I say, 'fuck me, I'm not surprised you've been driving like that whilst swigging down a bottle of Vodka', and we both laugh like loonies. He drops me back at the flat, giving me a parting hug, and goes home. I walk in to the flat and have to change my boxers just to be on the safe side of the crack.

John introduces Tony to Simon and Tony purchases four and a half ounces of cocaine for £5000 that tests at 78% purity. We then know we are dealing at the right level in the food chain.

John contacts me and says he's at the pub with Tony, who says he has a couple of stun guns for sale. I say that I will be up there soon. When I arrive, John and Tony are playing pool but stop when I arrived and place a rubber mat on the bar floor. Hysterically laughing, John tells me he and Tony have been testing the stun guns on each other.

Tony stands on the mat and John zaps him with the cheaper of the two stun guns. No problem. Then John zaps Tony with the expensive one and Tony jerks uncontrollably and falls backward. We are all laughing like children playing with a new toy.

John has a go with both and then I have a go with both. The pain from the better one is truly intense, but we are laughing so much we barely notice it and don't much care. Other people in the pub are stood there with their mouths wide open. Estelle says, 'are you three fucking mad?' And Tony says, 'Mad Jack McFucking Mad & his Mad Mates, at your service'. We all laugh hysterically.

There is another social night at the pub, and everyone is there, including Mitchell, who is with a couple of friends that we had never seen before. When Tony and I are walking in, I overhear Mitchell saying to his mates, 'There is a strong smell of pork in here tonight.

That is a reference to us possibly being pigs (cops), but I ignore the comment (but tell Tony at the end of the evening). Tony isn't happy at all because he and Mitchell have become quite close, and he has been to Mitchell's and Henry's homes a couple of times. Whenever Mitchell is in the pub alone, he would pick Tony as his friend of choice above everyone else there and offer to share his cocaine with Tony. Mitchell is a really heavy user and will go into the toilet six or seven times a night.

A couple of days later, I have forgotten Mitchell's comment and we go into another local pub for lunch. Mitchell is there holding court with about ten of the lads from the site. Mitchell shouts, 'alright boys, how are you doing?' And to my surprise, Tony says, 'don't talk to me, you two-faced snide cunt'.

At that time, the whole gang faces up to us and two of the lot produce knives. 'Do you want me to chiv (stab) him?' one guy says.

I'm thinking, fuck me, Tony. I know we can both have a row, but the odds are stacked against us here.

To my surprise, Mitchell says, 'calm down, boys', and he walks both of us back out of the pub -- with him walking forward and us walking backwards.

Tony says, 'you have been bad mouthing us in the pub and I'm fucking pissed off because I thought we were mates'.

Mitchell says, 'on my babies' eyes, I haven't been. I would never do that to you guys. I like both of you. If I've pissed you off, I'm really sorry. Come and have a drink'.

When Mitchell gives Tony a hug, his boys are watching as the doors to the pub have been held open. We go into the pub and Mitchell says to the barman, 'get my mates a drink'.

We spend the afternoon with them, and I must say, they are all complete gents from that point on. Tony and I say, 'you could teach a lot of people something about loyalty to each other and family values'.

In the film 'Snatch', they repeatedly say, 'I fucking hate Pikeys'. Mitchell point out they aren't Pikeys, they are showman, and there is a huge difference. One thing is a fact. Mitchell, his wife Karen and Henry never do anything that makes me believe what Mitchell says isn't true.

Mitchell did say to me that afternoon, 'Your mate Tony is ballsy; men have died for less''. I laugh and say, "yes he is, but I need to have a chat with him about timing', and we both laugh.

At the pub, I meet a guy called Dean who is selling handguns with ammunition for £1000 each; he had ten but he has already sold five. He has one with him that he shows me, but I think the price is too steep and knock him back. He leaves the pub and comes back later.

This time, he says he has a pump action sawn-off shotgun that he wants £700 for. I agree to buy it and arrange to meet later to pay and collect. We meet again and I purchase from him the pump action shotgun with a bag of ammunition.

Tony continues buying drugs from Terry, Nathan, Simon, Simons dad, David, and two new guys called George and Ricky. It's a family affair. The purity varies between 20% and 80% whilst the price remains between £30 and £50 per gramme and £1000 to £1200 per ounce regardless of the purity.

Paying more for the cocaine is no guarantee of purity, and all the people we deal with have no idea of how pure the gear is or isn't. Yet they are representing all they are selling is top quality. The best on the market.

I meet Dean again at the Pub and he offers for sale a sawn-off shotgun that belongs to a mate of his. He wants £400 for it. I agree to buy it and Dean sends one of his boys to pick it up. He return with it, and I have a look at it in a quiet area of the pub car park.

Dean can't open it as there is two cartridges jammed in the barrels. He starts banging it on the floor when the gun goes off, narrowly missing my legs. We both jump a mile and then started laughing. Dean finally gets the barrels open and ejects the cartridges. He wipes the gun down with a rag to get rid of fingerprints and gives it to me. He then recovers the cartridges that have been in the gun and put them in his pocket and gives me a box of cartridges.

One evening, Tony is at the flat on his own and decides to take a walk around the local park to get some fresh air. During the walk, he comes across a group of about eight 16 to 18-year olds who are smoking joints.

As he passes, the biggest guy in the group says, we

know your name... *wanker*.

Tony ignores him and continues walking, but the whippersnapper shouts even louder, 'we Know your name...*Wanker Wanker*.

Tony continues on but the fool then screams, 'oi, we KNOW your name...*WANKER WANKER WANKER*!!!

When Tony spins round and starts walking back, they all stand up like tough guys. When Tony reaches them, he says, 'Well, there is one of me mates and eight of you. I make that fight o'clock', mimicking the Pimm's advert.

Then he starts walking towards the biggest lad there. They all shit themselves and backed away. But the big lad says, 'Sorry, mister, sorry, mister'.

Tony points at his nose. 'You are a bunch of fucking cowards, and you will remember this day for the rest of your lives. The day one guy fronted all of you up and not one of you had the balls to have a go alone or together. Wankers all of you'.

He then turns and walks away. They don't know how close they came, each and every one, to being put in hospital that day.

John takes Tony to look at a Hydroponic Skunk (Cannabis) factory that he has set up and is running for another group of criminals in a couple of containers located on the docks. Tony says the set up is impressive and the skunk is growing like Jack's bean stalk.

Cheekily and cleverly, John is using the docks to provide the huge amount of electricity that is required to run a good hydroponics gig. He has run a cable off of the main supply to the docks and then split that into two, one for each 40- foot container. Without doubt, that John is a very clever man.

John says Tony and me are the only people he trusts enough to show the facility, that would clearly put Cheech and Chong in Seventh Heaven. Meanwhile, I plan to go home for some well-earned R & R, but before leaving, we tell the operational Commander about the Skunk factories.

He asks for my advice, and I tell him in no uncertain terms that John, Tony and I are the only people who know about it. If it was raided, I say, it would cause us a world of pain and would probably kill the operation.

The Commander agrees not to do anything about it, and I leave Tony at the flat and bounce home. I almost blow a gasket when Tony phones me up to tell me the team raided the Skunk factory the next day, contrary to my advice.

To say John is pissed off would wins understatement of the year. He wasn't there when they were raided the place, but as soon as he learns about it he goes to the pub and phones Tony. 'I need to speak now. Be at the pub in five minutes. I'm gonna kill some cunt'.

Tony again proves he has balls of steel by leaving the flat immediately to meet John at the pub. On the route over, however, he gets a phone call from the landlady Estelle. She is frightened. 'John is at the pub', she says, 'and he has a huge carving knife and he is stabbing it in the bar and telling everyone to fuck off out of the pub, that he is gonna kill someone'.

Tony tells her he's on his way. When he gets there, John is wired for sound. His eyes are wild as a Hyenas. When Tony walks in, John sticks the knife in the bar. 'Mate, I know it wasn't you as soon as you answered your phone'.

'What the fuck is going on?' Tony says.

'Only three people have been to the Skunk factory. Me, you and Gary the fucking grass', John says.

'Calm down, mate', Tony says. 'You can't say he's a grass until you know 100%.

'I know he is. I phoned him, he didn't answer, I left him a message, he hasn't rang me, and he hasn't fucking turned up. That is the actions of a grass and I'm gonna fucking kill him'.

Tony manages to calm John down. 'Don't do anything until Jack gets back from Holland and we can sort this out between us', Tony says. ' Jack's gone to sort out a big cocaine deal and he can't be having it fucked up just because of the Skunk'.

But John is still livid.

'Look', Tony says, 'there may be other reasons why the Skunk got raided, like the electricity wires. The power people could have gone snooping around or something'.

John still isn't having any of it. 'I know it's that cunt Gary, and it's not the first time I've thought he was a grass'.

I go straight back to work, and we have an urgent meeting with the operational Commander. My blood is boiling, but I remain calm but do speak candidly. 'There is no point in asking us for advice and then completely ignoring it. We are happy we can convince people we are not cops, but if you make us look like we could be a grass, you are putting our lives at risk'.

The Commander at first does not want to hear this reality-check.

'Your raiding of that Skunk factory could have caused the death of Tony. You have also now put Gary at risk, and he is not a grass at all. There literally is no bigger sin amongst organised criminals than being a grass'.

By now, I must have been getting on the Commander's nerves, but I carry on raving.

'I have known of people who have been maimed and killed who were not informants, but some criminal wrongly thought they were'.

The Commander holds up his hand. 'Fair enough', he says. 'I apologise, okay, and I promise never to jump the gun again. I don't want you placed at unnecessary risk. You're at risk as it is'.

Now things have changed. If the police receive information from any intelligence source that someone's life is in danger, even if they are a major criminal, the police must tell them they are at risk and that someone is gunning to kill them. This law is introduced by the European Court of Human Rights in 1998, ordering police to issue 'Threat to Life Notices' to people at risk of being killed.

I don't know what Gary is told exactly, but I know a notice to this effect is served on him. We don't see him for a long time on the estate, and John remained wrongly convinced that he was a police informant as a result.

Tony visit Simon's farm again and purchases cocaine at £1000 per ounce. He is also shown a rifle, which is ideal if Tony or I want to kill someone from a distance. They won't even know we are there, assassin style.

The rifle has a silencer and plenty of ammo. The rifle is test fired at the farm, and without any gunshot noise, the bullet hits a small target 500 yards away. Silent but deadly. Tony has paid £700 for it.

Tony is now buying cocaine in four-ounce deals from

Simon for £4400 or £1100 per ounce with a purity level generally of around 70%. The other dealers Tony deals with have varied purity levels, between 20% and 40%. When Tony buys nine ounces of cocaine, the price is then reduced to £1000 per ounce and Simon offers it for a kilo at £35,000.

The operational Commander decides that we have identified all the drug dealers and firearm's suppliers in the area, but he is concerned for Gary's safety. We are aware the if we are identified as undercover cops that it would cancel any rumour that Gary is a snitch. So the operational team start the arrest phase, and Tony and I go home for a well-earned break.

In the searches that follow, guns, cash and a couple of police uniforms are found. Tony and I receive a huge amount of thanks from Essex Constabulary at a number of levels. The last compliment, however, comes unexpectedly from John's wife, Donna.

Donna is glad we have put an end to John's unnecessary foray into the criminal underworld and hopes at some time in the future to get back the family man she loves. She goes on to say, 'in any other life, we all could have been good friends'. Apparently, she and John had even discussed me being a God parent to their son.

We have since heard that Mitchell died not long after the operation concluded, of heart failure. Both Tony and I are gutted to hear that, as he was far too young to die.

# TWENTY-FOUR

## The Hit Man and Hit Her

At the same time as this operation is running, I take on two additional operations -- one short term, as a contract killer, and the second, as a cold infiltration into an untouchable Mafia style family located in the midlands who are selling large volumes of cocaine and cannabis.

It is more common than people would think for disgruntled, generally law-abiding people to try and hire a contract killer to murder someone who they feel has wronged them, or purely to receive an insurance pay-out.

On this occasion, I am introduced to a couple who are convinced that a family friend has befriended their mum and is milking her of her entire life savings, in the region of a £750,000. As far as they are concerned, this is their future inheritance that is being swindled.

Using the name Chenty (a nickname from when I was a child), I meet them initially at Asda in Greenhithe and then in a layby on an industrial estate south of the Dartford tunnel. Shockingly at least to me, the woman, Cherie, is heavily pregnant, as this leads incongruously to discussions to end her mum's friend's life.

Cherie says the murder must take place as soon as possible, and that they would provide the Sawn-off shotgun to do this old fella in. She claims, rather callously, that if she weren't pregnant, she would do it herself. She admits she is a heartless, callous cow and claims that she could do my job.

I give them a number of opportunities to change their minds and not go ahead with the killing, but they insist that it must happen sooner rather than later. I'm recording everything they say to me, of course without their knowledge. Ultimately, they are arrested for conspiracy to murder, arrested, and put before the court.

A conviction should have been a foregone conclusion, but they are found not guilty. Had I not already seen the judicial system for the farce it is, I would have been gutted. This country gets the problems it deserves, and until the justice system starts working for the decent VAST majority, rather than the dishonest few, things will not change for the better.

# TWENTY-FIVE

### Whoa, We're Going to Barbados!

The next job running concurrently with the others is offered to another undercover officer initially, and he agrees to do it, but his wife says no way and he has to tell the control centre he must decline at his wife's insistence.

It is then offered to me, and I agree to do it. I know Denise would be completely against it, but I have been so many years putting up with Denise's jealousy issues that I have long since stopped pandering to her tantrums. If I minded an affair, there are ample opportunities for me to do so every day of the week.

This job involves infiltrating a criminal gang who has booked and paid for a holiday in Barbados. The infiltration is to start in Barbados and then continue when back on U.K. soil.

The reason the first guy bailed out is not about safety. This job deploys with an undercover female, and we are going to Barbados purporting to be a couple. I can hear the female readers, saying, 'I wouldn't let my husband do that in a thousand years – to Barbados with another woman in the same bed?'

I understand that thought process, but if your relationship is strong, there is nothing to worry about. Not all men are serial shaggers.

I have one meeting of four hours with the woman I will be spending the next year with as my partner, and we get on like a house on fire. She is bubbly, chatty, confident and I know she will be great on the job. Her name is Heather, and I'm using the name Gary. As a complete aside, she is also engaged to one of my best mates, who is also a top-drawer undercover operative.

Denise goes into orbit when I tell her about the job. She is a complete pain in the arse every day until the day of departure arrived.

We fly out to Barbados on Virgin Atlantic Premium economy. The main man, Richard, with his partner Stephanie are in first class, and the other gang members all travel economy. We have booked into the same hotel in the St Lawrence gap area of Barbados called 'Turtle Beach'.

Heather and I have the best room in the hotel. We see them and they see us in arrivals at Barbados, but we ignore them and make our own way to the hotel and check in. Heather has with her an expensive diamond ring (which she didn't wear at the start of the holiday) and which belongs to her mum.

We decide in the short term that we will make no effort to interact with the gangster family. The operational Commander isn't overly keen with this strategy, but we convince him that slowly, slowly, catch a monkey, is the way forward. I know his bosses would absolutely berate him if this strategy fails, due to the cost alone, and to be honest, I am shocked that he has even got this plan through; it's a testament to how much confidence his Chief Constable has in him.

There is a great deal of jealousy and cynicism around

expensive undercover deployments, with most senior officers thinking we are just on a jolly boy outing. But there is nothing jolly about going on holiday with someone who isn't your partner. You have to spend the next fortnight in their company 24 hours a day. That is a good test of any relationship, never mind a friendship that's four hours old.

Both of us have lively personalities, so it isn't long before other people in the hotel have joined us, and every night is loads of fun. I can see Richard and all his group are watching our group loving the holiday. On the beach, we go on a fast Hobe-cat Catamaran, and there isn't anyone on the beach who can't hear me laughing and Heather screaming in abject terror, as we rocket around at lightning speed driven by the captain affectionately known as Blackjack.

That is not because he likes the sweet, but he says he is a black version of Jack Sparrow from 'Pirates of the Caribbean', and has christened himself 'Blackjack' accordingly. After six days, the bossman calls us, and when we tell him that we have had only passing pleasantries with the gangster family, I can hear the panic in his voice.

Heather and I assure him we can pull it off, and by the time the conversation finishes, he has relaxed again considerably. One day, all the girls in the family are in the sea about waste deep, and Heather decided she will swim out further up the beach and then swim back to shore, going through them.

It is a great idea, but the current around this beach is far stronger than we have anticipated, and it isn't long before Heather is in some difficulty. I have to run into the sea and swim straight through them to save her, and then I pull her back into the shore coughing and spluttering. But it has the desired effect, and the girls started chatting.

We laugh about it that night though at the time it was far from funny. She was in real danger and could have drowned. It gradually becomes obvious to us that the girls are asking Heather questions on behalf of the boys, including Richard the gangster patriarch in particular.

I have on a solid gold Rolex worth £22,000, that has clearly drawn Richard's eye, so one evening, all the guests are invited to a cocktail party at the hotel sponsored by a local diamond retailer. When we attend, Richard and all his gang are there. We speak to them about the holiday, diamonds, fast cars and cannabis. You know, the subjects all posh people discuss when in Barbados.

As it turns out, Richard, Daniel and Pete are smoking joints constantly. Initially, Richard is quiet, but the more he smokes the more he starts to lighten up. He tells me he is loaded and has £125,000 worth of cars alone. I tell him I own my own boat and deliver boats from Southampton for a living.

Richard invites us to join the family for dinner at a local restaurant, and I pay for everybody there before Richard has a chance too (knowing he will owe us dinner). Then one evening I produce Heather's ring and propose to her in front of Richard's gang and other guests. This was a plan that Heather and I had conceived during the first week.

We have a huge party and retire to the room in the early hours, mortally wounded. A couple of days later, we are having breakfast. Pete, Richard's number one man, comes over and says, 'we are going diamond shopping, would you like to join us?'

We agree to share a ride into the main town, and once at the shop, Richard is trying desperately to show off and buy an expensive diamond ring for Stephanie, but his card keeps being declined. I'm sure it's only because it is an unexpected and huge transaction in a foreign country, and bank security procedures have refused the payment.

Richard is mega embarrassed, and I offer tongue in cheek to lend him the money £15000, but he won't allow that to happen. He decides to pay a deposit and organise the money over the next few days and pay the balance in cash. The boys offer me a joint, but I say I've never smoked though did have a heavy cocaine habit in the day.

For the remainder of the holiday, we socialise and chat, but nothing of a criminal nature is discussed. I tell the boss I am a good judge of character, and assessing the situation, and Richard will definitely want to see us back in the U.K. So the holiday comes to an end and we all return to the UK on the same flight.

Richard and Stephanie come down to sit with us and have drinks on the way back. We exchange numbers with everyone in the group bar Richard and agree to visit them in their hometown.

A couple of weeks later, Heather and I go to visit them for a social weekend. Richard arrives with Pete in Richard's new black Range Rover Vogue, driven by Muller who is Richard's regular driver. I have towed my 25-foot speed boat with twin engines so we can go out on a romp. Their eyes bug out when they see it.

We then go to watch Richard's football team, the 'Skinners' (a piss take on his use of cannabis play in a competition. It is a social weekend and nothing criminal is ever discussed.

The next meeting, I go on my own and am taken to Richard's home -- a mobile home on the grounds of his mum and dad. Richard and Stephanie have booked a trip to go back to Barbados for Christmas, and have paid £14,000 for the holiday.

In late September, I invite Richard and his driver down to Southampton for a weekend. He agrees to come, and I decide this is a good time to bring my old mate Tony into the operation. Then Heather and I are invited to a football presentation dinner, and we agree to go.

On the weekend of the football match, the girls and boys go out separately. While I am with the gang (other than Richard), I take a several 'fake' calls where I tell the person on the other end, 'everywhere is dry at the moment and I can't get anything for them'.

The boys lap it up, obviously taking that to be a drugs call, and I'm convinced they will pass that bit on to Richard. I also tell them I am owed £40,000 for some work I have done, but the guy is refusing to pay me. The inference being, that it is a movement of drugs by boat.

On a car journey, we have a general chat about the price difference for drugs in different areas, and I say that Southampton is generally expensive. We go to Richard's place in separate cars, and by the time I walked in, there is about £15,000 in twenty-pound notes sitting on the coffee table. And most of the people there are smoking joints.

Later, Muller Richards driver reveals to me that Richard is a major supplier, and if I need any drugs, to speak to Richard. When I do, I say, 'I didn't know I was dealing with a big honcho drug dealer', and he laugh and says, 'You didn't think I got all the money and car running a burger van did you?'

He does run a burger van, but it is purely a front to launder cash. Richard says he knows I was into drugs as soon as he saw my Rolex in Barbados.(another case of gangsters stereo typing people they meet) That evening, we go out in the main town, and it is apparent that all the pub bouncers are frightened of Richard's family.

There is no queueing to get in, and in some places, we don't pay for drinks. Later, when we pick up some food, we don't have to pay for any of it. I agree to take some drugs back to Southampton the next day, and get a nine-ounce bar of Cannabis for £240.

I start ordering drugs regularly from Richard, calling the cocaine champagne and a nine-bar of cannabis a beer. Initially, Richard offer me cocaine at £1200 per ounce, but I say, 'no thanks, that's too expensive'. He then says a kilo of cocaine is £32,000, but I say that I can't handle that much as my customers are all just rich yachties.

Whenever I order drugs on the phone and show up at the mobile home, Richard or one of his boys will always drive away on a quad bike and return with what I have ordered. So it is located elsewhere, hidden in the extensive grounds surrounding the house

Richard and Muller agree to come down to Southampton for a weekend with a couple of ounces of cocaine, and I am sworn to secrecy, not because of the drugs, but due to the young girls they are bringing with them. I book them into the best hotel in the area, with a top floor suite each.

In anticipation of them coming, Tony and I have been regularly drinking in two popular bars in the main strip.

As a result, everyone knows us. and because Tony is a good-looking charmer, attractive women are never far away. They arrive on Saturday afternoon and take the girls straight up to their rooms for some afternoon delight.

Before getting down to business, Muller gives Tony the two ounces of cocaine and a kilo of cannabis from a secret panel in the Range Rover. Tony and I agree to meet them later at Town Quay and give them a run out on my speedboat.

When we pick them up, Richard tells me the cocaine comes from his mum and I can have it for £1050 per ounce. The girls have gone off shopping in West Quay shopping centre, so we blatted round on the boat at speeds in excess of 40 knots, jumping over the wake of large boats and sometimes flying ten feet in the air.

They both hang on for dear life, but in the end, they say they love it and we agree to meet later for food and a night on the town. We speak about the money we have made in our lives, and Richard says he has more cash than he can cope with. He estimate he has over half a million pounds stashed near his home.

The night is a roaring success, and loads of people play an unwitting part in our deception by coming up and hugging and talking to us as if they had known us all their lives. The next day, the four of them head home, and Tony and I are reminded never to mention about this weekend in front of ladies.

I introduce another undercover operative to buy cannabis from Richard, as it isn't my scene, but Tony and I continue buying cocaine. I am introduced to Richard's family and learn that him mum and dad take ownership and control of the cocaine supply.

The entire family lives like kings with the front of the house looking like a supercar showroom. The house has been extended and modernised beyond all recognition from its original foot- print, and everything inside is dripping expensive and posh.

I am allowed to eat Sunday dinner with the family around the dining room table. I even ring Richard on the hotel phone whilst he was on holiday in Antigua, and when he realises it's me, he is pleased as punch to hear from me and says he looks forward to getting back for a night out.

When one of the cocaine deals is several grammes light, Richard's dad apologises and says he will make it up to me on the next one. On my next visit, Richard informs me that someone had stolen 10 kilos of cannabis from one of his stashes in the woods surrounding the house, and that he is mega pissed off.

I am glad I didn't know he was hiding it in holes in the floor in the woods. Richard believes some local pikeys have taken it, and says they will be sorted by the family in due course. 'That's a worry', I say. 'Could it have been the cops?'

'No, no', Richard says, 'They know what we do. They can't get near us, as we are too good for them'. I smiled inwardly.

Richard asks me if I would be willing to bring Puff (cannabis) back from southern Spain by boat. He offers to pay me £150 per kilo. I say, 'yeah, sure', as he reckon it is only £350 a kilo in Spain and portends to make a killing.

On one occasion, Richard isn't feeling well and his mother supplies me the cocaine wearing surgical gloves. She says, 'you can have four ounces at a time for £4000'.

I'm asked by the covert control centre to involve an Egyptian called Mo on the job, as he hasn't done any work for a while. I arrange a simple task for him driving up and collecting some drugs for me. My agreement to use him is definitely a huge mistake. He's a complete liability, having no experience with writing evidence.

Not to mention, he gets totally lost, can't find Richard's place, and comes across as a complete buffoon. Mo clearly cannot be trusted to organise a piss-up in a brewery! I wouldn't trust him to buy a kilo of sugar, never mind cannabis or cocaine. The only thing he is useful for is being Egyptian. That's where his qualities start and end.

Unfortunately, there are some undercover operatives who have been recruited purely for their ethnicity rather than their abilities. Don't get me wrong, though. There are some amazing undercovers from a non-white background, but Mo is most definitely not one of them. He reminds me very much of the fake Sheik that worked for the Sun newspaper, but without the successes. Because Mo needs wet nursing even to get himself dressed, and I vow never to use him again.

We continue to buy cocaine and cannabis from the family, with Tony ultimately purchasing nine ounces of cocaine from them. The arrest phase then follow, and we are all commended by the Chief Constable and the Crown Court Judge for the arrests and convictions of a prolific, previously untouchable family.

The Essex job and the Midlands job come first and second in the government's awards for most successful, well executed drugs operations of 2005.

# TWENTY-SIX

## If I Could Turn Back Time

In 2005, Denise, the children and I discover Turkey. I have been all over the world, and Turkey is by far the safest place with the friendliest people I have ever visited. I cannot for the life of me understand why it has a bad reputation in the U.K. as somewhere not to holiday or visit.

We have gone to the same resort every year from 2005 onwards because of the value for money and idyllic setting which is Olu Deniz. A lot of the resort areas are empty during the winter months, because it is very cold.

A large number of Kurdish men travel from their homes on the borders of southeast Turkey, and work in the hundreds of restaurants and bars for the summer season, returning home in November. I originally thought they were Turkish, but now I know the Turks hate them with a passion and accuse them of destroying the Turk's reputation internationally.

Every time we visit Turkey we eat in a lively restaurant/dance bar and become friendly with the staff. A waiter called Mustafa, who is Kurdish, always makes sure we are well fed and watered, and over time, he joins us for a drink at the end of the evening.

In summer 2007, he asks Denise and I if he can have

our email addresses and correspond over the winter period. We give them to him, and not long after we return home, he emails Denise, thanking us for using the restaurant and offering to find us cheaper accommodation next year if we come back.

He asks if we can chat on messenger, and we do a couple of chats, but my keyboard skills are crap and I quickly grow bored of it. Occasionally, I will come home from work, and Denise would say, Mustafa has been online and tells me what he has been up to. And I don't think anything of it.

One day Denise says, 'Mustafa told me he's been kicked out of his flat and living rough. He wonders if we can lend him £600 as a deposit for another rental'.

'No', I tell her, 'we don't really know him and that is a lot of money for a Turkish rental'.

Denise isn't happy with my stubborn stance and accuses me of being cruel and heartless. She continues talking to him over the winter, and often when she's online to him, I go to the Gym. Our computer is in the spare bedroom, so occasionally I will pass some pleasantries to him whilst Denise is chatting with him, as she's a speedy typer.

A couple of months later, Denise show me a picture of Mustafa with black eyes and cuts to his face. He looks like he's been in a fight that he lost, or has been tortured. He has told her that he fell down a flight of stairs and he needs £1000 for hospital treatment, and wonders if we can lend him the money.

Again, I say, 'absolutely not!'

At the time, I'm earning £40,000 per year, Denise is at £12,000, and we simply do not have £1000 laying around.

I get to thinking, however, that if he has been in a fight, he's not that good a friend. This is a turning point for Denise and I, as she 'secretly' sends him £200 from our joint account (thinking I would not notice).

I do notice a change in Denise, but I cannot put my finger on it. The penny drops, so to speak, when I walk into our house and find Denise chatting on MSN Messenger to Mustafa and she immediately closes the conversation screen down.

I say nothing and pretend I don't notice. The next time I'm home alone, I retrieve all the historic conversations, and it makes for shocking reading. Over time, he has been saying what an arsehole I am working long hours and I don't deserve her. Can you believe it?

Amazingly, he has told her that he has fallen in love with her and is encouraging her to get as much money as she can and run away to Turkey with him. Not kidding! She is being coy about it but not dismissing the idea at all. And he has persisted for months without her shutting him down.

We are due to arrive in Turkey for a family holiday in August 2008, and it is all paid for. I continue to monitor the conversations, which are hurtful to me, without letting Denise know, of course. She has been giving him small amounts of money regularly, apparently, which I never noticed.

I know he is scamming her, but declaring what I know wouldn't have changed the outcome -- and now I have a bigger picture to think of regarding my whole relationship with the mother of my children.

In late June-early July conversations with him, she says she is going to tell me she is going clothes shopping whilst I am round the pool with the kids. She will come and meet him. He then asked her if she would have sex with him, and she has agreed. That conversation is terminal for our marriage.

Even if Denise saw him for what he was, a romance scammer, and stopped all contact, as far as I am concerned, our marriage was over. She has been accusing me of being unfaithful all our married life, and I never thought we would end up here, with her embarking on an affair with a Kurd.

I am surprised for obvious reasons, but also because Denise's dad had an affair which mentally broke Denise's mum and caused her to be sectioned. Denise has never forgiven her dad for that, and I put her insane jealousy down to her poor experience with her dad.

At the time, we have two huge German Shepherd dogs, and to kennel them for two weeks costs over £500. I tell Denise that it is too expensive, so I can stay at home and her brother's ex-girlfriend Rita can take my place on the trip.

Denise practically bites my hand off to accept the change of plans, and tells Mustafa, whose first response is, 'make sure you bring plenty money'. I have thought many times what made Denise so blind to his true intentions, and to this day, she has never offered a clue as to an explanation.

Believe it or not, the conversations continue, plunging deeper into the rabbit hole with graphic accounts of what they want to do to each other. I'm thinking, meanwhile, we, she and I, used to do those things years ago. What went wrong? Truth is the great leveller, though. How do you stop your girlfriend from giving you a blow job?

Answer: Marry her.

August comes and Denise, Rita and the kids go on their getaway holiday. When I drop them at Gatwick Airport, I say to Denise , don't do anything I wouldn't do and keep your panties up'.Feigning to be stunned, she looked at me and says, 'Don't be ridiculous. What do you take me for?'

I wave, thinking, you don't really want me to answer that question. Any doubt as to what she did while in Turkey is resolved when she returns from holiday. The conversations resume in great and grotesque graphic detail.

I snore quite badly, and Denise has always complained about that, so I take the excuse to move into a spare room to spare her. Truth is, I have no intention of having a sexual relationship with Mustafa's left-overs, for fear of catching an STD.

I'm convinced Denise is not the only woman Mustafa is ripping off, as it does not make sense. Nowadays, there are tons of examples of so-called romantic fraud, made possible by the internet. Fooling love-sick British women into sending money abroad is far more prevalent than I would have thought. Now it has become such a problem the Metropolitan Police have formed an international task force to deal with it.

As the affair gathers steam, Denise becomes aware that the chats are stored on the computer, so she madly start deleting everything before logging off. I decide that if tell the children that mum is having an affair, it could have a detrimental impact on their futures. Louise is studying for her A-Levels and Ella is studying for her GCSE's, so I decide to keep the affair to myself.

I buy a computer spy program called Spector-Pro and install it on every computer in the house. Whenever Denise is online, I get an email of every conversation she has, and every three seconds I get a screen shot of exactly what she is looking at.

Keeping on top of all that, as well as working long hours, is gruelling and extremely stressful. To combat the stress, I join a west London Boxing Gym and start White Collar boxing. I figure that I have some pent-up anger to expend, and this is a good way of getting rid of it.

I absolutely love the boxing and wish I had gotten into it years ago. I become, for the first time since running Field Gun in 1982, a lean, mean, fighting machine. Boxers are a breed of their own, knocking lumps out of each other and then, at the end of their bouts, hugging each other as only good friends do.

It isn't long before Mustafa is asking for money again. This time he says that his father has died, and as the eldest boy in the family, he has to pay for the funeral. He wants £3000 and Denise says there is no way she can give him that level of money without me knowing.

His response is brutal, as he thinks he has her wrapped around his gnarly finger: 'if you don't get it, you will never see me again'.

Any sensible person would say adios, amigo, but 'love' is blind and to my utter surprise Denise says, 'Don't say that. I love you and I'll get the money from somewhere'.

The next screenshots I receive is of Denise making a loan application for £3000 to the Halifax Building Society. I immediately contact Halifax and tell them what is happening. They decline the loan without her knowing why.

Denise tries other routes, but with my intervention, the result is always the same. 'Computer says NO'.

When she tell Mustafa, he goes into orbit and stop talking to her for a week. It is pitiful to see Denise begging him to come back online like some love-struck teenager.

# TWENTY-SEVEN

## SOCA or SHOCKA

At some point before the 1st of April 2006, a panel of halfwits decides it would be a good idea to amalgamate staff from The National Crime Squad (Police) with Her Majesties Revenue and Customs (LUBS, i.e., lazy useless bastards), and MI5 (Government intelligence gathering. i.e., Spies).

Whoever sanction this half-baked plan needs taking out to the garden for a proper slap. I'm hoping it is Michael Gove, after a heavy night on the Charlie. At least then I could understand the fuck up, but I don't really know. It couldn't possibly have been anyone who has ever worked in either organisation at grass roots level, because we all knew we hate each other with a passion.

Notwithstanding that on the 1st of April 2006, the Serious Organised Crime Agency is born. Maybe more an immaculate conception. Although that couldn't be right either, because there definitely isn't three wise men or a virgin at the top end of this farcical union. Publicly known as SOCA, to all the cops that work here this triumph of foolishness is known as SHOCKA.

I pride myself on never prejudging anything or anybody, so before the amalgamation starts, I make a point of meeting some of Customs Beta Projects staff.

They are the staff that The National Crime Squads' covert unit will now be working hand-in-glove with, from the very same office. To their credit, they have lorries, boats, and a fleet of cars that any prestige showroom would gladly market.

They also have storage units and offices that make the National Crime Squad look like a tin pot outfit. They have every conceivable toy, with the exception of Captain Barbosa, but to a man and woman, they are completely fucking useless. You wouldn't ask them to complete a street level drug bust, never mind an infiltration into organised violent and dangerous criminals.

Without a doubt, the amalgamation is a fuck up of epic proportions. I go from being one of the busiest successful undercover operatives in the country, to virtual unemployment overnight. Point blank, I definitely would refuse to walk into a crowd of villains with anyone at the Beta Projects' team. And I would lay money on it, that, without Captain Barbosa, their successes could have been written on a postage stamp with a pickaxe.

I hear that three of them have spent 18 months in Northern Cyprus allegedly infiltrating ex-pat organised criminals. At the end, there isn't a single seizure of drugs attributable to them. There isn't even anything that could link them evidentially to a crime or criminal act. In fact, the only thing they buy, without being accused of being law enforcement, is an ice-cream on the beach, which, I've been told, they did daily.

Actually, all joking aside, the only useful thing they bring home is a tan. Value for money? Beta Projects definitely is not. They even use untrained staff on their jobs, and I've been told they take their girlfriends on jobs with them to boost their credibility. That is a complete taboo and could lose people their jobs or much more. Only an idiot would take an untrained person on a covert deployment.

SOCA recruits managers from outside of law enforcement. So now we have managers from retail food outlets deciding whether or not they would sanction a covert deployment. I remember one such manager asking, 'how long do the covert operatives stay dug in the ground for?'

'What the fuck?' I say. 'Sorry, Boss, wrong department? We don't live in holes in the ground spying on gangsters. We socialise with the gangsters and live in flats and houses'.

His response: 'I'm not putting my name to that. It is dangerous. Permission denied'.

The scene is set for covert operations on SOCA to be as scarce as rocking horse shit because spineless managers were more interested in protecting their promotion rather than the public we are paid to protect and serve to the best of our ability.

To be fair, SOCA did have some successes and rightly they should have. If you give the Flying Squad unfettered access to GCHQ, with all the things they and MI5 have access to, there would not be an organised criminal walking the street anywhere within the M25. Country wide, if the Flying Squad were allowed to extend their area of accountability, it would be Katy Bar the Door for all organized criminals.

The office has a job running from the National Crime Squad side, involving infiltration of a Colombian drug cartel. The cartel is importing large quantities of cocaine by secreting it in plastic pineapples that are cleverly hidden amongst 40-foot containers of real pineapples.

We rent an office at Tilbury docks, and I am driving regularly a container-articulated lorry to collect goods from the port and deliver them around the U.K. To make sure we are legitimate, the Columbians have insisted we take one delivery a month which only contains proper pineapples. And we have to pay the import costs.

Initially, we are picking up their load from Columbia and giving the pineapples free of charge to a pig farmer in the midlands. He says his pork has never tasted better and butchers can't get enough of it. All operations are costed, and I decide rather than give the pineapples away we should sell them and recover the money we are losing for the importation.

I visit Covent Garden Market, a major hub for vegetables and fruit, and find a trader who is willing to pay cash for our entire load. This results in us breaking even on our costs and satisfying operations we can afford to keep going.

Excessive drinking and rarely eating take a heavy toll on my mum, and eventually her bowels pack up completely. She has to have a colostomy bag fitted, and is no longer able to drink alcohol because she can't bear the effect it has on her taste and smell.

As the realisation kicks in, she wean herself off drink, and the lovely woman I remember as a child comes flooding back. I am so pleased that people who had only known her as a complete arsehole got to know the person she really was. I don't blame my mum at all for what happened. Being a lone female, skint with seven children, and one severely physically and mentally handicapped, would even put a saint into an early grave.

I don't believe there is an afterlife, but if there is, my first port of call will be to find my dad and kick the grade-one bullshitter hard in the balls. In fact, if I started, I imagine I would never stop kicking him. When my brothers Charles and James, had cleared his flat after he died, and they discovered that he had another wife in Malta with children from him, and another wife again in Wales who also has children from him.

I have no wish to know any of these children, but they do have my total sympathy.

Mum dies of natural causes in hospital on the 22$^{nd}$ December 2007. I am with her with my brothers, and we thought she was getting better and made the decision to all have lunch. She died whilst we were away.

We organise the funeral for January, and I return home to Denise and the children. However, I don't tell them about her death until after the New Year so as not to put a downer on our Christmas celebrations. By contrast, her funeral is well attended with both friends, relatives and family present.

# TWENTY-EIGHT

On the 1st of October 2008, I am sleeping in the lorry at Thurrock services when I receive a call from a friend of mine. He says he was driving to work he learned that Denise had been involved in a car crash whilst driving my daughter Louise's Citroen Saxo. Rob, she's terribly upset but uninjured, thank God', he says. I say I'll come straight home.

After I take my lorry back into the docks and park up it, I commence my route home. The M25 motorway is slow moving, and one hour later, I have only travelled about 30 miles. When going past Clackett Lane services, my phone rings and I answer it.

'Where the fuck are you?' Denise yells. 'If you don't get here in an hour, Louise will be dead before you arrive'.

I had no idea Louise was even in the car, and my friend who called me didn't either. Obviously, Denise had been too shocked or worried to admit to anything.

'Where are you?' I say.

'QA hospital'.

'I'll be there ASAP'.

Gripping the wheel hard, I swerve onto the hard shoulder and barrel down the freeway at speeds up to 120 mph. As I am sobbing uncontrollably, the other drivers must have thought I was a mad man.

It isn't long before I'm heading south on the A3 through Guildford. The traffic slows but there is no longer a hard shoulder so I commence weaving in and out of traffic like a scene out of Fast & Furious 6, only to slam on my brakes to avoid slamming into a white transit van who stubbornly refuses to let me pass and keeps swerving in front of me.

I eventually squeeze past him at the Hogs Back and then he starts chasing me, shaking his fist. When the traffic stops again, I notice that the bloke has gotten out of his stupid van and is marching towards me. Bristling for a fight, I get out of my car quickly and high step it towards him.

He throws a haymaker punch that misses, and I drop my weight quickly and I kick him hard in the groin. Stupidly he leans forward, so I leverage a wicked uppercut that knocks him out spark cold. As he lays on his back in the carriageway in front of his van, I spin round, get back in my car and speed off.

Twenty minutes later I'm at the casualty department of QA Hospital. Louise is on a bed and her face is a mess. Her head has a huge gash in it, and she is unconscious and connected to a life support machine. Denise is unhurt but crying incessantly.

It transpires that Denise was driving Louise to college in strong winds. She lost control of the car on a tight bend and hit a tree. No alcohol or drugs were involved. All the impact was on Louise's side of the car, however, so she rammed the window screen despite wearing a seatbelt.

Miraculously, the first person at the scene - after my friend who left me the message – is a brain surgeon. Without a doubt, that is the only reason Louise is alive today. Within five minutes, she is transferred to Southampton Brain Injury Unit, where she is stabilised, undergoes major surgery, and then is transferred to intensive care.

I agree to stay overnight, and Denise goes home to look after Ella. I am gobsmacked and livid when, a mere two hours later, I receive an email notice showing that Denise is online, talking to Mustafa about the crash. Hey, she should have asked him for money to cover the surgery, but apparently this slips her mind.

I don't remember the exact words that Mustafa uses, but they're to the effect, 'I don't give a fuck about Louise. She has nothing to do with me and don't call me again until you have sent the money I asked you for'.

When he hangs up and cuts the conversation short, my blood is boiling over. Denise begs him to come back online, but he is so ruthless that he does nothing.

We have agreed that I will do all-night shifts with Louise until she is allowed home, and that Denise will sit with her during the day when I'm needed at work. This is another incident where I have to compartmentalise what is happening, because I know if I started thumping Denise, wild horses will not be able to pull me off her.

After about five days, Louise's consultant tells me she is well enough to be transferred to a general ward, but advises that if we can cope with all of her medications, she will recover much quicker ensconced within the peace and quiet of her own bedroom. We take his advice and take Louise home.

After about three days, Louise wakes up. 'Dad', she says, 'I can't open my right eye and I've got a whooshing noise in my ears'.

Feeling nervous, I take her straight to our local GP for an emergency appointment. The GP informs me that the closed eye and whooshing noise is just a by-product of the accident and advises me to monitor it and bring Louise back in a week if things don't improve.

As we're driving back home, I say to Louise, 'I'm not happy with that advice'.

'Okay', I say, 'then I'm taking you back to the Brain Unit at Southampton'.

I relate my intention to Denise and drive to Southampton General at breakneck speed. Marching Louise straight into the consultant's office, we explain her symptoms and instantly he presses the alarm. Louise is then whisked away for emergency treatment, including an MRI scan.

It transpires that Louise had a previously undetected fracture behind her right eye which was bleeding into her brain. If I had not taken her back, she would have died. The consultant informs me Louise is going to have an emergency coiling operation, which involves going in via the femoral artery in the right leg and stopping the bleeding behind the right eye.

Son of a gun, I think. But without hesitation, I sign the consent form and the operation goes ahead. Thankfully, it is a complete success. Louise is still alive today thanks to the Brain Unit at Southampton, but my faith in GP services has been completely destroyed.

If you google 'whooshing sound in your ears', it says, 'turbulent blood flow around the brain'. This is quite an odd and definitive set of basic symptoms. Why the GP didn't recognise them will remain one of life's mysteries (especially when she could have just googled it like I did).

During the crash, Louise also lost one of her front teeth – which means, I have to pay £1300 to have the gap bridged. The insurer pays out on the car, and when I call them to enquire about the £1300 dental repair, they advise me that Louise would have to sue her mum.

The notion is that the insurance company would allocate and pay for a solicitor to thrash out the claim and agree a payment. So I put the claim file together, submit it and promptly forgot about it. Over 2 years later, I get a call from Louise's solicitor.

'We have a settlement offer from Denise's insurance solicitor', he says. I have already decided that I want the whole £1300 back, and to my surprise, she says, 'They have agreed to £50,000'. Though I nearly fall off my chair, I say without even thinking, 'I'm sorry, that's not enough', and put the phone down.

A couple of days later, Louise's solicitor calls back. 'Okay, full and final settlement £65,000'. I agree to accept the amount and put the phone down, almost wetting myself laughing.

Once the cheque clears into Louise's bank account, I ring Louise's insurers and say, 'No wonder our premiums are so high. If you had said yes, Mr Sole, we'll pay the £1300 dental bill, when I originally called, it would have been done and dusted'.

I can't even hazard a guess as to how much the solicitors had been paid for dealing with this claim. The world has gone mad, but I'm not complaining. It has allowed Louise a foot on the property ladder much earlier in her life than would have been possible without the payment.

# TWENTY-NINE

I continue on the Columbian job working as a lorry driver. Eventually our efforts pay off when the Columbians tell us the load of cocaine is on the way. A container arrives with 300 kilos of cocaine secreted in plastic pineapples amongst the twenty-tonne genuine load. The plastic pineapples are so good it is impossible to tell the real thing from Memorex.

However, our old friend the drugs dog isn't fooled one bit. He sniffs them out with a twitch of a rabbit's tale, much to the delight of his handler. Another undercover operative proceeds to call all the intended recipients to a meeting to collect what they have ordered, and the arrest phase then starts in earnest.

This is the only SOCA covert operation that I am involved in during my three years at SOCA. I have been told the National Crime Agency was formed because of government disenchantment with SOCA's lack of success.

But the truth is, unless managers with balls of steal and just as many guts as some of the operatives are put in place, I'm predicting undercover work will be consigned to the history books.

Goodbye, 007!

After that, over a period of time I team up with a great

undercover operative whom I'll refer to as Pete Beal (from a fictional character in EastEnders). Pete and I make SOCA's covert haulage facility fit for purpose and capable of carrying out legitimate work.

But what Pete doesn't know about trucks and haulage isn't worth talking about. We put in place a driver training programme which hopefully is still being complied with, but I'm not holding my breath. Most of the decent operatives see the writing on the wall and leave out of sheer boredom and greater frustration.

Meanwhile, back at the ranch, Denise continues her strained long-distance relationship with Mustafa, the money grabbing feign without a wit of morals. And it becomes a full-time job ruining her attempts to give him large amounts of cash, even though he keeps asking for reasons that get more and more absurd.

I decide that when Denise and I finally divorce, I will visit this thieving little fucker and teach him a lesson that he will never forget. Therefore, I continue boxing and over time get better, fitter, healthier, and meaner than I have ever been in my life. Unfortunately, in the process, it also becomes an addiction.

I'm doing some kind of physical training mixed with fighting 14 times a week. Once at 5am every morning, and once in the evening. I decide that, at the first opportunity but without blowing my Spector-Pro secret, I will confront Denise. That opportunity comes on New Year's Eve 2008/2009.

I decide to stay sober and drink shandy all night whilst Denise gets more and more pissed. We are at a friend's house party, and at midnight after singing "Auld Lang Syne," everybody is elated and phoning family and loved ones. At about 2am, we return home, with Denise mortally drunk. She collapses on the bed, and I take her phone out of her handbag and check her messages.

There are a few from her to Mustafa, and one reads, 'I can't wait to leave Rob and be with you, I love you, I will get Rob to buy a flat in Turkey then leave him and we can live there together forever'.

Boy that hurts deep, not only because she is planning to leave me, but she intends to rip me off to the tune of about £80,000 for good measure. I forward the texts to myself and then sleep on the sofa. Because the kids are at friends' houses, on New Year's Day all hell breaks loose in the marital home.

In a final stab of desperation, Denise initially denies the affair until I throw the phone on the sofa and say, 'read aloud the last message from you to Mustafa at midnight last night'.

She reads it to herself but can't bring herself to utter the actual words of the message. It takes all my self-control not to beat the living daylights out of her, and I know people who have since heard the story that say they would not have dealt with the affair as calmly as I did.

I warn her that disclosing the sordid affair will probably destroy the kids at a crucial time in their lives, and they may never forgive her and may even stop talking to her. Therefore, we agree that our marriage is over and that we will formally divorce at the first opportunity. Meanwhile, we will commence a two-year separation period that coincides with Ella leaving school in August 2010.

I tell her that I had been recovering and collecting all the MSN chats before she started deleting them, and that

I know about the money she is giving, and plans to give, to the scoundrel and thief that is Mustafa. I tell her that her money is hers and that henceforth that mine was mine, so if she wants to give him her money, fine with me.

I also tell her that Mustafa is nothing but a conman, and as soon as the money stops flowing, he will hop over to one of the other beds he is also lying in. Denise is an intelligent woman, and she must have known in her mind that what I am saying is right, but her heart is stealing the day (no pun intended) and my words of caution land on stone-deaf ears.

In the next conversation she has with Mustafa online, she tells him I know everything, and that she has had to confess everything about everything to me. He throws a tirade of abuse at her and then stops speaking to her for a long time. She goes online nightly, begging him to answer, and it is pitiful to read these messages. but it gives me a rest from wading through reams and reams of garbage.

After a while, she messages him and says, 'Rob and I are getting divorced, and we have agreed to sell the house and split the profits 50/50'.

Stone me when he answers right away and expresses his undying love for her after days of radio silence. Love truly is a powerful thing, and he works it like banshee, gushing at how much he loves her in every single conversation. Of course, he also keeps asking her when she will have the money, and she keeps bullshitting him for fear that he won't wait until October 2010.

In the meantime, she starts giving him small amounts of money because that is all that she can afford. Every now and then, however, his true character surfaces, and he will say, 'I want more, steal it from your cunt of a husband'. Denise tries to convince him she can't, but he refuses to believe her.

Surprising Denise, I agree that we can all go on a family holiday to Turkey, and surprising her even more, I say she is free to trot over to see the miscreant as long as she is discreet with the kids. If our daughters find out, I tell her, all hell will break loose and I don't want any part of it.

If she ever had a doubt, I make it crystal clear that we are totally finished, which works to put her between a rock and a hard place: If her relationship with Mustafa doesn't succeed, she will have thrown her family away for nothing.

In my heart of hearts, I have already decided their fate, because the Rottweiler in me is already plotting Mustafa's demise. This is one I have to think about long and hard, though, because there are no rules of evidence that anybody truly cares about in a place like Turkey.

In Turkey, the police and legal system in general are quite corrupt, and they have a lock-you-up and throw-away-the-key mentality, particularly if you are a foreigner. For any doubters, watch the film classic based on a true story called 'Midnight Express'.

We go on holiday in August 2009 with Denise's brother, Louise, Ella and her boyfriend Jonathon. True to form, Denise is indiscreet, and Louise finds out about Mustafa and then goes to tell Ella. It turns out that Ella had already known for couple of months. Denise had foolishly given Ella her mobile to play a game on, and whilst using it, Denise had received a sexually explicit text from Mustafa.

Apparently Ella has decided that she can't tell me because she is frightened about what I might do. Sometime afterward all this, Mustafa has a huge argument with Denise whilst we are still there, because she doesn't have the money he wants. As a result, he gives her a proper beating in the way only the Kurds have the reputation of doing.

When Denise tells me of her beating, I say, 'Why are you telling me? I don't give a fuck. You have made your bed, now you have to lie in it'.

We return home at the end of the holiday, and Denise goes back into overdrive trying to scrape up money to loan Mustafa. Not knowing that I'm secretly thwarting her efforts, he becomes more and more irate. 'If you come to see me without £5000', he threatens, 'I will beat you like a dog again'.

Instead of Denise telling him to fuck off as any sane person would have do, she promises to redouble her efforts to find the money. I am absolutely gobsmacked by her behaviour. I have been with her for 22 years and never laid a finger on her. Incredulous that she is accepting this verbal and physical abuse from him does not begin to describe my feelings.

Conversations with Mustafa become more and more infrequent because he has asked Denise straight away whether she has his money. When she says no, he just goes offline instantly. Eventually she tells him that, because of English law, the divorce decree will not become final until the 1st of October 2010.

At that time, she will receive £10,000 cash immediately, and upon Ella's 18th birthday in 2012, she will also get fifty per cent of the profit from the sale of our home, making her a reasonably wealthy woman, by British standards, and by Kurdish standards, absolutely minted.

Meanwhile, their conversations have become more and more sporadic. Frequently they engage in arguments over money and then he just disappears, not coming back online with her for weeks on end.

As October 2010 approaches, I tell Denise that I'm going on holiday with my brothers to Spain, but in fact I've booked a week away on my own to Turkey. Louise and Ella have completely stopped talking to Denise, so life in the marital home for Denise is at best unpleasant.

The decree absolute comes through on October 1$^{st}$ and she gets her money, exactly two minutes before I walk into the restaurant where Mustafa works. While outside the restaurant, I do encounter a group of five men that, my years of working undercover, tell me are crooks.

As I walk in, Mustafa is sitting at a table holding hands with an English woman. He recognizes me and freezes after letting go of her.

I sit down and quietly tell him in no uncertain terms that his relationship with Denise is over. In front of this girl, I also tell him that there will be no more money coming from my ex-wife. The girl slaps him hard, and it immediately becomes apparent that he is taking money from her as well.

'You thieving bastard', she says, and walks out the door.

Mustafa, who by now is shaking, swears on a stack of Korans that he will never speak to Denise again. With a sneer, I show him some explicit pictures I have of him masturbating on the web cam.

'If there is any more contact between you and Denise', I reiterate, 'I will distribute these pictures to every restaurant and bar in the resort. And if you don't think I'm serious, I have printed up 1000 fliers with you wanking in technicolour'.

He is thoroughly aghast when I proceed to tell him, 'My advice to you is to pack a bag and go home, 'because I genuinely believe your life is in danger and you will be dead by the end of the season'.

To his dismay, I then ask him to tell me who the owner of the restaurant is. Quickly he points to a thick set man holding court amongst the five crooks that are hanging around outside the restaurant. Approaching him, I say, 'Excuse me, are you the owner?'

When he affirms, I say, 'can I have a word with you in private?'

With Mustafa still at his table, we return to the restaurant and sit down a few tables away from him. I tell him the story about Mustafa and Denise and the money he has stolen from me with her help, and then such sit back, lifting my chin in conceit.

He's been listening to me intently, and then he says, 'I like you, my friend, because I can tell you are a real man. You haven't come here shouting your mouth off, throwing your fists around, because if you had every one of those four men outside has got a gun and you would be fucking dead'.

I lift both eyebrows high at the thought.

'My name is Hassan', he says, 'and I am the head of the Kurdish Mafia in this area. Nothing happens here without my sanction'.

I nod and he summons Mustafa to come over.

Suddenly Hassan stands up and gives Mustafa a wicked back-handed slap. Then he says to Mustafa, 'get a bottle of Jack Daniels and two glasses for me and my good friend Rob here'.

Mustafa promptly fetches the bottle and the two glasses, Hassan tells Mustafa to set them down and fill them, and Hassan and I proceed to down the two glasses. Looking straight at Mustapha, he says, 'You are my nephew, but if you speak to this man's wife ever again, or take a penny from any other woman, I will personally send you back home in a fucking box'.

All colour drains from Mustafa's face until it is white.

'Go!' Hassan says, dismissing him.

And I have to say, I breathe a sigh of relief myself.

This could have gone so wrong for me. I attribute what saves me to years of undercover experience, and the resulting instinct not to behave badly and instead seek out the owner and have a rational discussion with him, rather than going berserk.

We drink together for about an hour, shake hands and part company, but not before he gives me his mobile phone number and says, 'you are welcome to eat and drink for free in my restaurant, and if you ever need help, I will be there for you'. I thank him and leave.

At the end of the week, I return home. The only emails have popped up in my inbox are of Denise trying to contact Mustafa. I have achieved my goal of blocking this crook from receiving the £10,000. Despite what Denise has done to me, I do not want pond scum taking everything from her and sending her home with zilch in the bank and bloody heartache on her sleeve.

Mind you, not just for her benefit, but for the benefit of our daughters as well. A fate which has befallen quite a few naive females who stupidly think they are the only one in these guy's lives, and that the bullshit these guys are spouting is true.

I inform Denise and the kids exactly what I have done. Predictably, she goes into orbit, calling me everything in the farmyard but a duck wad. I would like to think now that she knows she has had a lucky escape and could have ended up with absolutely nothing but the clothes on her back. She has never to this day thanked me for intervening, but hey hey for the monkees. That's life.

A postscript is that one of the divorce conditions requires Denise to move out of the marital home. She rents a bedsit on her own about three miles from our home. That must have been a sobering experience for her after living for 16 years in a beautiful four-bedroom house with an in-ground heated swimming pool.

Live and learn, baby cakes. Live and learn.

# THIRTY

There is a reason that old men don't box.
Yet I continue white collar boxing in West London and often go around the country taking part in shows in front of sell-out crowds. My trainer Les thinks it would be a good idea to take me onto a west London Pikey site where they have a makeshift ring that can accommodate a couple of training fights.

When we pull in, I say, "Are you fucking serious? What happens here if I win?'

He tells me not to worry, that these are lovely people, and to be fair, he is absolutely right. I'm made to feel more than welcome. And I win all three of my fights, to boot. By the time of the second and third fight, most of the people are cheering for me, not their hometown man. We have an amazing night.

Next, I am due to fight at a major event. My mates and brothers are travelling to watch me, and they pay £60 a ticket for a boxing dinner. The week before, on the Saturday, I arrive for training and only three of us boxers from Les's stable have bothered to show.

Les says there is no point having a fitness session, so he asks a professional boxer who is at the time shadow boxing if he would do three light rounds with each of us. The boxing rules disallow him to hit us as he is a professional.

On the other hand, we must try our best to hit him, the thought process being he will easily be able to keep us at arm's length, and at the same time, we will get experience in the ring with someone who moves and defends well. When the first fighter, George, goes into the ring, it is virtually three rounds of shadow boxing, with neither hitting the other.

I am next, and over years of fight training, I have developed some very quick hand movements. In the first ten seconds, I tag him hard on the nose and I can tell that it hurts him. More out of natural reaction than spite, he retaliates and hits me about eight times in lightening succession.

When he's done, I don't know whether I'm Arthur or Martha. I manage to stay on my feet, but after three rounds my head is spinning like Linda Blair in the 'Exorcist'.

The training session comes to an abrupt end, and I go home with the mother of all headaches. A week later, when I'm at another show, I lie to the doctor and say that I'm feeling fine and fit to fight. What I haven't told revealed is that I have the mother of all headaches.

As I wait outside of the door close to the ring, I hear my opponent being introduced. He comes out to the song 'Eye of the Tiger' from the movie 'Rocky' and receives a thundering applause from the crowd. Next is my turn, and the announcer introduces me as, 'Fighting out of the blue corner is Rob Sole, who is our oldest fighter at 50 years of age'.

The crowd immediately starts booing and shouting, 'no way' and 'bollox'. Then my music comes on as, 'One foot in the Grave', sung by Victor Meldrew. I bounce through the door and up to the ring and the entire crowd stands up and claps and cheers, turning me on. I vault the ropes and take off my boxing top like I'm King Kong.

A former boxer himself, the compere says, 'Fuck me, I didn't look like that when I was 18 years old, ladies and gentlemen. This is going to be one hell of a fight'.

As billed, we both knock lumps out of each other, and I take a couple of hard head shots that rattle my brain. The fight is declared a draw by the ringside judges, but I must say I've never been happier to get out of the ring as I am on that night.

After the fight, the fellas all want to go out to have a few lap dances and get mortally pissed. I shake them off, saying I feel rough as rats and am going straight home to lie down.

I fall asleep at about 11.30pm that Saturday night and don't wake up again until the following Thursday evening. When I do, my head is banging like a rough sea on a rocky beach, and it's five days later. Eventually I can't take the pain any longer and report to casualty with great reluctance.

I am admitted immediately, with a suspected bleed on the brain. The consultant tears me off a stripe for not coming sooner, and he informs me in no uncertain terms that my boxing days are over. To be honest, I'm glad. The injuries last much longer and hurt much more when you are older than they ever did as a young man.

When I am discharged, the doctor tells me I can't fly, despite my planned holiday in ten days' time. He says bed rest is a must. What happens next is something I wouldn't wish on my worst enemy. Within three months, I become clinically depressed and my bodyweight drops from 13 stone 7 pounds of solid muscle, to 10 stone 7lbs of skin and bone.

It's so bad that I am frightened of going out. Whenever I do, I have major panic attacks whilst food shopping, and driving my car becomes increasingly difficult, magnified tenfold if I put any music on. So over the next six months, I become a total recluse.

At the time, my daughter Ella is living with me. Louise is living with her partner and Denise is still in her bedsit. Ella tries to get me to see a doctor, but I won't go. Eventually I agree and am asked what I would say to quotidian 'list of questions for mental illness'.

There are ten questions, and they are all answered on a scale of 1-10. I answer most of them as high numbers, but the final question "on a scale of 1-10, is how likely am I to commit suicide'. I always say I'm not at all likely.

I now know that is the crucial question. If you are not going to kill someone else or yourself, you will not get help other than some form of tablet. I'm sure someone will say it's down to resources or funding, which I fully understand, but please stop the bullshit and rhetoric about how much we care about mental health.

The truth is that the truth hurts. Truthfully, the government and NHS don't give a flying fuck or rat's arse, if there is such a thing (maybe it's Rocky the Flying Squirrel!). What happens to me is nothing short of disgusting, and I remain in a chronically depressed state from 2011 all the way through to 2013.

To be sure, I am given strong medicine -- anti-depressants called Venlafaxine. But they do nothing for me.

On the other hand, on my medical file, it states:

This man isn't mentally unwell; he is doing this to punish his ex-wife for having an affair (a line written by a GP who really needs to find another occupation unrelated to the practice of medicine).

This man needs hospitalisation (written by the same GP who clearly had forgotten his earlier comments or confused one of the two comments with another patient).

Yet neither are correct. In fact, I am extremely unwell and remain so for two years, being left to rot by the NHS. At no time are their recommendations to hospitalise me acted upon.

Yet, I grow a mountain man beard and don't shower for months.

Yet, my bedding and house stink.

Yet, the swimming pool in the back garden has gone dark green and become a frog pond.

I try numerous times to cut through my femoral artery in the groin area with a carving knife, but the pain is so excruciating that, if I'm honest, I haven't got the balls to kill myself.

People say suicide is the coward's way out. I can assure you it takes immense guts and determination to take your own life. Because I have tons of guts and maniacal determination – and still, I could not do it.

At my family's request, doctors come to see me at my home, but my answer to question 10 remains the same: 'Me? Kill myself? Never'.

After two years of hell for me and my family, I finally say, 'Rob, if you can't kill yourself, you are going to have to get better'. So I drag myself out of bed and set about making improvements.

When I look at the swimming pool and am able to get

it working again, the dark green liquid includes rats, frogs, and newts inhabiting the murkiness, some dead and some alive.

I empty the pool's contents with a bucket, one gallon after another, from 5am to dusk every day for a week. That's what it takes. I have to refill the water to get the pool clean and running again.

Now I feel elated. When I go to see my GP, I'm wearing a superman onesie and eating a bacon baguette. I tell him I feel much better. A shrewd man would have sat me down and kept me there until a mental health expert arrived, but he just packs me off home with a pat on the back and strong whiff of I can't be bothered with you lot.

Louise and her husband have bought their own house and now have a baby. Denise is still living in a bedsit and Ella is still with me but having an awful time. Neither of my daughters are talking to their mum because they both blame her for my condition. Denise isn't even allowed to see the baby.

One night Denise calls me. She says, 'say goodbye to the girls for me and tell them I love them', and then she hands up the phone.

I reflect on what she's really doing and realise she may well be wanting to top herself. So I drive round to her bedsit and double-knock the door. When she doesn't answer, I kick the door in and find her lying on the bed with half a bottle of paracetamol tablets next to her.

Shit! I drag her body into the kitchen and force my fingers down her throat until she vomits and becomes violently sick, upchucking the contents of her stomach. I sit and speak to her until she falls asleep, and then sit up with her the entire night on the sofa watching her breathing.

The next morning, she wakes up as right as rain, thanks me and goes into work. I return home and decide to ring the most senior manager for civil staff in Hampshire Constabulary, where Denise works as an admin clerk. I speak to the head of section, Emma, and tell her that Denise is suicidal.

Emma can't be bothered and is completely uninterested. She advises me to ring someone else (who actually cares). I ask this person to get Denise some help and send her home on compassionate leave to sort herself out. This person says it's not her problem.

Mega miffed, I tell her that if Denise commits suicide, blood will be on her hands. I then ring Bob, Denise's line manager, following Emma's advice, and he too is equally disinterested.

Then I blow a gasket. 'If anything happens to Denise, you lazy fat cunt', I tell him rather unkindly, 'I'll come down there and rip your head off and shit down what remains of your neck'.

I ring Hampshire Complaints Department and am unmercifully fobbed off, so I decide to ring the chief Constable, a fellow named Andy. His staff won't let me speak to him, so I wait a couple of days then ring him back. This time I say, 'it is detective Superintendent Sole from internal complaints in the Metropolitan Police. We are just about to arrest a couple of Hampshire police officers for corruption. Can you please call me ASAP?'

Within ten minutes, my mobile rings. It's Andy. He had been in a high-level meeting in Yorkshire and came out specially to ring me. I immediately declare who I really am and explain myself. 'Denise, a member of your staff, is suicidal'.

He goes into orbit and shouts at me for deceiving him.

I retort, 'You attitude does you credit, sir, but you have a duty of care to your staff'.

He terminates the call.

Very soon afterward, police from Winchester Police station are dispatched to my address and I am forthwith arrested. The cop who arrests me doesn't know why he is arresting me, but he has been told to do so ASAP due to 'some kind of harassment'.

It would be correct to say, at this point, that I am suffering from early stages of a manic episode. My senses are heightened, and I have an extremely short temper. I say whatever I want without thinking about the consequences and my attitude is bloody cheeky.

My recollection of all the law training I have had comes flooding back to me, and I can quote points of law for specific offences – essentially, the Police bible of do's and don'ts for dealing with anyone brought into custody.

At Winchester Police Station, the staff ignores my protest at being detained without proof or evidence I have committed a crime. The arresting officer is sent away to find out why I am here, which is contrary to the rules. He comes back a while later, still none the wiser, and my detention is still authorised without any evidence being given. I am thereupon locked in a cell and my mobile phone seized.

If any of the custody sergeants who deal with me had read the codes of practice, they choose to ignore it. I am held in custody for hours and start making a fuss and threaten to make a complaint. Laughingly, the Asian custody sergeant says words to the effect: 'I have loads of complaints and they always get dropped when I pull out the race card'.

Eventually, when a ginger-haired, fat detective from Basingstoke comes to see me, I give him both barrels (because people in custody for major crimes are dealt with quicker). Later that evening, he comes back to interview me, but he is absolutely useless. I am shocked that a detective is dealing with what is essentially a minor crime that is normally dealt with by uniformed officers.

It transpires that I am being accused of harassment against Emma and Bob, Denise's line manager. Apparently, showing concern for someone who is suicidal can never amount to harassment in and of itself, because the statute states that the harassment of a person must be on more than one occasion -- and that has never happened here.

After the interview, he points his little fat fingers at me and says, 'if you had put your hands up, I would have let you off with a caution'.

I counter his nonsense with a few words designed to make his day. 'To give a caution, there has to be some fucking evidence you useless fat wanker, and you haven't got any'.

A report as to whether or not to charge me is submitted for an urgent reply to the Crown Prosecution Service, and they say there isn't any evidence to charge me with anything. Hampshire Constabulary, being a law unto themselves, ignores the CPS and charges me anyway with two counts of Harassment under the 1998 Harassment Act.

I am also charged with being rude to the fat ginger detective who I have nicknamed FLUB (Fat Lazy Useless

Bastard). The saying, 'if the CRAP fits, wear it', springs to mind. Oops, sorry, CAP. If this sorry sack is a typical Hampshire detective, the force is in trouble.

Clearly, the staff at Winchester Police Station who have dealt with me have no concept of the evidence required to prove the offence. I have said previously that Hampshire is the laziest force I have ever dealt with, and now they are winning the competition for being the stupidest. In my humble opinion as an ex-Flying Squad member.

I am held in custody about 18 hours for this offence and bailed to appear at Basingstoke Magistrates Court at a day and time in the future. In the meantime, I have made a complaint against everyone who has dealt with me to Hampshire Constabularies Complaints Department.

Once all the facts come out, Hampshire Constabulary apologises for the way I have been dealt with and gives me £7500 compensation for my troubles. It is my opinion that all the people who choose to ignore the rules and deal with me abysmally, were acting on behalf of Andy, the Chief Constable. Clearly, he wanted to teach me a lesson and felt he could abuse his power by doing so.

The Asian Sergeant resigns immediately to protect his pension, and the others are given words of advice. In addition, the court case against me is dropped by the CPS. 'Case dismissed, you maggots!'

Meanwhile, I am taking a high dose of Venlafaxine that I really should have been told to stop taking immediately. When I start going out again, friends ask me if I am taking cocaine because I am always so 'connected'. I have no clue what they are talking about and dismiss the thought out of hand.

My behaviour deteriorates rapidly, and I become very argumentative and threaten to poleaxe a few people who piss me off. In my local pub, three guys are very lucky to be going home in a car rather than an ambulance when they think it would be funny to drink my pint and nick some chips off of my plate.

When I challenge them, they all get up and start getting lippy with me. Eventually, one says, 'come outside and I'll fucking do you'.

I say, 'mate, your mouth is writing cheques that your body won't be able to cash. Sure, why don't you and your mates go outside and I'll give you all a fucking kicking'.

They go quiet and then the leader says, 'Sorry, mate, we were only joking. We will get you a pint and some more chips, okay?' I sit down to a fresh pint and a new order of chips.

It's not like me to have a short fuse, but again, I am unaware of the totality of my circumstances. However, my children notice a change in me, and on one occasion, Ella says something out of turn and I spin round and slap her hard in front of her friend, who is looking at me in complete disbelief.

'If you don't like it, fuck off home now', I say to her friend.

Generally, I am sleeping for no more than two hours a night, and for the remaining 22 hours following the slap, I am a total madman. When I go to Asda, I start laughing and joking with women in the queue and without warning grabbing their breasts. Fortunately for me, they are so shocked they are speechless and just walk out.

On other occasions, I get in my car, a Mazda MX5, and drive around Portsmouth at 2am spoiling and looking for fights. You can smell my brakes when I stop I'm going so fast. I'm even pulling in front of other cars and saying, 'Get out of the car, you cunts, and I'll kill every mother fucking one of you'. The only reason I'm not doing life for murder right now, is that nobody dares to get out of their cars.

I can't remember exactly how it happens, but I end up with an appointment to see Dr Minshall; he's the consultant Psychiatrist for our area based at The Parkway Centre Havant. Right away his pegs me as a narcissistic who is *not* actually mentally unwell.

When I hear his diagnosis, I'm thinking, really? Is he for real? Did he get his qualifications by submitting the requisite amount of Kellogg's cornflake packet tops?

My behaviour continues to get worse, and one night I play loud music until 2am. When someone has the audacity to complain, I threaten to tear them a new arsehole. Meanwhile, either that night or another, Ella and I have a huge argument about the state of her bedroom. 'Enough is enough!' I proclaim. 'You can fuck off and live with your boyfriend if you want to live this way'.

Whilst Ella is away at college, I empty the entire contents of her bedroom into black bin liners and throw it all on the drive at the front of the house and lock the doors. 'Good riddance!' I scream to no one in particular, just to get my jollies off. Then I go back inside with a wide Jack Nicholson grin.

At 2am in the morning, I pitch up to Louise's house, bib the horn, and shout, 'Come on! Get the kettle on. I'm gasping for a cup of tea'. She politely tells me to go away and come back at a reasonable hour. With a cheeky grin, I roared away into the night sky.

Gradually, the nickname Mad Jack McMad starts to have the ring of truth to it. Eventually, Louise, fearing for my sanity, calls The Havant Mental Health team, getting me another appointment to see Dr Minshall. I'm interviewed by him and a female colleague.

This time, the penny drops with him that I am not 100% right. I'm a live wire and am quickly bored of chatting to him and get up and walk out. And I have since seen his report about my visit. With the information he had before I arrived, a more clever man who knew his tradecraft would have had things in place to section me, because I desperately needed to be.

Instead, he just writes a report giving chapter and verse the symptoms for a mania episode: grandiose, pressured speech, sexually uninhibited, and on and one.

Truth is, I'm barking mad, but he doesn't see those symptoms because I present as an intelligent, cocky, gobby, wanker (symptoms which, if sectionable, would result all British rock stars and celebrities being locked up in institutions).

I return home, I find that I am not happy with the bathroom. Whereupon, I smash the whole thing into smithereens -- sink, toilet, all the tiles off the walls, and lastly, the floor tiles, rendering the whole kit and kaboodle demolished.

Now I'm living in a single room surrounded by expensive things I have purchased online and in stores. Surrounded by bags and bags of completely useless items, I am. And I'm not getting into bed for the two hours that I am sleeping. Instead, for some bizarre reason, I'm sleeping on a mattress on the floor which I've removed from the bed.

One day, Alan comes to my house to pick up a fridge that I said he could give to his mate. When the police randomly arrive, they think he's me and don't believe his denials to the contrary despite the fact he is small five foot eight inches tall, when I'm over six two and built like a brick shithouse.

They are just about to cart him off when his friend arrives and confirms that he is who he says he is. I've always considered it good police practice to make sure you know what the person looks like before you go to his house to arrest him.

Training memo to Hampshire constabulary: You never know when there may be more than one person at home, and people don't always tell the truth.

Better late than never. Finally, two men from the Havant Mental Health team arrive at my house to assess my mental health, and thankfully I'm still at home. At this time, I would like to publicly apologise for my behaviour, because there's no two doubts about it: I'm rude and obnoxious and completely out of line.

Skip Bawa, who is the leader and senior member of staff at for the Havant Mental Health Team, asks if the team can come in and talk to me about my mental health (essentially, talk me out of my tree before I hurt myself or someone else).

'No, you can't, you paki cunt, and if you don't fuck off immediately, I will put both of you in hospital', are a few of the choice words that I pick out from approximately 600,000 words that I have to choose from in the Oxford English Dictionary.

They return later with two police officers, and this time the police take the lead. But not to worry. 'If one or all of you put one more foot forward', I say, 'I will beat the crap out of all of you -- now fuck off!'

And from here, dear panel – I take a Kingly bow - I am sectioned and now appear here to tell my grandiose story, so as to gain my freedom and save the British taxpayer any further expense that might be unnecessarily born on my behalf.

# A LONG WAY HOME

# ONE

Thankfully, the Panel sees right through Dr Patel and Gabija Knights' report and testimony, both of whom trash me and opine that the Bucklebury Psych Ward should keep me there and throw away the key – no, actually, in fairness to them, they recommend further confinement to the ward without any basis to do so.

After temporarily adjourning, the Panel reconvenes. As far as I'm concerned, this is Judgement Day. If I am confined against my will further, I would be in trouble with a capital T.

The important individual is in attendance on Judgement Day, and I don't mean the Panel, Patel, Knight or me. That person is the same Skip Bawa who intervened at my home and sectioned me – the same fellow, in other words, to which I roundly spewed: 'No, you can't, you Paki cunt, and if you don't fuck off immediately, I will put both of you in hospital…'

The Judge overseeing the Panel says, after clearing his throat, 'Mr Sole is not presenting to us as a man who is mentally unwell'.

I smile, but then he addressed Mr Bawa. 'Sire, if you saw Robert Sole now at home – honestly, my ears are ringing from my blood pressure going through the roof - or on the street, would you section him now?'

'No, I couldn't and wouldn't', Mr Bawa answers, to his enormous credit. Because, if he had had it in for me, he could have said anything, and I can only repeat, if he had voted for further confinement, I would be dead today.

'Mr Sole', the Judge proclaims, 'you are free to go'..

Unable to anything more or less, I give Mr Bawa a huge kiss whilst fighting back tears of joy. He has just saved my life, and I will never forget that as long as I live. And now I know how the Indian Chief felt in 'One Flew Over the Cuckoo's Nest', when he broke out and ran off into the hills.

How do I know? Because, after my small celebration in front of Panel, I return to the Ward, where I am told a friend from Portsmouth can come to pick me up.

'Can I leave?' I say. The staff person replies, 'you can just wait here for your friend, but if you want to, yes, you can leave now. You are free to do, sir'.

It only takes a split second for me to make up my mind. I chose to pack and leave immediately, preferring to stand in the car park at Thornford Park in the bloody pouring rain, rather than risk them changing their minds or me being involved in an incident with Linford Christie whilst waiting.

\*\*\*

Hallelujah! Hallelujah!

It's 2014 now and I'm free and out in the community, where I make a full and swift recovery. And I have lived a full, industrious, and amazing life ever since. To be sure, I do have to take the drug Lithium for the rest of my life to control my bi-polar tendencies, the clinical diagnosis placed on my condition.

The fact that I fully recover at home with no intervention, just the occasional visits from Skip, prove beyond doubt that Dr Patel and social worker Knight either had no clue what they were talking about, or lied deliberately for the financial benefit of the Priory Hospital/Company, or somewhere in between.

Who would have believed that, at the ripe old age of 50, having served a stint in the British Navy and 25 years fighting organised crime throughout the UK, I would have been done in by a white collar boxing match?

To be fair, I was an extremely violent, out of control and obnoxious man when I was sectioned, and nothing like the person who I was before that fateful boxing match. Nevertheless, I do blame it in part on the NHS, because if my depressive state had been dealt with even remotely properly, I probably would have made a full recovery two years earlier. But that was not the case, and instead I found myself institutionalized.

The report I had written about Andy Marsh and Hampshire Constabulary persecuting me, ironically, was used as grounds for confirming I was not operating with a full deck (persecution complex, etc). But in fact, both of those statements were and are factually 100 per cent accurate. I would go further and say the mental health care arena is full of the blind leading the partially sighted, and when you know that not all of the inmates are truly criminally insane, that is truly disturbing.

I have never understood why there is such a clamber to reduce the prison population. It is the only punishment that really works, for the plain and simple reason that you cannot burgle houses, rob shops, assault or rape decent people going about their normal lives... when you are locked up. And most of these people are repeat offenders.

It normally takes quite a while to be sentenced to a term of imprisonment, and by that time, just as an honest person will have decided what course their life and employment will take, the same is true of a criminal. The liberal left is deluded if they think that rehabilitation works. In every police area, the same people commit 90% of the crimes. If we grasped the nettle, locked them up, and threw the key away, crime rates would plummet.

I'm sure the hospital records will show differently, but the fact is a lot of what has been written about me (and most other inmates) is either regurgitating historic information that is sorely outdated, or that is complete bullshit in the first place. The staff at all levels thinks, because you were mentally unwell, you also have no brain between your ears, when in fact, the opposite is true...and the staff might be called out for their pure daftness.

Since my release, I have read reports written by my keyworker, who spoke to me on a one-to-one basis once in three months. His reports were not worth the paper they are written on, or he simply did not know me.

In my opinion, that constitutes a fatal error of judgement, and despite deserving to be there on admission, the honest truth is that within three weeks I was fully in control of my actions and faculties and not likely to repeat. And because I kept notes. I know who talked to me, who tested me, and who saw me and who didn't.

In addition, clearly the SOCA did not feel it had a duty of care to its former employees -- even those who had lived the life I had since 1992. The bosses at SOCA, in my humble opinion, should be thoroughly ashamed of themselves and waterboarded (just kidding). They can't say they didn't know I was there, rotting in the psyche ward, because it was the topic of frequent conversations for obvious reasons.

All in all, this is the final chapter lived of an extra ordinary life, if I don't say so myself. It's true that I am widely regarded as mad as a box of frogs, as the saying goes. But honestly, have you ever seen a mad frog? I have always been told that it's the frog that actually turns into Prince charming.

Ironically, in 2013, I did go properly mad, not as a frog but as a human being. The mind is a complex piece of equipment, more powerful than I had ever comprehended before I went mad. I admit that I am madder than the character from the Mac'adder clan, made famous by Rowan Atkinson in his hilarious comedy Black Adder.

By UK standards, my life began in unimaginable poverty, in housing the government wanted to knock down to build slums. Truth is, the government doesn't build slums; it's the feral people who rent them that make them that.

Its 2023 and I'm 64 years old. I now live with the woman called Jane who is what every woman should try to be. Kind, giving and constantly looking for ways to make me smile. I reciprocate that behaviour, and utopia prevails. I feel like I've died and gone to heaven. If such a place exists.

I think you make heaven here on earth by the way you deal with everyone you meet regardless of race, colour, creed or sexuality. But part of me wishes heaven were real and that there is an afterlife for the following reasons: (1)

To give my dad a swift kick in the balls, which he richly deserves, and (2), to give Jane back to Keith, her husband, who died at 53 of Cancer which robbed him of a full life with this amazing woman.

That is all I have to say, for now.

> Don't forget to live before you die.

# ACKNOWLEDGEMENTS

I want to thank Tony Thompson, the author, for not dealing with me in an Honest way. This book would never have been this good if you had written it. Stick to promoting racial Hatred in the Police.

Thank you to Steve Eggleston, who made it all possible.

Thank you to John Stockley for the book cover – amazing artwork.

Thank you to India Roberts for putting the finished book together.

# ABOUT THE AUTHORS

ROBERT SOLE was brought up in the North East, in an area in which the council were knocking down houses to build slums. As one of seven children under 10 years old with alcoholic parents, every day was a struggle, exacerbated by his sister being both physically and mentally disabled.

Faced with two choices, The Navy or Jail, he chose the former, and embarked on a journey which will never be equalled by anyone else.

His Journey proves nothing is out of reach if you want it badly enough. Giving up is not an option.


STEVE EGGLESTON is a law school Valedictorian, former law professor, author, lecturer, and colourful trial lawyer. In his renaissance life, he has launched a hip-hop start-up, produced feature films, helmed a rock 'n roll magazine, booked 1000+ live shows worldwide, and managed Grammy-winning artists. As an international bestselling author, he is published in fiction and non-fiction and lives with his family in Somerset, England, where he draws and paints in his free time. Steve's business can be found on steveegglestonwrites.com.

Printed in Great Britain
by Amazon